HAD SHE
BUT KNOWN

HAD SHE BUT KNOWN

A BIOGRAPHY OF
MARY ROBERTS RINEHART

CHARLOTTE MACLEOD

THE MYSTERIOUS PRESS

Published by Warner Books

A Time Warner Company

Copyright © 1994 by Charlotte MacLeod

 Mysterious Press books are published by Warner Books, Inc.,
1271 Avenue of the Americas, New York, NY 10020.

A Time Warner Company

The Mysterious Press name and logo are registered trademarks of Warner Books, Inc.
Printed in the United States of America
First printing: April 1994

10 9 8 7 6 5 4 3 2 1

Library of Congress Cataloging-in-Publication Data

MacLeod, Charlotte.
Had she but known : a biography of Mary Roberts Rinehart /
by Charlotte MacLeod
p.   cm.
Includes bibliographical references.
ISBN 0-89296-444-8
1. Rinehart, Mary Roberts, 1876–1958—Biography.   2. Novelists, American—
20th century—Biography   I. Title.
PS3535.I73Z76—1994
813'.52—dc20
[B]   93-38776
CIP

Book design by Giorgetta Bell McRee

*Lovingly and gratefully dedicated
to my sixth-grade teacher at
Bicknell School*

ALMA ROCHE DRISCOLL

INTRODUCTION

In 1989–90, American mystery fans joined their British counterparts for a long, gala celebration of Dame Agatha Christie's hundredth birthday. In 1976, America let the centennial of its own Mary Roberts Rinehart slip its collective mind. The fact that the country happened to be celebrating the two-hundredth anniversary of its founding that same year may be taken as a mitigating factor, perhaps, but it was still a pretty shabby way to treat the memory of a compatriot who, over a span of half a century, was the best-known, best-loved, and by far the best-paid writer America had ever known.

Like Christie, Mrs. Rinehart wrote many books and several plays, some of which were box-office successes and one a long-running smash hit. It's interesting to note that Mary's bonanza was *The Bat* and Dame Agatha's *The Mousetrap*. Later playwrights might ponder whether inserting small mammals in their titles might be the key to success in modern mystery drama.

Like Christie, Mary wrote many short stories, straight novels, and an autobiography that dealt more with her family life and travels than with her writing. Like Christie's, her mystery novels are still in print, although her other writings have to be tracked down in used-book stores.

Totally unlike Christie's reticence was Mary's magnetic attraction to public life. Young Mary Clarissa Agatha Miller yearned to become a professional musician but was too shy to perform before even the smallest audience. Mary Ella Roberts played the piano every morning to accompany the hymns with which her fellow high school pupils were required to start the day. As the youngest probationer in Pittsburgh Homeopathic Hospital's nurses' training school, quarantined at Christmastime with a wardful of riotous male smallpox patients, Nurse Roberts played carols to quiet them down while a hot-tempered young bachelor surgeon named Stanley Marshall Rinehart led the singing in a magnificent baritone voice.

Mary also played the piano for her first publisher on that fateful occasion when he'd come to find out how many more potential best-sellers this unassuming little doctor's wife might have tucked away in the bottom drawer of her secondhand desk. That evening he sang, she sang, her husband sang, their three small sons and the family dog all sang together. And well they might, for a mystery novel more beguiling, more innovative, and more amusing than any that had gone before was soon to leap off the booksellers' shelves and fling itself into the welcoming hands of the great American reading public.

Mary's overwhelming success as a writer, along with her insatiable urge to be in on whatever was happening, led her onto strange paths. She trod them with equal parts of zest and decorum, in flowery hats and ladylike frocks sewn by herself or her talented mother until she got rich enough to afford a dressmaker. Going overseas during World War I as a correspondent for the *Saturday Evening Post* and an inspector of field hospitals for the Red Cross, she packed her furs, her jewels, and a white velvet evening gown along with her khaki trench suit and notebook. She did zealously inspect field hospitals in France and Belgium, she did reach the front lines, to the chagrin of less favored correspondents, and she did exchange her muddy trench boots for her furs and elegant costumes when she met with kings and queens and lesser dignitaries.

Back in America, Mrs. Rinehart was asked by Secretary of the Navy Josephus Daniels to visit the Atlantic Fleet and write it up for propaganda purposes. That led to a request from Secretary of War Newton D. Baker to report on conditions in army camps around the country. Invited by noted guide and sportsman Howard Eaton to join a grueling trail ride through newly opened Glacier National Park, she donned her riding boots, mounted her horse, and wound up acting as unofficial ombudswoman for the Blackfoot Indians.

And on she went, always writing, always finding something new to write about. Inevitably, Mary Roberts Rinehart was not universally adored. She was too prolific, too free with her opinions, too damnably successful for too long a time. As the old lioness went into her final decline, some of the lesser Felidae began to move in. Her style was passé, they said, too fraught with emotion, too inhibited by outworn mores.

They joked about her penchant for moving the action forward by inserting little previews of coming attractions. "Had she but known . . ." How could Mary's heros and heroines have got into the pickles she so adroitly contrived for them, had they but known that the bloom was off the rose, the fat was in the fire, and somebody's goose was about to be cooked? After her death in 1958 at the age of eighty-two, certain critics showed a tendency to dismiss Mary Roberts Rinehart as a joke in rather poor taste.

Not so the many writers who recognized their indebtedness to a true mistress of the mystery; not so her fans, among whom I enthusiastically include myself. Mary and I go back a long way together. I clearly recall spending part of a summer sitting on the floor behind a standing bookcase in the North Weymouth branch of the Tufts Library in Massachusetts, reading snatches from a new book titled *My Story* that I was not yet old enough to take out. After I got to high school, I could and did borrow all her mysteries, most of them rebound and showing signs of heavy use. Later I bought copies of my own, in paperback or secondhand, and read them over and over. I still do.

It must have been in the summer of 1987 that I got such a hankering for a new Rinehart mystery that I tried writing one myself, siting it off the Maine coast, where Mary had spent happy summers during her later years. Coincidentally, *The Gladstone Bag* would appear in 1989, the year when everybody else was getting worked up for the Christie centennial. It was then that my urge to attempt a little public-relations job for my old and valued book friend really took hold.

Writing is largely a matter of small miracles. *The Gladstone Bag*, for instance, was sparked by seeing a bright red truck with GLADSTONE painted on its side. Then one thing led to another and lo, a book was born. *Had She But Known* happened much the same way. I mentioned to my beloved editor, Sara Ann Freed at Mysterious Press, that I was thinking about a biography of Mary Roberts Rinehart. Sara had just met Frederick Rinehart, a grandson of Mary's eldest son and himself a publisher. He put me in touch with his father, George, who gave me iced tea with fresh mint from his garden, some interesting reminiscences about Grandmary, as he'd known her, and the addresses of other family members. Betty Rinehart, widow of Mary's youngest son, her daughter Connie, and Connie's husband, B. Albert Burton, treated me to lunch and provided me with valuable material from the family archives. Gratia (Mrs. Gordon) Montgomery, daughter of Mary's middle son, added further insights. My grateful thanks go to them all.

It was an eye-opener to discover that, while books about Agatha Christie were proliferating like hamsters, only one biography of Mary Roberts Rinehart had been published since her death. *Improbable Fiction*, written by Jan Cohn, then chair of the English department at George Mason University, appeared in 1980 from the University of Pittsburgh Press and has since been reprinted, as well it deserves to be. Dr. Cohn's zeal to preserve as much information as possible about one of the most charismatic women this century—and the last quarter of the century before—has ever known, plus her diligence in tracking down and setting forth information that would otherwise have been lost about Mary the woman as well as Mary the public figure, merits both praise and thanks from all who value our literary heritage.

Jan Cohn's book is particularly rich in material pertaining to the later years, obtained from members of the immediate family who were still alive when she began her research. *Had She But*

Known deals largely with the years before Dr. Stanley Rinehart's death. A book has to stop somewhere, and it would have been both presumptuous and superfluous for me to attempt a pastiche of what Dr. Cohn has already done so well. I do hope she won't mind my having made use of her superbly organized chronology, which saved many hours of repetitive research on dates and payments.

During the three years or so since I began this project—warned by my agent that it would take about three times as long as I thought it would, and how right he was!—I have been pleased to see further stirrings of interest in my old friend Mary. In 1992, *Crown of Life*, a young adult story about Mary by Sybil Downing and Jane Valentine Baker, was released by great-grandson Frederick's firm, Roberts Rinehart Publishing. It is to be hoped that there will be more to come. A life so long, so full, and so lavishly documented deserves to be explored from many directions and various points of view.

Warm thanks are due to Mr. Charles E. Acton, Jr., at the University of Pittsburgh Library, Rare Books, and his coworker Eleanor R. Ferber, for their kindness, helpfulness, and forbearance in offering access to the Rinehart archives. Especially heartfelt thanks to bibliographer Ellen Nehr, who did the rummaging. Mrs. Nehr has been of great service in tracking down Rinehart-related writings and photographs, not to mention lending a sympathetic ear to my frequent whimperings for aid and comfort.

Thanks also to Betty G.Y. Shields, executive director of the Sewickley Valley Historical Society, for information relating to the Rineharts' years at the Bluff, and most particularly to my good friend and fellow writer Barbara Paul, who stayed me with flagons, comforted me with haute cuisine, and let me watch her Marx Brothers tapes during my stay in Pittsburgh.

My sister and secretary, Alexandria Baxter, has by now word-processed so many drafts that it seems almost unfair to make her punch out the praise she has so greatly earned for her patience, perseverance, and pep talks during what has sometimes seemed an endless run of writing and rewriting. But here it is, kid, and you might as well finish the job.

So much interest has been shown and so many good people

have contributed in one way and another to the writing of this book that it would take reams of paper to write a proper acknowledgment. I can only hope that all who helped will take the wish for the deed, accept my sincere gratitude, and enjoy the results of our combined efforts.

—**CHARLOTTE MACLEOD**
Durham, Maine, August 17, 1993

HAD SHE BUT KNOWN

CHAPTER 1

As the Twig Is Bent

How the tree inclines may depend on who gets to bend the twig. Some precocious seedlings may prefer to handle that job themselves. Take, for instance, Mary Ella Roberts, born in what was then the city of Allegheny, Pennsylvania, on August 12, 1876, under the sign of Leo. The infant Mamie, as she was dubbed, could not have picked a more congenial zodiacal sponsor. A little over three decades later, as Mary Roberts Rinehart, wife of a hardworking doctor and mother of three little boys, this chubby, blue-eyed baby was to become the most lionized woman in America.

It is doubtful whether, on their firstborn's natal day in the centennial year of the United States, any thought of future glory flitted across the minds of Thomas and Cornelia Roberts. The young parents must have had more immediate concerns, such as whether their wee bundle of joy was going to yell all night and keep the whole household awake. Well might Tom and Cornelia worry, for the old gray brick house on Diamond Street was crammed to the eaves with Robertses.

As to who was head of the house, there could be no question.

Tom's mother, widowed since 1863, had supported herself and five children by taking in sewing, one of the few employments by which a respectable woman could make a living. By now her business was thriving, her children grown up and able to lend a hand. Both sons had white-collar jobs. Tom was the eldest of the brood, but his brother John was the real go-getter. He and his beautiful though delicate wife Sarah, called Sade, were already settled in the spacious front bedroom on the third floor when Tom won the heart and hand of pretty Cornelia Gilleland, a farmer's daughter who'd come to the city to get away from her new step-mother.

A young clerk on small wages was in no position to set up housekeeping on his own; Tom followed his brother's example and brought his bride home to mother. This was common practice then, as it seems again coming to be; families stayed together, pooled their resources, and rubbed along until the inevitable breaking point. Tom and Cornelia were cheerfully allotted the front room on the second floor, one flight closer to the workroom where Mother Roberts had set up a few treadle sewing machines and hired seamstresses by the day to help fill her customers' orders.

Mary's earliest memories of Cornelia Roberts, related in her delightful biography *My Story*, were of a high-colored young woman with a magnificent head of curly hair and a warm contralto voice. She sang all day, and why shouldn't she? Tom's three sisters had welcomed her with open arms. Sade, though less demonstra-tive, was by no means unamiable. Mother Roberts must have been glad of an extra pair of capable hands in a big old house without running water or central heating, where the laundry was done on a scrubbing board in a washtub, where tea leaves were sprinkled over the carpets to keep some of the dust from flying up under the vigorous but not terribly effective assault of a corn broom in a housewife's hands, where the ever-present clouds of coal dust wafted over from the Pittsburgh steel mills and settled on the white lace curtains that had to be washed and stretched by hand every few weeks.

All these tasks were jam to a farmer's daughter. Cornelia worked and sang with equal fervor while Tom went off every morning in the boiled shirt, starched collar, and top hat that she laid out for him, mulling over his increasing solvency, making plans to start his own business and move his wife and child to a house they wouldn't have to share with anybody. Though his wife seemed in no great hurry to leave the family enclave, Tom himself was finding his mother's domination increasingly onerous.

Both the Gillelands and the Robertses had sprung from Covenanter stock. The Covenanters were stern Presbyterians, Robert Burns's "Orthodox wha believe in John Knox." They had supported Oliver Cromwell against Charles I in the Civil War of 1642–48 and held to their convictions during the Restoration despite sometimes brutal oppression. Many of them had emigrated from Scotland to Ireland; it was from there that Mary's ancestors had pushed on to Pennsylvania.

The Gillelands had evidently stuck to farming; Mary seemed not to know a great deal about them except that they were respectable folk who had worked hard and done well. The Robertses had been mostly teachers and preachers, although one, a postmaster, had run a profitable sideline selling liquor to the indigenous population. Tom might have inherited a few genes from that wicked postmaster; he liked to remind his mother that, while he and his siblings could claim blood relationship to Scotland's great Argyle family, they were also descended from a notorious buccaneer, Bartholomew Roberts.

For Mother Roberts, life was real, life was earnest. The seventh day of the week was for her not the pagan Sunday but the Sabbath, always the Sabbath. Keeping it holy meant not playing the piano, not playing cards, not doing much of anything except behaving yourself and trying to stay awake during the sermon. The household went faithfully to receive their weekly ration of religious uplift, all but Tom. He, to his mother's deep distress, was an avowed agnostic. He did obey the biblical injunction to go forth and multiply, though; when Mary was four, she acquired a baby sister.

Olive's birth raised the family nose count to ten; for the time being nobody seemed to mind. Life in the old brick house went on as usual, cheerful and noisy. On weekday evenings, the three young aunts, Tom's sisters, entertained their gentlemen friends in the parlor, where the old-fashioned rosewood sofa with its slippery horsehair seat must have contributed to an ideal ambience for togetherness. Maybe it was the horsehair sofa that hastened the final breakup. Tillie, Mary's favorite aunt then and forevermore, got herself a new beau; and this one had serious intentions.

Until now, Tillie had stayed home and kept house while her mother sewed. All of a sudden, here she was, swishing through the back parlor in a beautiful gown of dark red taffeta while the minister waited to perform the ceremony and little Mary peeked out from behind the assembled skirts. No eyebrow was raised at Tillie's red wedding dress. In those days a bride-to-be did not have to proclaim herself a virgin by wearing white; it was taken for granted that she wouldn't dare be otherwise until the wedding night.

So Tillie was united with her Joe. The marriage was blessed with nine children and lasted for sixty happy years.

Maggie, the middle sister, never married. She was happy for many years at her job in a department store, except for the time when her boss, described by Mary as a middle-aged man with a roving eye, presented her pretty teenaged niece with some silk stockings. Mary never mentioned to her aunt that he'd also offered to help put them on. She might have been naive, but she certainly wasn't stupid. Maggie stayed with her mother until the household was finally broken up, then she and Mrs. Roberts went to live with Tillie, Joe, and their multiple progeny. As a husband and provider, Joe must have been among the all-time greats.

Not so the cad whom Tish, the eldest sister, got stuck with. He was a floorwalker in the store where Tish clerked for a while, was about twice her age, had already married three wives in succession and cheated on every one of them. He cheated on Tish also, and sponged on the whole Roberts family for money to cover his rubber checks and sundry other defalcations. He really cooked his goose with Mary when he telephoned her husband-to-be before the wedding, pleading for bail money to keep him out of the jail where he surely belonged.

Tish must have had superior powers of self-deception. However outrageous her husband's behavior, she went back to him time and again, believed he meant it when he told her she was beautiful, and mourned him when he departed for that bourne whence none returneth. She taught herself to believe that the checks Mary sent were in fact dividends on her own investments. She also believed that she had been Mary's inspiration for Letitia Carberry, the imaginary Tish who, in a long series of short stories, was to keep America in stitches for years to come. Granted, Mary's Tish had her eccentricities, but she'd at least have known better than to tie herself up to a no-good moocher.

One way and another, the clan was branching out. John's wholesale wallpaper business was making money hand over fist; Sade wanted a home of her own and, of course, got it, a tight little house just around the corner from Mother Roberts. Its great advantage was the stable at the back. Sade, for all her delicacy, was a fine horsewoman, and John was as good or better. They kept a trap in the summer, a sleigh in the winter so that Sade would get to show off her new diamond ring and sealskin coat in fine style. After a while, they moved out of the city to a much nicer house in Sewickley, where Mary was often invited to spend weekends with them.

It was from John that Mary received her love of horseback riding and her loathing of trotting races. Watching Uncle John drive his two-wheeled sulky along a racecourse for hours on end was a desperate bore; getting to sit in her aunt's sidesaddle on John's big bay, Charlie, was a thrill beyond belief. For Mary's debut as an equestrienne, clever Cornelia had fashioned a miniature habit with a long skirt and a fitted basque but had given no thought to those starched ruffles on her daughter's little underdrawers. Mary returned from that first ride badly blistered but once the agony had passed, she was quite ready to try again. In years to come, her uncle's early lessons were to serve her in good stead.

CHAPTER 2

Breaking Up and Moving On

John Roberts showed his Covenanter blood more than his siblings did. He'd grown up tall and thin, dour and reserved, inflexible, sometimes irascible. Nevertheless, John was the one whom everyone else turned to in a pinch. These pinches were usually financial, and John never refused to shell out; though sometimes his words to the wise were sufficient. In later years it would be sensible Uncle John who steered Mary on the course that would bring her fame and riches.

The exodus from Diamond Street continued. Cornelia was becoming eager for a change, a second daughter in such close quarters was definitely one too many. Tom was his own boss now; he'd taken on a sewing machine dealership. The ladies who sat in his downtown showroom, shirring and topstitching to demonstrate what fun it was, had been attracting new customers. This was definitely the time for a move.

Like John, Tom didn't take his family far, only to another little brick house a short walk away. One of four in a row, the house he'd rented looked to the casual outsider much like the other three. To Mary there was all the difference in the world.

She could not recall the actual moving, but she retained a vivid memory of being there by herself in the new house. Her parents had parked her in front of the kitchen stove to keep warm and out from under their feet while they dealt with the agonies of getting settled. The stove was new and shiny black. Burning coals glinted from behind the half-open slits in the damper slide. She could smell the linseed oil from the new oilcloth on the floor. Now, she knew what the word *home* really meant.

Looking back, Mary wrote that she thought her father had instigated the move in order to get away from his mother. That seems likely, although all the young Robertses must have felt the constraint of living with so implacable a conscience. Mary remembered an awesome encounter she'd had with her grandmother when she was very young. She'd woken up late one night and wandered out into the sewing room, startled to find the old lady still sitting there with a piece of unfinished work in her lap, holding a needle up to the light from the overhead gaslamp. Mrs. Roberts's one good eye was squinted up in a painful struggle to see the tiny hole into which she must poke the thread. Her blind eye, reduced to a whitish blur by some old injury, stared straight ahead. She might have been one of the Norns. Mary sneaked back to bed.

Until Olive came along, Mary had been the only child among a congeries of generally well disposed grown-ups; she must have had her share of petting and spoiling. Still, the bars were always around her. She mustn't go uninvited into other people's bedrooms, she mustn't bother the somehow frightening hired seamstresses of whom she caught glimpses sometimes through the open door of that cluttered, ill-lighted back room where the sewing machines were kept. She must be a good girl at all times, particularly on the Sabbath, when everybody was expected to remain aloof from worldly diversions.

His mother's house rules must have rankled Tom especially. Although Mary in her memoirs called her father an agnostic, Tom sounds more like an atheist, as rigid in his own way as Mrs. Roberts was in hers, refusing to entertain even the possibility of a deity or an afterlife, setting himself in vehement opposition to his mother's unswerving belief in a God of wrath who kept a fiery pit well stoked for the unredeemed.

Tom might rail as he chose, but Mother Roberts knew where the pitchforks were kept, and why. How could Mary ever be good enough to escape the fearsome fate that awaited bad little girls? As children do, she invented small terrors to mask the big one. In the new house, her inner panic settled, not surprisingly, on the back bedroom.

There were three upstairs rooms. The biggest was where her parents slept, in a grand new walnut bed with a dresser to match. The second was shared by Mary and Olive. The third and smallest was where the hired girl slept, when Cornelia had one. When she didn't, it was used as a storeroom. That was when the ghosts moved in.

Live-in maids were not then a luxury reserved for the ultrarich. Lots of immigrants' daughters and raw girls just in from the farms were glad enough to do housework for board and room and a dollar or two a week until they found better jobs or more lenient employers. Few girls could come up to Cornelia's standards, so the little back room was often empty and Mary would rush past its door with her heart in her mouth. She never mentioned her private nightmare, but somebody else found it out.

Tom, by nature and inclination an inventor, a muser, and a ponderer, was always open to new ideas. One day he brought a phrenologist home to supper. Phrenology was quite the vogue in that late-Victorian period; the theory was that, by feeling his subjects' cranial bumps and hollows, the practitioner could diagnose their psychological strengths and weaknesses. Which bump tipped this man off, he never revealed. But he really rocked young Mary back on her spring heels when he told her there were no such things as ghosts, and she'd better remember it.

He could also, he said, determine whether a little girl truly loved her parents. Since the phrenologist was the Robertses' dinner guest, since Cornelia was a truly magnificent cook, and since Mary had been taught to behave herself in company, he could hardly not have awarded her full marks in filial piety. That was when Mary began to think he wasn't so smart as he claimed to be. Of course she didn't dare say so.

Parents brought up in the old Covenanter tradition, along with a good many who weren't, still believed that to spare the rod was to spoil the child. Devoted mother though she was, Cornelia kept handy a small whip for educational purposes. Considering how many clothes children of that time and class were made to wear, her chastisements may not have been all that painful. Still, to be struck by a grown-up, whatever the provocation, is a hard thing for a sensitive child to handle. Each flick of the switch only reinforced Mary's secret dread that she wasn't good enough and never would be.

Despite the punishments, Mary and Olive had it better than many others of their generation. They were comfortably housed and generously fed. They were dressed like young princesses, thanks to their mother's skill with the many sewing machines at her disposal. Though Mary couldn't remember ever once having seen her mother sit down to read a newspaper or a book, Cornelia must have been a remarkably clever, creative woman. She was a cook and homemaker par excellence. She could sew just about anything, including a whole menagerie of stuffed Noah's ark animals to set around the base of the Christmas tree. The elephant, fashioned of gray flannel with knitting-needle tips for tusks was, to Mary's mind, her mother's *chef d'oeuvre*.

After her offspring had fled the nest, Mother Roberts had filled their emptied bedrooms with boarders. Her rooming-house venture must not have lasted long, though, for Tom and his wife soon fell into possession of the old rosewood parlor set on which his sisters had flirted with their beaux. Cornelia was well enough pleased to inherit the chairs and sofa, but a housewife who not only gave the whole house a turnout and rearranged the furniture every Friday but also sent the hired girl of the moment out to scrub down the brick sidewalk and give it a fresh coat of red wash with her second-best broom was not about to sit still for that dingy old black horsehair. Cornelia put up with it just so long, then she shut the parlor door and warned Tom, Olive, and Mary to keep out. Days later, she flung open the portals and herded them in to view her handiwork.

They saw a lovely new carpet, with lanes of cotton crash tacked over it to be walked on till the first flush of newness wore off. The old parlor set had been transformed by charming slipcovers of rose and white linen. Both the mantelpiece and the piano that Cornelia had bought on the installment plan over Tom's objections were draped in elegant silk scarves. And on the mantel sat two terra-cotta figures. One was a replica of the Greek Slave, the other was Eve. The girls were ecstatic; Tom only smiled. Eve had her apple, the slave had his bonds, but certain visitors suggested that perhaps those accoutrements were not enough. Much as she hated to, Cornelia added swaths of satin, artistically arranged to strike an acceptable compromise between aesthetics and what was then conceived as morality.

Moral teachings of the time leaned heavily on the Ten Commandments but trod lightly around the eleventh. People who obeyed Jesus' admonition to love one another had to be extremely careful how they went about it.

Mary heard many sad stories, though she didn't understand most of them until she was grown up. She was fully occupied with her own little world and its small diversions. One of these was, of course, Olive. Four years is a long span between young siblings; Mary was very much the elder sister, but the two of them played together amicably enough. Some of the time, anyway. They folded little wagons out of paper, hitched caterpillars to them with thread, and watched their wagons being slowly pulled around. One could not, after all, depend on a caterpillar to exert much speed. They put their dolls to bed, they cut paper dolls out of fashion magazines. When the girls each got a nickel, they ran to the ice cream parlor and splurged. If they had only one nickel between them, they asked for a single dish and two spoons.

There were no playgrounds in Allegheny, and there were many restrictions. Even the children's clothes were restrictive. They wore long black stockings and spring-heeled, high-buttoned boots all year round. Thrifty parents bought the boots a size or so too large so that their little ones' feet could grow into them.

Feet grew to the right size and kept on growing; by the time the boots wore out, they were usually at least one size too small. As a result, most adults suffered from corns, calluses, and bunions that they'd acquired as children. Mary was to have trouble with her feet all her life long, not that it slowed her down any.

Whatever the weather, children were dressed according to the calendar; or maybe the almanac, Pennsylvania being the state whence had first come those helpful pamphlets that were wont to be hung by a string near the kitchen stove: Bradford's starting in 1687, the famous *Poor Richard's* beginning in 1732. However the yearly date was determined, it came to pass infallibly that upon a certain morning in September, though the mercury might be trying to splash out the top of the thermometer, every child within grabbing distance was buttoned into itchy, long-sleeved underwear that covered him or her from neck to ankles.

Girls suffered the extra misery of thick flannel petticoats that had a nasty way of bunching up into hard wads over their knees if they tried to run, or even to walk fast. Both sexes scratched their way through the winter, and kept on scratching until the official spring robin announced that today was the day to shed your woollies.

Parents had somewhat more latitude in their mode of dress. While Cornelia Roberts wouldn't have been caught dead with a rouge pot in her possession, she was not above helping nature along with a few subtle touches. Mary was enchanted to watch her mother, splendid in a black taffeta evening gown, patting not only her face but also her neck and arms with a powder puff before going out to a party with Tom.

Now that they didn't have to be quite so well behaved, young Mr. and Mrs. Roberts were enjoying themselves in new ways. One night they went to see a play—a not very proper play—called *The Black Crook*. Presumably the hired girl of the moment baby-sat Olive; Mary was to have the special treat of a night on the town with Aunt Ella, her mother's sister.

Ella and Mary's goal was the Pittsburgh Exposition, which was being held in Allegheny. Some wooden halls had been flimsily thrown up for the purpose down by the river, on flatland that would be covered with water in flood time. Tom was one of the exhibitors—he had saleswomen at the sewing machines, shirring and ruffling to the wonderment of many onlookers. Always innovative, he'd included in his display an added attraction, a glass case that contained a little ship on a bright blue ocean. When wound up with a key, the waves would rise and the toy boat would rock and dip just like a real ship at sea. Spectators crowded to watch, and Ella and Mary grew sick of the crush and climbed to the balcony.

It is not known why any exhibition manager in his right mind got the idea that the pianos should be displayed on a jerry-built balcony, or why the merchant who owned the pianos had been fool enough to agree, or whether it was divine judgment or plain bad luck that set Mary and Ella among the pianos just as the balcony's too-fragile supports gave way. Why they weren't both killed is anybody's guess. Ella sustained a badly broken ankle. Mary crashed facedown on a low spiked fence that surrounded a first-floor display. One of the spikes pierced her chin and came out just under her lower lip. The scar remained, but could not have been very noticeable, as it does not show up in the many photographs that were taken of her in later life. Her worst injury was a broken femur that would keep her on crutches for quite a while.

Many people must have been injured in such a debacle. Mary and Ella didn't even rate an ambulance—they were driven home sitting upright in a doctor's buggy. After some time, reparations were granted. Whatever amount Ella got couldn't possibly have been enough to compensate for the limp that plagued her the rest of her life. Mary was awarded the magnificent sum of $300 to be put against her education. Mother Roberts drew the natural conclusion that the injuries were a judgment against Tom and Cornelia for their willful flouting of the Eternal Law by going to see an immoral play.

That the sins of the parents might be so spectacularly visited on their daughter could have been of little solace to a young child who already held a pretty dim view of her grandmother's vengeful deity. Mary did get some comfort, though, from an unexpected source.

While she was still fretfully trying to mend, a Russian woman who had done some sewing for Grandmother Roberts came to call and brought her husband, a black–bearded giant with gentle blue eyes. Cornelia was in some doubt as to whether the husband ought to be allowed near her little girl, for he had a dreadful reputation. Whatever a nihilist might be, he was one of them, he'd even been exiled from Russia for being it. Cornelia was, however, broad–minded enough not to hold his strange affliction against him; she rose above her doubts and he became a faithful visitor to the small convalescent, even making Mary a lovely doll's bureau out of cigar boxes. The varnish he'd put on always got a bit sticky in damp weather, but Mary cherished his gift for years.

Perhaps it was to get the children away from the perils of the big city that, once Olive was old enough to leave her mother, she and Mary were sent to spend summer vacations at a farm owned and run by a Gilleland aunt and her spinster daughter. Getting the sisters to the farm was no great feat. Cornelia's cousin, another Maggie, often drove into town; she could pick the girls up in her buggy. Once outside the Allegheny city limits, they were in the country. Somewhere along the road, they went up a grassy lane that led to a low, remote little frame house built on to one large room with an outer wall of logs. This had been part of the original dwelling. Inside was a ladder that led to a loft where the boys of the family had slept.

Now the boys were all gone from the farm. Only elderly Aunt Mary and her daughter Cousin Maggie were left, raising their vegetables, fattening their pigs, driving their cows to be milked, setting the milk in the cool springhouse for the cream to rise so that Aunt Mary could thump away at her barrel churn, working the dasher up and down, up and down, until after a long, long time the butter came.

Mary knew well where the butter went after it had come. Every week on market day, Cousin Maggie came into Allegheny with neat yellow pats to sell, along with eggs and other good things from the farm. Cornelia would come with her market basket on her arm and a daughter or two at her skirts, to buy the week's groceries and enjoy a brief chat with her cousin. It was interesting to be on the supply side for a change. The two girls would go out with a basket and gather the eggs that the hens laid in the mangers.

There were other small diversions. Mary made whisks out of old newspapers that she cut in strips and wrapped around a piece of broom handle to shoo away the ubiquitous flies. Twice a week the butcher's cart came up the lane and Cousin Maggie haggled with the butcher for some thin round steaks fried in batter. (Decades later, Mary would still order them once in a while, just for a taste of the past.) With a bent pin for a hook, Mary fished for minnows in the creek across the road, and brought them back to swim in the rain barrel. Regrettably, they always turned belly-up and she had to scoop their little corpses out the next day, but those minnows made a fisherwoman out of her, then and forever more.

Sometime during one of her later visits, Mary discovered a cache of dime novels inside a bench in the kitchen. At once she settled down in the rocking chair beside the oil lamp—there was no gaslight at the farm, of course—and proceeded to take another giant step along the road she was to travel.

CHAPTER 3

School Days, Rule Days

Mary couldn't remember when she learned to read, but she did retain a distinct recollection of her first day in school. This was a memory she could have done without.

All she did was pick up her slate pencil. Then—whap! The teacher was behind her, rapping her over the shoulder with a ruler. Mary Roberts, barely six years old, had committed the enormity of using her left hand! Being born left-handed could hardly be called a sin, but it was treated like one in the classrooms of the time. Pupils wrote with the right hand, and that was that. However great the struggle, the aberrant child must be forced to conform to the norm.

Mary did learn to write with her right hand. Over her long lifetime she was to pen miles and miles of manuscript—short stories, poems, articles, plays, novels, travelogues—always at top speed with a strong, rightward slant, dipping her fountain pen into the bottle when the ink wouldn't flow fast enough to keep up with her. Regardless of how her multitudes of readers ate up her output and clamored for more, Mary seems too often to have been beset by a feeling that whatever she did wasn't quite good enough. She, the ultimate workhorse, must keep trying harder, taking on more responsibilities, pushing herself to the ultimate limits until she collapsed under the strain and had to have another operation.

How much of this endless driving was due to that first-grade teacher's sense of duty, how much to Cornelia's little switch, how much to Grandmother Roberts's pitiless credo, how much to an innate something in Mary herself, can never be sorted out. Pretty soon Dr. Freud would be pioneering the concept that great neuroses from little traumas grow. Freud may have reckoned without the saving grace of humor. Certainly Mary's funnybone was well developed.

However, she found little to laugh at during those early years at school. The rickety wooden firetrap where she spent a sizable chunk of her childhood was probably less noisome than the average lazar house but, from Mary's description, not much. Classrooms were poorly ventilated, inadequately lighted, indifferently cleaned. Sanitation in the true sense of the word did not exist. Open toilets in the small bricked-over school yard were the children's only recourse; how they managed on stormy days is perhaps best not dwelt upon.

Any notion of trying to make the classrooms attractive and inviting would have been dismissed as sentimental balderdash. Children were not to be coddled, not to be nurtured as individuals. They were simply receptacles into which a certain number of facts had to be stuffed each weekday from nine to twelve and from one to three. When they got into the upper grades the afternoon hours became one to four. And they were to sit still and behave themselves the whole time, or else. Eventually some progress-minded humanitarians pushed through the innovation of a fifteen-minute recess. This sent the whole school crowding together out into the inadequate school yard. With barely room to move, much less to play, they stood around like sheep waiting to be called back in.

Compared to big, dirty Pittsburgh, Allegheny was something of an upper-class community, and upper-class communities did not neglect the arts. Once a week, therefore, old Mr. Flack with his long white beard and his tuning fork came to give the kiddies a music lesson. Somewhere along the line, Mr. Flack must have retired or died, or else he only taught the smaller children. Great was Mary's surprise on her wedding day some years later to discover that the big, jolly Mr. Rinehart who had supplanted Mr. Flack during her high school days was one of her new brothers-in-law.

Music lessons were probably the bright spot of the school week; for Mary the writing teacher's lessons were the darkest. Even after she'd conquered the problem of right hand versus left hand, learning the Spencerian system was for her unadulterated torture. Spencerian script was pretty to look and easy to read, but it strictly forbade any hint of individuality. To achieve this splendid nullity, the forefinger must be curled just so, the wrist kept flat as an ironing board, the Saturn, Apollo, and Mercury fingers must rest lightly but not too lightly on the paper.

This period was the only time of the week when inkwells were filled and steel-nibbed pens passed out. Woe to any rude boy who yielded to temptation and dipped the end of a girl's pigtail in the ink or flipped a spitball from the end of his pen! He would be marched forthwith to the principal's office and given a thrashing with the long rattan that played so large a part in the educative process. It was, in fact, generally assumed by the pupils that the principal's sole function was to keep the pant seats of young miscreant males well-dusted. Girls, of course, wouldn't dare misbehave in any serious way; their minor infractions could be dealt with easily enough by the teacher's ever-ready ruler.

As far as fact-stuffing went, Mary conceded that her school didn't do too badly. A pupil who made it safely through the lower grades could read, write, and cipher; most could spell at least the easier words. They knew a little bit about geography, they could see on the map that other countries than their own came in different colors. As to where they actually were and whether Allegheny had any real connection with a larger world, none of them knew and few stopped to wonder. Their history lessons taught that the British were mean and wicked and the Indians no better; Mary felt it her patriotic duty to hate redcoats and redskins alike. It took her years to realize how wrong both she and her teachers had been.

This sort of teaching allowed no room for original thinking. The star pupils were those with the most retentive memories. To a quick-witted, imaginative child like Mary, the average school day must have seemed like a foretaste of the Bad Place her grand-mother preached about. And when she got home, she had to sit down at the scarf-draped Hardman piano and practice for two hours.

Mary thought then and later that she'd have been far better off being given the chance to stay outdoors and play. Of course she would have, but mothers were assumed to know best. A parallel might be drawn here between the piano lessons and those starched ruffles that had wrought so cruelly on little Mary's nether regions during her first riding lesson. Cornelia wanted not only the necessities but also the frills for her pretty daughter, the advan-tages that she herself, growing up on a farm, had never been able to obtain. That an advantage might involve a sacrifice seems not to have occurred to her.

Mary, in her unpublished manuscript *To My Boys*, told a pathetic story of coming home earlier than usual after school one day and finding her mother at the dining room table with a strange man sitting beside her. He was a penmanship teacher; this was a respected occupation in that heyday of the curlicue when being able to write a beautiful hand was a mark of distinction. Some who mastered the Spencerian hand went on to become virtuosos of the swoop and swirl, to invent embellishments, even to raise the written work to an art form by, for instance, writing out the words of the Gettysburg Address so as to form the unmistakable shape of President Lincoln's face.

Cornelia's aspirations probably did not go that high. Mary was old enough by then to understand why her mother aspired at all: At this time, Tom Roberts's work took him out on the road a lot, and his letters home were written in an elegant, flowing hand. Cornelia, a lover of beauty, had been ashamed to reply in her unformed schoolgirl scrawl. She did learn the Spencerian method but she executed it in her own distinctive way, perhaps because the teacher thought Mrs. Roberts too grown up to slap with his ruler. Instead of connecting the letters with the mandatory swinging curves, she left each perfectly formed character sitting in its own little space like a miniature picture at an exhibition, to be viewed and admired for itself alone as she herself might have liked to be.

Getting back to basics, Mary received another and a potentially grimmer lesson before she ever entered the classroom. She was sitting on her grandmother's front steps one day, dressed up like a china doll as usual, when a strange woman came along and stopped to ask if she'd like some candy. Naturally Mary wanted candy, so she took the stranger's proffered hand and off they went, much farther than the little girl had bargained for. And still no candy. Mary grew tired, she began to cry. At that, the woman relieved her of a little turquoise brooch and ring she was wearing, shoved her into an old privy, and ordered her to stay there.

Mary was not all that docile a child, and an abandoned backhouse is not an amusing place to be. She stood it as long as she could, then, still crying, wandered out into the road and found a policeman to lead her home to her frantic parents. A few days later she was taken down to the mayor's office and shown some photographs. One was of a woman named Kate, whom the grown-ups seemed to think was the guilty party. What did Mary say?

Being an amiable and obliging child, she said what they wanted to hear and Kate was duly arrested. For a long time afterward, though, Mary was to wonder whether she'd fingered the wrong woman.

Maxims of an improving nature were rife in those sententious days, so Mary must surely have heard that a burned child dreads the fire. But the words took on new meaning for her one Saturday night. Cornelia's zeal for cleanliness applied as much to her young daughters as it did to her lace curtains. Every night of the week they got sponge-bathed in the china bowl from the washstand, standing up in it when they were small enough, doing the best they could as they grew bigger. But Saturday was real bath night, when the tin bath was set up in the kitchen, the water in the stove boiler was heated, and the little girls were given a thorough scrubbing.

One night, as Mary climbed out of the tub, her wet foot slipped on the shiny linoleum. She sat down hard on the red–hot stove, and dreadful blisters arose. For what must have seemed like ages, she had to lie on her face in bed, having her burns surgically dressed by the family doctor on his rounds while little sister Olive told everybody who'd listen precisely what had happened. When the sufferer was finally able to go back to school, she got awfully tired of being asked by the boys if she wanted a cushion.

Generally speaking, Mary seems to have retained few memories of her early classmates, except that some were white and some were colored (her word), and that none of them seemed to notice or care who was which. She did retain a vivid impression of a certain girl with the enchanting name of Birdie Berry, however. Birdie was the local bread baker's daughter. One day she and Mary were walking home from school, quite amicably until they got to a house where the Scottish maid once a year hired a bagpiper to parade back and forth on the pavement, making incredible sounds (again Mary's words). At that point, Birdie wheeled around and landed her classmate a stinging slap.

Mary never did find out what prompted the blow. She wondered about that slap off and on for the next seventy years or so. To add to the mystery, Birdie was always affable as could be when Mary got sent to the bakery shop for a loaf of bread and Birdie happened to be serving behind the counter. Evidently the baker's daughter had no qualms of conscience about the scar she'd left on poor Mary's tender young psyche.

CHAPTER 4

Life and Death Along the River

As a child, Mary seems to have been remarkably apt at soaking up the minutiae of her ambience. Her ability to create the atmosphere of a place, to humanize her characters with believable details, would play no small part in her development as a compelling novelist. Thanks to her reminiscences, we have a clearer picture of the Allegheny that used to be: a tidy city, even tidier after clean-burning, inexpensive, virtually work-free natural gas had replaced smelly oil lamps and messy, smoky, heavy-to-lug soft coal. It was a red-letter day when Mary watched her mother fill a coal grate with whitewashed bricks and turn on the new gas log.

Admittedly, with horsecars and horse-drawn carts, carriages, wagons, traps, sulkies, and buggies for transportation, with cattle still being driven through the streets to the abattoir, the streets could hardly be called pristine despite the legions of sparrows that did their willing best to dispose of the heaps of droppings. However, the litter that accumulates on modern city streets was not seen then, largely because packaging was still a thing of the future.

There were no beer cans to toss around; beer was sold over the bar, or in bottles, or else you brought your tin pail to the family entrance and the bartender pumped you a dime's worth for home consumption. Newspapers were too precious to throw away, for they came in handy in many ways: as insulation, as fly swatters, as tinder to start a fire, as temporary mats to protect a fresh-scrubbed floor from muddy feet. They got cut up for dress patterns or to make spills. Mary remembered cutting papers into strips, then rolling them into long, tight spirals. A jarful of such spills sat on everybody's mantelpiece, to be used for lighting the gas log or a father's after-dinner cigar.

Everything at the grocery store was sold in bulk, measured out from a bin or a barrel with a scoop or by the handful, weighed on the grocer's scale, and wrapped in paper or dumped into a brown bag that would be recycled in one way or another. As the family errand girl, Mary went often to the grocery store to buy some needed item, such as a replacement for one of the gauzy little mantles that diffused the gaslight so prettily but were prone to catch fire from the candlelike flame inside if they got tilted the least bit askew.

Sometimes Mary was on an errand of mercy. Cornelia was prone to violent sick headaches, which we today would call migraines. The grocer had one of the few telephones in the neighborhood, and luckily the doctor had another. After Mary sent her message, the doctor's horse would come trotting up, the doctor would climb down from the buggy with his scuffed black leather satchel in his hand, sit down beside the bed, take the patient's pulse, and say, "Stick out your tongue."

Old habits die hard. Decades later, the famous and distinguished Mrs. Rinehart shocked a renowned New York doctor by automatically offering to stick out her tongue.

Despite its tidiness, despite the boon of natural gas, the lack of man-made litter, and the notable housekeeping of its energetic housewives, Allegheny was still not a clean city. There was always that great cloud of soot belching over from the steel mills across the Allegheny River and up the Monongahela. Well protected as they were by long black stockings and high-buttoned boots, Mary's and Olive's feet were always black by nightfall. At the turn of the century, when fashion decreed that a woman's skirt should trail the ground regardless of what she might have to drag it through, there must have been a small horror story under every ruffled petticoat.

But a dirty city was a wealthy city. The Pittsburgh mills were going full blast and more labor was needed to work them. Immigrants were arriving by the trainload, lugging the featherbeds and other oddments that they'd managed to bring from the old country. Speaking no English, they looked blank and confused, easy prey to the company men who rushed to herd them into the less than hospitable company houses and got them signed on to the payrolls before they realized what they were letting themselves in for.

The men soon caught on to the hard, dangerous work; learned how to survive among the roaring blast furnaces, the great cauldrons of molten metal, the red-hot ingots. They learned never to sit down on anything before spitting on it first, to speak a little English, to drink their liquor steelworker-style, a slug of whiskey then a gulp of beer. As time went on, they formed committees, started small newspapers in their own languages, joined the National Amalgamated Association of Iron and Steel Workers as pioneers in the trade union movement. It was in Homestead, a borough of Allegheny County that had been intended as a lovely residential area and taken over by the mills, that their union struck against the Carnegie Steel Company.

The year was 1892, the strike went on for 143 days, one of the longest and most doggedly maintained strikes in American history. On July 6, exasperated by the workers' continued demands for a living wage and less inhumane working conditions, the company bosses sent in two hundred men from the Pinkerton National Detective Agency. In the ensuing riot, seven men were killed and twenty or more wounded. The governor mobilized the entire state militia and marched it into Homestead. The strike was broken, the smokestacks belched again, and the workers picked up their lives as best they could. In years to come, Mary Roberts Rinehart was to express herself publicly and forcibly on the side of the millworkers.

For now, her world was her neighborhood. Next door to the Robertses lived a bearded, gentle man with a lovely smile. He was deaf and dumb, nevertheless he was an insurance salesman. His spinster sister kept house for him, he wrote out policies in a clear, elegant hand—Spencerian, no doubt—and carried a little pad of paper and a pencil with him at all times. On meeting a neighbor, he would jot down on his pad an appropriate comment about the weather and hand it over in smiling expectation of a return comment. This could be a trial for young Mary, who was then still struggling with her left hand–right hand problem. She used to avoid the deaf man whenever she could, but she was always ashamed of herself afterward.

The last house on the row was rented by the Farleys, a family of four curmudgeons who never spoke to anybody, never sat out on their front steps in hot weather as was the custom among their neighbors, never did much of anything as far as Mary could find out. Her curiosity about the surly Farleys was never to be satisfied.

Next to this house of mystery sat the steam laundry, where a girl sat feeding collars and cuffs into a mangle, hour after hour. Mary heard her screams the day she caught her hand between the hot rollers, and ran to see what was happening. After that, Mary often saw the girl through the window, her sleeve pulled down over her stump, doing what tasks were possible to a person with one hand.

There was also a butcher shop, where an amiable German and his wife doled out thin slices of sausage to children who came in on errands with their mothers. Their daughter was less amiable; one night she chopped both her parents to bits with a cleaver, anticipating the Lizzie Borden tragedy by a decade or so. Mary reached back to this episode many years later in 1933, when she was writing *The Album*.

Between the friendly insurance man and the inscrutable Farleys lived the Millers, a middle-aged couple with a single child, a girl just about Mary's age, which was then about seven. Sallow, thin little Bessie wasn't much to look at, but her parents loved her dearly. They must, Mary realized later, have found the contrast between their lone chick and her rosy, chubby, energetic playmate something of a trial. The father, called Clem, was a Civil War veteran, one of many in the area at that time. Somehow, he had survived not only the Confederate bullets but also near starvation in dreaded Andersonville Prison. He'd even learned in that hellhole how to play the banjo, but the songs Mary heard him strumming were all sad ones.

There was also an Aunt Norah, who suffered dreadfully from asthma and made noises that were hard to bear. To get away from all this melancholy strumming and wheezing, the two little girls invaded the Robertses' shed, where the hydrant stood and where Cornelia kept her washtubs. Outside of having to vacate the shed on the days when Mrs. Klotz came to do the laundry, they were free to play house as they chose. They scrubbed the splintery wooden floor, they bedded their dolls down in the washtubs and treated them for imaginary ailments, got them up and gave them dolls' tea parties.

Then one day Bessie didn't come out to play. She was sick in bed, and Mary was not to go near her. Mary never did see Bessie again; she watched in tears from an upstairs window as the little coffin was taken out of the house to the hearse waiting outside. But children have to get on with their own lives. Regrettably, Mary was not thinking about her long-ago playmate a dozen years later when she happened to plan her wedding for the same April date on which Bessie had died. Mrs. Miller never spoke to her again.

Being a child was a dangerous business in those days, full of pitfalls that nobody even knew existed. There was, for instance, the river. Floods were almost routine in the springtime, there where the Allegheny and the Monongahela roared into the mighty Ohio with their waters swollen by melting snow and April rains. Floods could even be fun. During the epochal Pittsburgh flood of 1884, Tom Roberts, correct as always in his high white collar and high silk hat, took his family for a little cruise, rowing them right through his Sixth Street office from the front door to the back.

Their own house stood high and dry above the floodplain but Mary knew well enough how the poor people in the cheap-rent district along the riverbank dealt with the yearly inundation. Even if *The Case of Jennie Brice* were not a splendid mystery, the book would be worth reading for Mary's descriptions of life along the river in floodtime: the widowed boardinghouse keeper calmly taking up her carpets and moving the kitchen stove up to the back bedroom, mooring her rowboat to the newel post as the water flowed in through her front door, tying it higher up the banister as the floor continued to rise, finding it gone when the Good Samaritan arrived in his own boat loaded with raw liver to feed marooned and starving dogs and cats, and took his part in the macabre plot.

Far more macabre were the real-life outbreaks of typhoid fever. Residents seem to have considered these more or less acts of God; a likelier cause would have been the pollution of human and animal waste washed from open privies and fouled streets into the river that was also the city's drinking-water supply. Just how Olive Roberts managed to contract typhoid fever while the rest of her family stayed healthy can only be conjectured; it would have been easy enough when foodstuffs lay open to contamination in the markets and nobody had ever been told to boil the drinking water. Whatever the cause, Olive was suddenly a very sick little girl, and the doctor's orders didn't make her any better.

While a cold should be stuffed, according to the canon of the time, a fever must be starved. This meant giving the four-year-old patient barely enough gruel and calf's-foot jelly to keep body and soul together. Most importantly, Olive was to have no water to drink, not so much as a sip. No matter how high her fever raged, how heartrendingly she begged and screamed, the only relief she got was a teaspoon dipped into a glass of water and put in her mouth to suck on. Finally one night Cornelia could withstand her child's frantic entreaties no longer. Feeling like a murderess, she filled a tumbler to the brim and held it to Olive's parched lips. In spite of all that medical science could do, Olive got better.

The aftereffects of Olive's ordeal were felt for a long time. For one thing, she was thenceforth considered delicate. Like Aunt

Sade, Olive must not be expected to do anything she didn't want to do. Even when she got old enough to run errands, these were still routinely handed over to Mary. Not to omit any of the barbarities that went with treating a fever, the doctor had decreed that her head must be shaved.

Nearly bald, reduced to skin and bones by her starvation diet, Olive Roberts was the living picture of a pathetic little waif. As children will, she made the most of it. Cornelia was naturally anxious to get a little meat back on the convalescent child's bones, but Olive had always been a fussy eater. Now she developed a new idiosyncrasy: for a whole year she absolutely refused to eat at the family table if her father was present.

Nobody knew why. Tom Roberts had done nothing to hurt or frighten her. On the other hand, Mary's autobiography doesn't contain any tender mention of a doting daddy dandling a winsome wee one on his knee, much less haunting the sickroom to agonize over his desperately ill younger daughter. Even a four-year-old can recognize and resent a parent's indifference. But this is only a hypothesis. Olive's recalcitrance may have been some leftover fantasy brought on by the fever, or simply a ploy to keep on getting the extra attention she'd had from her mother during the bad time.

Whatever the reason, Olive stuck to her guns. For a solid year, Cornelia Roberts was constrained to toting supper trays up to the bedroom that Olive and Mary had continued to share even during the worst of the fever. There she stayed, coaxing and wheedling, while the little tyrant took her time picking disdainfully at the food in which her mother had invested so much love and care.

Just how and when this small melodrama came to the end of its run is not specified. Maybe Olive got over her fixation, more likely she just got bored with the game. She certainly would not have received so much coddling had the family doctor's view of the matter paralleled that of the man Mary later married. When asked how he'd have handled the situation, Dr. Rinehart replied, "Let her starve." A four-year-old child who'd been able to manipulate her parents so effectively was, in his opinion, capable of anything. Mary, on the other hand, seems to have taken a certain amount of pride in her little sister's stubbornness and even profited on occasion from Olive's example.

Take the incident of the bicycle. This has to have happened sometime after 1885, though probably not a great deal later. Mary would have been eleven or so. Bicycling had already caught on with boys and men young enough and agile enough to have mastered the Ordinary, the original high-wheeled boneshaker that had made its first appearance in Britain four years before Mary was born and had been manufactured by the Pope Company in Boston, Massachusetts, since 1877. The Ordinary was not for the unadventurous. But in 1885 came the Safety, the precursor of the modern bicycle. With both wheels the same size, it was low and dependable enough to be mounted and ridden without serious risk to life or limb. The company was even offering a model with a dropped frame suitable to be ridden by females, depending on how one defined "suitable."

One of Mary's friends had a father who owned a toy store. He must have been doing well with the immediately popular men's Safety, for in a moment of daring he'd ordered two of the dropped-frame models, one for his own daughter, the other for whoever had the intestinal fortitude to buy it. Mary had the fortitude, but she didn't have the money.

So she did what Olive might have done. She kept hammering at her parents night and day until at last they gave in. She got her bicycle, along with a good deal of flak from the neighborhood. Bicycle-riding by young girls was not at all the thing. It was dangerous, it was unladylike, it was downright indelicate, and the Robertses ought to be ashamed of themselves. Tom was not one to care what the neighbors thought. He was always receptive to new inventions; why shouldn't his daughter move with the times?

Cornelia did mind the talk, but even she came around after a while and made Mary a natty dark blue cycling suit with brass buttons. The skirt would create no hazard—schoolgirls' skirts weren't very full and reached only to their boottops. Besides, there was a wire guard to keep her clothes from becoming entangled in the rear wheel. The bicycle was further equipped with hard rubber tires, a bell on the handlebars, and a will of its own, as Mary discovered during her first attempt to ride it. She was riding down a path in the park near her home when she suddenly found herself heading straight for the (fortunately shallow) lake. She got half-way across before she fell off, which wasn't bad for a beginner.

Once she'd mastered the principles of riding, Mary had lots of good times on her bicycle, but she never explained what became of the bicycle later. Perhaps Olive took possession when Mary left home, or perhaps the two-wheeler had been sold by then, for strange things were happening at the little brick house. Some-where along the line, Tom Roberts's sewing machine business, like his daughter's bicycle, had faded into oblivion.

It must be remembered that the sewing machine was no recent invention. By the 1880s there were numerous models on the market. Tom had been carrying the Domestic Sewing Machine, a brand that must have faced stiff competition from better-known companies like Singer, founded in 1851 and still, at the time of this writing, a leader in the field. Furthermore, adaptations of sewing machines to industrial use had created a growing business in ready-made clothing that was cutting into the home sewing market. A sewing-machine dealer catering to homemakers must have been under constant pressure to keep up with his competi-tors. Tom was no supersalesman; whether he quit or got fired is moot. The one relevant fact is that, once he'd got through at Domestic, nothing at the Robertses' was ever again the same.

CHAPTER 5

A Great Deal to Learn

To young Mary Roberts, her father was just a man whom she didn't actually know very well, even though she could remember him in his nightshirt, back when they'd lived with Grandmother Roberts, fanning the coal grate with a newspaper to get the fire going. He was fair, good looking, medium tall. Lately he'd grown a mustache, perhaps to compensate in some measure for his receding hairline. When he was home, he read books and chewed tobacco, a habit that disgusted Mary, particularly when she got old enough to take on the revolting job of cleaning his spittoon. For as long as she could remember, he'd crossed the bridge to his Pittsburgh office every morning, dressed in the clothes Cornelia had laid out for him: the studs already fixed in his clean shirt, the links in his stiffly starched detachable cuffs, his folded handkerchief laid ready on the bureau. When he was about to leave the house, Cornelia would hand him his shiny black top hat, always carefully ironed by her own wifely hand.

Mary had never seen her mother kiss her father good-bye, however. As far as her daughters could tell, Cornelia never kissed Tom at all. The two seemed to be contented in their marriage, even though they had little in common except their home and their children. Tom was not ill-disposed toward his daughters, Olive's megrims notwithstanding; he used to bring home a dozen bananas and a box of candy every Saturday night as a special treat. But children, like housework, were a woman's responsibility. Tom's spare hours were more apt to be spent inventing an improved glass insulator for the telegraph lines that were by this time crisscrossing the country or pondering how to convert slag from Pittsburgh's blast furnaces into a usable form of building cement. Playing with his offspring came low on Tom's list of priorities. What finally drew his attention to Mary as a person was *Foxe's Book of Martyrs*.

Since she was about eight years old, Mary had been a faithful patron of the town library. Mr. Benny, the one-armed librarian, seemed never to notice, much less care, what she took out. Neither did her father, until he discovered her one evening scaring herself into fits over Foxe's grisly illustrations of early Christians being tortured to death in various imaginative ways. Forthwith, Tom ordered the book returned to the library and suggested that Mary instead turn her attention to Dickens and Thackeray.

Mary took her father's advice gladly enough. Dickens and Thackeray disposed of, she went on to read Zola, Victor Hugo, Jules Verne, Dumas, Balzac. She wept over *The Duchess of Malfi*, she read Eugène Sue's *The Wandering Jew*, she explored *Through the Dark Continent* with Stanley and discovered Dr. Livingstone. Tough meat some of this for a girl still in grade school; but a far more worthwhile education for an embryo novelist than Mary had been getting from the boring, straitjacketed curriculum at school. She claimed never to have gone back to any of these books in later years, not even to have reread her own novels once she'd seen them tucked safely between covers. Nevertheless, what she gained from her early raids on the library stuck with her forever after.

Mr. Benny himself was never one of Mary's heroes, although she did get a new perspective on him one Decoration Day when she saw him in a faded soldier's uniform, marching through the cemetery with a number of fellow veterans. Mr. Benny was the flagbearer, steadying with his one hand the staff that fitted into a leather socket at his belt. The drums were beating, the pipes were shrilling. For some reason she couldn't explain, his dedicated but undevoted young patron burst into tears.

These men would have been Civil War veterans, of course. Decoration Day, later Memorial Day, had been instituted once the shooting was over as a time to deck the graves of those who had died on both sides of that terrible struggle. The outbreak of the Spanish-American War doesn't seem to have meant much to the Robertses. They were surprised to learn that a neighbor of theirs who they hadn't realized was a naval officer had been killed in the war.

Tom was even less interested than his wife and daughters in what was happening around the neighborhood; his inventions were engaging more and more of his attention. He had a financial backer, a man whom the children were taught to call Uncle Joe Moffatt, though "Uncle" was only a courtesy title. Joe Moffatt had put up part of the money Tom needed to take out a patent on his most potentially profitable invention, a rotary sewing-machine bobbin. Of more interest to Mary were the plants and seeds that Uncle Joe sent from his own garden to beautify the Robertses' backyard.

Until now, the place had been what Mary described as a weed-grown no-man's-land, merely two strips of unthrifty vegetation on either side of a brick path that led to the privy that leaned up against the back fence that separated the Robertses' back lot from the prison yard. For his daughter, it was a revelation to see Tom Roberts, whose well-tended hands were unused to manual labor, turning over the soil and whitewashing the fence. She was happy to work with him, setting out plants, sowing seeds, running string up the fence for the morning glories to twine on. To their mutual astonishment, the plants throve. Tom tended them like children, better, in fact, than he cared for his own children, as Mary recorded somewhat bitterly in her unpublished memoirs.

Watching her father out on the path holding a hose, watering his garden bit by bit, Mary got the bright idea that he might run a perforated pipe along the fence from the hydrant. In that way, the entire garden could be watered at once, just by turning on the valve. Tom didn't think a young daughter's suggestion worth pursuing, however, and somebody else got to cash in on the sprinkler systems that have been so widely used during the past century.

Mary was growing up, shedding her baby fat, getting ready for high school. From Tom's garden, the Robertses had watched the old prison behind their house being torn down and a new high school being erected in its place. This was the school Mary would enter. She was horrified after it opened to realize that one of the classrooms looked directly down on her own family's privy.

This new high school was in no way like the stultifying old grammar school. Its curriculum was stiff but stimulating, more like a junior college. Courses were long and tough: algebra, geometry, English literature, rhetoric, and science, which was mostly limited to physics. The Latin teacher, a Dr. Gibbons, was a graduate of Amherst College. He had a heavy head of hair, which he was apt to tear at in anguish at his pupils' stumbling attempts to scan Caesar and Virgil. The teachers were, without exception, men; although shortly after Mary had been graduated at the age of sixteen, a young woman named Willa Cather would break the all-male precedent by teaching at Allegheny for a year.

The principal, James Morrow, whom everybody called Jimmy behind his back, was small in stature but great in achievement. His son Dwight became a lawyer, won many honors for distinguished service to government and charitable institutions, and was ambassador plenipotentiary to Mexico under Presidents Harding and Coolidge. Another son, Jay, a colonel in the U.S. Army, was an engineer in the building of the Panama Canal and served as the canal's governor and president of the Panama Canal Railroad from 1921 to 1924; he went on to hold other distinguished positions and honors. Dwight's daughter, Anne, married the famous pioneering aviator Charles Lindbergh and herself became an acclaimed author.

In addition to his administrative duties, Jimmy Morrow taught senior mathematics. He himself was an arithmetical wizard. During a spare moment, he liked to pop into the algebra class and invite a student to write two long rows of figures on the black-board. He'd glance at them for a second or so, turn his back to the figures, multiply them mentally, and reel off the total in a flash. Mary complained that Principal Morrow had given her an inferiority complex, but at least she'd learned to add in her head by the time she received her diploma.

High school was also teaching her some extracurricular lessons, chiefly about boys. Mary confessed later that her sudden interest in attending the young people's Sunday evening services at church was not due to a spurt of religious zeal. Like the rest of the attendees, she would listen with something less than half an ear to the sermon, the larger share of her mind being focused on whether some reasonably personable member of the opposite sex would ask to walk home with her.

The system was pretty well organized. Boys would duck out first and form an impromptu stag line. Girls would linger to straighten their hats and pick up their muffs, then saunter decorously past the boys, pretending they weren't there until some fiery young blade got up nerve enough to step forward and make his pitch. Being approached by the right swain was bliss, the wrong one was tragedy. No boy at all was utter despair, at least for the moment. These walkings-home amounted to exactly that, there would be no hanky-panky along the way. The boy didn't even get asked in for a cup of cocoa unless the girl had reached sixteen, at which magical age she was entitled to pin up her hair, let down her hems, and serve the cocoa.

Even sitting alone together on the front steps under the watchful eyes of parents and neighbors was taboo; but love, or its reasonable facsimile, would find a way. A few boys would band together like young Don Juans with their mandolins and banjos and stroll down the road, stopping under what they believed to be a girlfriend's bedroom window and assaulting the night with what they further believed to be melody. Oftener than not, they'd choose the wrong window and get a dousing from the washstand pitcher of some wrathful father.

Perhaps Mary got serenaded, or perhaps Cornelia decided that the bird's-eye view of the privy did not reflect a proper image for her blossoming daughter. Mary had always been the pretty one, and her fond, ambitious mother envisioned for her daughter the ultimate happy ending: marriage to a nice young man of good family and comfortable fortune, or at least to a decent Presbyterian with a reasonably steady job and no great yearning to be an inventor. Again, she decided it was time to move.

So Cornelia went house hunting. It didn't take her long to find what she wanted. The new house was on the north side of the park, a better location from an upwardly mobile point of view, though less desirable in other ways. For Mary, getting to school would no longer mean just a pop around the corner but a long walk around the park; in wintertime she'd arrive at class numb with the cold. But this house was bigger than the old one, it had a genuine bathroom with a built-in tub, and, for the first time in their lives, Mary and Olive would each have a bedroom to herself.

Cornelia had the same insouciant attitude toward money that Mary was to display with such éclat during her later life. She trained her elder daughter to say sweetly, "Mother isn't in just now," when a bill collector came knocking at the door. She sold Mother Roberts's nice old rosewood parlor set for twenty dollars and splurged on a fashionable new plush-covered parlor suite with a matching fringed scarf for the mantelpiece. Once she'd got everything arranged to her liking, the parlor was so elegant that she kept the blinds down lest the upholstery fade and never let anybody sit in the chairs for fear of rubbing the plush.

Mary said later that this house was the only mistake Cornelia Roberts ever made. The loving daughter might have erred a bit on the side of charity with regard to some of her mother's decisions, but Mary was certainly not wrong about the move. By the end of the first year in their grand new quarters, the Robertses were feeling the pinch. Tom hadn't found another steady job. He was earning some money, but not enough. Uncle John would have helped, but soon John himself was in bad trouble. His big wallpaper warehouse, the fount of all financial blessings, caught fire. Standing on Liberty Street, watching rolls of flaming wallpaper shoot out like skyrockets as the streams from the fire hoses hit them must have been like gazing into the Fiery Furnace that Mary had worried so much about as a child. Firemen, black as coalminers, were stationed on the roofs of surrounding buildings, wetting them down, trying to save them. The air was full of charred paper scraps, which blew into the spectators' faces. By the time the fire was under control, the building had burned to the ground.

It stands to reason that a canny Scot like John Roberts would have carried insurance on his business, but no sum is ever enough in the face of such a disaster. John must have had his own financial problems, and big ones; nevertheless, Mary's description of her father's setting up a wallpaper showroom suggests that her uncle was still trying to help his brother. Tom had a stand in his family dining room that held the samples. When a customer came along he would flick them over, one after another, with those aristocratic white hands his daughter so often mentioned.

Maybe Cornelia resented having her new house turned into a shop; more likely the scheme just didn't work. Soon Tom Roberts was out on the road selling wallpaper, mainly to dealers in Ohio. To the end of her days, Mary could recite a litany of Ohio towns from which her father had mailed home the exquisitely penned notes and postcards that she was to gather together and burn on the day of his funeral.

John's fire marked a turning point in several ways. Mother Roberts and Aunt Maggie left Diamond Street for Tillie and Joe's big house in the suburbs. Left to manage without their friendly support and with Tom away on the road, Cornelia broke down from strain and overwork. Mary and Olive, aged fifteen and eleven, took care of their mother and managed somehow to keep the house running without letting the neighborhood know that there was no money to hire a helper.

Mary had for a long time been in the habit of spinning romantic daydreams inside her head. Now she decided to recoup the family fortunes by writing down her tales and selling them. A local newspaper had been advertising for readers to send in short stories one column in length; Mary wrote three and saw them all published. She was paid a dollar apiece. Thanks to her recently acquired arithmetical skills, she figured out that, at this rate, a literary career was not the road to riches.

Her father's wallpaper venture was not doing too well, either. Later he switched to peddling a soft drink called Nux Phospho. Finally Tom took on a product that few people had ever heard of and almost nobody wanted to buy. It was called a cash register.

At this time, small merchants were still using the old-fashioned till, an open invitation to human error and petty pilferage. A cash register would keep the money safe in a closed drawer, it would produce an accurate total. The customer need wait no longer than a minute or so for a clerk to ring up the sale and count out the change.

But cash registers were expensive. They took up too much counter space. Clerks and cashiers were vociferously hostile, seeing the new machines as aspersions on their honesty and ability; Tom Roberts was not the man to talk them down. Mary thought her father's basic problem was simply that he hated asking anybody to buy anything.

Surely the problem must have run deeper than that. Selling had been Tom Roberts's career for pretty much all his working life. He was experienced, personable, well dressed thanks to his wife's solicitous valeting, well educated through his extensive reading. With so much going for him, why couldn't Tom himself get going? If he didn't like what he was doing, why not get into some other job such as bookkeeping or banking, where he wouldn't have to ask for money because it was already there?

The answer may lie in that seldom-used word *hubris*, the overweening arrogance that carries around its edges a dark hint of unhappy endings to grandiose dreams. Tom Roberts, like Pip, had great expectations. One day, he would be recognized as a famous inventor; one day he would command wealth beyond the dreams of avarice without having to demean himself by collecting it bit by bit like a common peddler. Mary's reminiscences of her father give an impression of one who considered himself a gentleman and a scholar, sitting a bit aloof from his family, turning the pages of some learned tome with those white hands that had never done a day's hard labor, honing his intellect as he spat gobs of tobacco juice into his well-burnished cuspidor.

The cuspidor rather spoils the picture, but Tom wouldn't have noticed. Intellectuals were entitled to their small indulgences. They could flout a mother's most sacred beliefs, they could reward a wife's many hours of toil at turning a dismal parlor into a decorator's dream by allowing her one brief, patronizing smile and not a word of comment, much less praise. They married and had families because that was what manly males did, but they didn't have to pay much attention to their children, that was the woman's job. A man's was to provide the housekeeping money, which meant having a source of income, and therein lay the rub. One job was as boring as another, so why try to change? Until his ship came in, he might as well stick with what he knew.

The life of a traveling salesman is never any picnic. Cheap hotels and bad food must have been particularly hard on a man who'd been pampered all his life, first by his mother and sisters, then by that quintessential helpmeet, Cornelia Gilleland Roberts. The proud dreamer was getting a bitter taste of life on the downside. Mary drew a sad picture of him coming home on weekends, always tired, sitting glum and silent at the table, letting his coffee cool off. He never liked to drink it hot.

Cold coffee was not the only beverage Tom fancied. For so long as he'd lived under his mother's roof, he must perforce have shunned the demon Alcohol. Once free of her domination, he and Cornelia had been able to relax a little. Mary could recall being sent with a dime and a pail to fetch beer from the local saloon when company dropped by; there was surely no great harm in that. Once away among strangers for the first time in his life, though, increasingly depressed by one turndown after another, with nowhere to go for solace but the YMCA or the corner gin mill, Tom would more likely than not have opted for the latter.

Even getting a drink posed its problems, however. The redoubtable Carry Nation, relict of a drunkard, was already out swinging her hatchet. Legions of women who had seen too many children go ragged and hungry while their fathers drank up the week's wages had begun marching in temperance parades, exhorting youths to join the Band of Hope. A few even grabbed their own hatchets and joined Mrs. Nation in her saloon bashing.

Prohibition was to become the law of the land in 1919; the temperance marchers and a new legion of bootleggers would rise up and call it blessed. Cornelia Roberts wasn't waiting thirty years or more for such a law to be passed. Her Covenanter blood was up, she was already running her own temperance campaign, with her husband as its sole target. Cornelia wasn't a complete prude— she didn't mind keeping a little beer on ice for hot summer evenings—but she did make her feelings known without inhibition whenever she found out that Tom had been nipping at the hard stuff.

Tom Roberts was not one to brawl, he simply tuned her out. One way and another he was detaching himself from a reality too grim for an idealist to handle, retreating into his private world of inventions and daydreams, earning less, drinking more. On his weekends home, he and a crony who also liked the bottle too well for Cornelia's taste would sit hour after hour at the dining room table with plans and figures spread before them, counting the riches that would be Tom Roberts's once his patents were adopted and that overdue gravy train rolled into the depot, getting richer with every swig.

Tom was by no means a fool. His inventions did have merit. His idea of making cement from the slag thrown out from the steel mill furnaces was valid, as witness the vast amount of cinder block and cinder concrete used in construction today. His glass insulator for telegraph wires probably would have worked as well as most of the other designs that still show up as collectibles at flea markets and yard sales. Again, his problem was the competition. The nineteenth century was a time of exploration and discovery on many fronts, the U.S. Patent Office was routinely buried under submissions ranging from world-changing to totally mad. Many were variations on previously issued patents. The first patent for a sewing machine had been issued in 1755, Tom Roberts's patent was one of thousands in the same category.

Tom's invention was a rotary bobbin; he may not have known that a rotary hook-and-bobbin device had been patented in 1850 by another American, Allan B. Wilson. Wilson's concept had not caught on, however; the sewing machines that Tom Roberts sold from his showroom had been constructed on the same principle as the weaver's loom: a treadle-powered shuttle moved back and forth under the needle, spinning out thread from a slender bobbin that fitted inside the shuttle. This was a good, reliable design; such machines worked well and stood up to long use. Their one drawback, and the one that inspired Tom's invention, was the tiny pause that resulted every time the shuttle must alternate from back to forth, or forth to back, thereby limiting the speed at which the machine could perform. Tom reasoned that a bobbin spinning around and around without pause would make for a smoother, faster, more efficient operation.

He was quite right. A manufacturer saw his design and offered him $10,000 for the patent. That was a lot of money in those days, but Tom turned it down. If his patent was worth ten thousand, it was worth a million. The manufacturer didn't agree. At this stage, John Roberts would have dickered for something like $15,000 and a small percentage of the profits, and eventually done very nicely out of the deal. Tom was adamant, and got nothing. One has to wonder which he really wanted, the money or the dream. By the time Tom's patent came up for renewal, Joe Moffatt was dead and the inventor dead broke. Unrenewed, the patent went up for grabs, and the rotary bobbin became standard throughout the sewing industry. Mary kept her father's hand-carved prototype bobbin to remind herself of how idly rich she and Olive might have become had Tom Roberts only known how to close a deal.

CHAPTER 6

Where the Brook and River Meet

Despite the decline in the family fortunes, life at the new house was still not all doom and gloom. Cornelia was no Sade—she shook off her illness and got back to work, shifting Mary's belongings in with Olive's, renting out the bedroom that Mary had enjoyed for a scant year to two young men who came and went on silent feet, helping to keep the wolf from getting too close to the door. Cornelia also began to take in sewing, though she was less open about doing so than her mother-in-law had been.

She was still determined to keep up appearances. The doorstep must be scrubbed, the windows washed, the silver knives and forks must be warmed in the oven before the Sunday roast was served even though there was no longer a maid to wash and clean and wait on table. Mary's piano lessons had gone by the board; she was spending her after-school hours helping Cornelia with the chores and wondering what would became of her once she'd taken her small part in the graduation rites that were swiftly approaching.

Mary was popular in high school. She worked on the school

paper, she played the assembly-room piano for the hymns that were an invariable start to the school day. Sometimes she got invited to parties. Allegheny was an affluent community, and even young people's at-home dances were taken seriously as social events, with real dance programs, favors, elegant refreshments, a hired musician at the piano and another playing the violin. White cotton crash tacked over the double parlor carpets provided a smooth surface for boys and girls to glide over, trying to remember what they'd learned in dancing class, while the chaperons looked on with benign but vigilant eyes. Mary was always as well dressed as any, Cornelia saw to that, but no party would be given for her at the Roberts house. So darling Aunt Tillie gave one instead, dance cards, favors, musicians, and all. Mary never forgot Tillie's kindness, for this was the only party she'd ever had.

Mary was sixteen now, and the boys were noticing, and not just boys, either. She set the whole school buzzing one day when the new Latin teacher, a good-looking young bachelor who was studying to be a lawyer, took her out to lunch. Perhaps Jimmy Morrow put a *pulex* in the teacher's ear, for he didn't ask her again, but that didn't matter. Next in line was a blue-eyed, blond-haired boy to whom Mary became secretly engaged. They kissed once or twice in a chaste and respectful manner. He gave her a ring set with her birthstone, a sardonyx, the ugliest stone there was. She wore the token around her neck under her blouse for a few weeks, then handed it back. The rejected lover sulked for a while, but there were other pretty girls in Allegheny and young males' hearts can be turned as easily as their heads. Mary was sorry to have upset her blue-eyed swain, but she had more pressing matters on her mind.

All through high school, even during the worst of the family upheavals, Mary had been operating on the premise that, one way or another, she would be able to attend college. During her senior year she'd been getting special tutoring from a friend of her father's named Mitchell. She had a firm goal in mind: She wanted to become a doctor.

This must have seemed crazy in a period when the medical

field was considered an all-male enclave, especially by the males. Mary, however, had precedent on her side. Not long after her family had moved to their first real home, a small brass plate had appeared one day on a house down the street. It read C. JANE VINCENT, M.D.

This was the first time anyone in the neighborhood had so much as heard of a woman doctor, much less found one living next door. For a while, nobody went near Dr. Vincent. Then patients began drifting in, mostly parents bringing children. Having a woman treat a young child seemed less bizarre than letting her work on adults. Dr. Vincent was neither young nor beautiful, and her manner was somewhat forbidding, as well it might have been considering the battles she must have had to fight; but she'd caught Mary's imagination.

Doctors were persons of consequence. Allegheny housewives would get out of a sickbed to scrub the doorstep and put on a clean nightgown rather than be shamed when the doctor arrived. Doctors had buggies to drive and mysterious satchels to carry, they knew how to take your pulse and make you say, "Ah." It may also have occurred to Mary that they were healers of the sick. In any event, she had clung steadfastly to her childhood decision. Now here she was, ready to start but not knowing where to go.

Mary knew better than to expect any financial aid from her father and mother. They had all they could do in those tough times just to pay their butcher's bill. Uncle John wouldn't be able to help because the panic of 1893 was affecting his struggle to recoup from the warehouse fire. Even if she'd had the money she wouldn't have known where to apply. Most medical schools wouldn't even let a woman through their doors, and they certainly wouldn't admit a girl under eighteen. But Mary couldn't sit around the house spinning vain hopes for the next two years, and she was certainly not about to take in sewing.

During Cornelia's illness, the family doctor had remarked that Mary was a good little nurse. Mary knew that the Pittsburgh Homeopathic Hospital had recently established one of the few schools of nursing in the whole United States. A nickel for the streetcar would take her there. Training as a nurse might be a step toward becoming a doctor. At least it wouldn't hurt to go and ask.

When Mary broached the notion to her mother, Cornelia threw a fit. Girls of good family did not become nurses. Waiting on the sick was almost worse than being a domestic servant. Was this what an underappreciated mother had worked and scraped and hoped and prayed and made all those pretty dresses for?

Mary had never been the most docile of daughters. She argued back. Arguing was not Cornelia's forte. She had no gift of words like her daughter. She went into one of her silent sulks.

Mary could handle a sulk. She let down a tuck in her new flowered dimity, pinned up her hair for the first time in her life, sneaked a dusting of her mother's face powder, donned her white summer bonnet with the rose on the side, picked up her ruffled parasol, and tripped off to get a second opinion.

Her old friend the family doctor was not in his office. He'd gone off for the summer and left someone else in charge. This doctor was a much younger man, even younger than Mary took him to be. His gold pince-nez had lenses of plain glass; its sole function, had Mary but known, was to make him look more grown up. Ditto the small mustache, black like his hair and his eyes. His complexion was dark, and dark was the look he bent upon this sweet young thing in her ruffles and roses once she'd told him what she'd come for.

So Miss Roberts thought nursing was romantic, did she? She pictured it as nothing tougher than smoothing pillows and stroking fevered foreheads, did she not?

No, she did not, Mary averred stoutly. She'd had nursing experience, she knew what tending a sickbed was like. She was not afraid of hard work, she could do whatever needed to be done. What was an inexperienced young doctor do with so intransigent a young lady?

This one reacted much as Mary's Latin teacher had done. Perhaps it was her zeal for learning that caught his fancy, more likely it was the rose on her hat and the winsome face under the brim. Since she was so stubborn, he'd take her around the hospital where, he confessed, he'd only just finished his internship, and give her a taste of what nursing was really like. He knew every rathole in the place, he added by way of reassurance. He set an appointment for the following day and finally got around to telling her his name. He was Dr. Rinehart, Stanley Marshall Rinehart. Rather a euphonious name, Mary thought. Her dream was beginning to show a slight, very slight, sign of becoming a reality. Partly thrilled, partly scared, she picked up her parasol and went home to supper.

While they were washing the dishes together, Mary told her mother what she'd done that afternoon. Cornelia broke down and cried. Gone were her dreams, her hopes, her plans, all vanished like soap bubbles from the dishpan. Mary tried to show a proper degree of sympathy, but she kept her appointment with Dr. Rinehart.

The hospital seemed an alien place, dreary and mysterious; Mary was disconcerted by queer smells and strange, echoing sounds. In *My Story*, she described even the nurses as figures of mystery, moving so briskly and so quietly in their crisp uniforms and odd little caps. An ambulance arrived, a stretcher was carried in. On it lay something covered in a gray blanket. Was this a real person? Was it alive? Was it dead? No matter, it was awesome. It was intriguing. It was something she wanted to be part of.

At this time, Mary had no concept of a nursing career as a commitment to human service. That would come later. For the moment, she was seeing the hospital as an adventure, a new experience, a means of solving her present dilemma about getting on with her life. She asked Dr. Rinehart where she could apply as a student nurse, and he showed her.

Miss Marguerite Wright, superintendent of nurses, was a figure of majesty. Mary described the great lady as she was to see her so many times in the exhausting days to come: her white hair dressed high in the pompadour style that was then just coming into fashion, her black taffeta dress rustling along the ward floors as she made her morning rounds with her always-present assistant trotting dutifully behind her. She must have had a closetful of those dresses, always the same, always in perfect order. The new probationer would learn to quail at the mere swish of a taffeta skirt.

Today, however, sitting behind the desk in her private office, Miss Wright was all affability. She did cast a dubious eye at the ruffled parasol and that skittish little rose on Mary's hat.

"Miss Roberts," she asked, "how old are you?"

Good question. Mary paused to reflect. Well, it was almost July and she was going to be seventeen in August, so why be nitpicky? "Seventeen," she replied.

"And when is your next birthday?"

"August twelfth," said Mary, thereby docking a year out of her life, as far as the hospital records were concerned. When she entered the hospital as a probationer six days after that equivocal birthday, her age went down on the books as eighteen.

Student nurses were not supposed to wear uniforms until after they had got safely through their three-month probation period. Mary was told to bring whatever simple, washable dresses she had, with some aprons to wear over them. Cornelia, resigned by now to the ruinous course that her wayward daughter had set for herself, whipped up a couple of dark blue cotton frocks, gathered very full in front to create the illusion of a grown-up bosom. She cut out a number of aprons from the finest handkerchief linen and sewed them all by hand. If Mary was determined to take the downward path, at least she'd be properly dressed for the descent.

Late on the afternoon of August 18, 1893, Tom Roberts escorted his elder daughter to the gloomy, dark red brick building where she was committed to staying for the next two years, provided she survived her probation. Whatever might have been in the father's mind, he didn't confide it to Mary. He just handed her bagful of hand-sewn aprons to the doorman and went away.

The doorman was affable enough, but he had his own job to do. He showed Mary into a waiting room, set her bag on the floor beside her, and left her alone. She'd put on a rosebud-patterned blue foulard silk dress and a broad blue hat to boost her morale for the occasion. It felt odd to be sitting here by herself, dressed like a fashion plate, smelling the iodoform that hung so heavily in the air. Why didn't somebody come? All at once a wave of terror swept over her, her hands began to shake. Mary was to wonder later why she hadn't thought to pick up her bag and flee.

A millennium or two later, or so it seemed to the quaking neophyte, the assistant supervisor came in. This was a brisk little woman wearing the skirt of her immaculate uniform an inch or two off the floor to reveal tiny shoes with ridiculously high heels. Mary would learn to resent those heels. How could this ancient crone of thirty or more click along so briskly hour after hour, day after day, when Mary's own young feet were always so sore and swollen? Sometime later, the assistant would move to the Philippines and marry an army officer. On this fateful occasion, she merely showed the new girl to a tiny, high-ceilinged bedroom and left her there to settle in.

The room held a narrow iron bed, a bureau, a small table, a rocking chair, and a straight chair. Its small closet contained a laundry bag. The single window looked down on a paved court-yard that was bounded on three sides by the hospital wings. On the open side, at one corner, was the stable that housed the ambulance and the horses that drew it. Mary would get used to hearing the furious clang of the bell and the pounding of the horses' hooves at any time of the night or day—they were the bane of every off-duty nurse trying to get some sleep.

Suppertime turned out to be outrageously early, five o'clock for the first seating, five-thirty for the second. Dawdling was not encouraged. Mary ate a meal that must have been a letdown after a lifetime of Cornelia Roberts's cuisine and went back to her room because she didn't know what else to do.

Pittsburgh can be scorching in August, and Mary had left her door open for a breath of air. At seven o'clock, she began to see the night-shift nurses passing by on their way to the wards. Rubber heels had yet to be invented, so some had the heels of their shoes tied up in bandages to silence their tread. All of them looked dragged out. They could not have got much sleep on a hot summer day with the windows open and traffic noises ricocheting up off the pavement. These nurses would be on duty for the next twelve hours with a short relief for a midnight supper, provided they could grab enough time to eat it.

At a quarter past seven, Mary heard new sounds welling up from the nurses' parlor on the floor below. This, she would learn, was evening prayer. Nobody had explained that she was expected to attend regularly. When she dutifully showed up the next evening, she was startled to see the other nurses kneeling in front of their chairs. As a Presbyterian, she'd always stood up to pray; now here she was in a hotbed of Episcopalians. What would Grandmother Roberts say, had she but known that her granddaughter was kneeling in public?

This first night, after the sound of hymn singing had died, Mary heard a firm step in the corridor and a brisk voice demanding to see the new probationer. It was Her Majesty the superintendent, head high, shoulders back, black taffeta train swirling about her feet. Mary found out later from the other nurses that Miss Wright had come from a fine family and been among the first graduates from the training school at Bellevue Hospital in New York.

Mary also learned that Miss Wright was an absolute autocrat. She made her rounds of the hospital twice a day, always with her high-heeled acolyte clicking along behind, then she went back to her office and issued her orders, which had better not be disobeyed or slackly followed up. When Miss Wright was not on the floor, the assistant served as her eyes, ears, and mouth; another lesson Mary soon absorbed was to watch her step when the assistant was around.

Tonight, Miss Wright had been downstairs reading the evening prayers and was about to check the diet slips for the following day with the nurses in charge. Her visit to Mary didn't last long. She just wanted Miss Roberts to know that she would have two hours off each day, not counting sleep time, and a half-day once a week. The following morning at seven o'clock, she would report to Ward E.

Mary didn't get much sleep that night. The bed was harder and narrower than she was used to. At one point, the patrol wagon drove into the yard, clanging frantically. She'd drop off for a while, then start up in a panic, light the gas, and look at her watch to make sure she hadn't overslept. The watch was really her mother's, a nice gold one that must have been bought in a more affluent time. It had a second hand that the new probationer would be needing to count pulses, if she ever got the chance.

All Mary's worry about oversleeping had been a waste of time. At six o'clock in the morning the night watchman, a little old Welshman named Davis Davis, came pounding on doors, shouting out the time. He'd been on duty all night long, working his slow elevator up and down, ferrying the emergency cases and the tired doctors who would have to cope with them. Once Davis had got the day shift stirring, he could eat his breakfast and go to bed. Mary put on one of her new cotton dresses and tied over it a gauzy apron that would soon meet a sad fate in the hospital laundry. She ate what little she could choke down of a hurried breakfast and crept to the door of Ward E. She gazed timidly at the patients, and they gazed dully back at her.

She'd been assigned to the women's typhoid ward. That was a slight relief. After Olive's long illness, Mary did know something about typhoid. This was the season for it, when rivers that had flooded in the spring were running low under the blazing suns of a hot summer, concentrating their pollutants to peak performance. Nobody was blaming the rivers, of course. Even Miss Wright and the doctors still considered typhoid fever an act of Providence.

Mary counted fifteen tall iron beds, each with a little stand beside it, each with a card hooked to its bottom rail telling the patient's name, sex, age, occupation, religion, and next of kin. There was one splash of color in the middle of the room, a round table with a red cloth on it. Wherever they could be fitted in, small cots had been set up to hold those patients for whom there were no other beds; every one of them was occupied.

The sight was almost overwhelming: twenty-odd sick patients, some of them even more skeletal than Olive had been by the end of her ordeal, some raving with fever, some, mercifully, showing signs of recovery. Each patient had to be bathed every day, some of them every few hours. Beds had to be kept spotless, long hair combed and braided, mouths cleaned of fever sores, temperatures taken, medicines and nourishment given, all this by only two nurses and one badly frightened probationer.

As it turned out, Mary didn't even get to braid a pigtail.

Novices like her were assigned the most menial jobs, including tasks that even the night soil man of her early youth would have gagged at. She wept sometimes, but she kept on working. At the end of her ten-hour stretch, the head nurse patted her arm and told her she'd done well.

That evening Mary knelt among the nurses. Their aprons were stained, their caps askew, their faces pale with fatigue. She was one of them now, she was committed. She would work as hard as they did, and she would be as good as the best.

CHAPTER 7

Nurse Roberts Wins Her Cap—and Sets It

That first day on the wards might have been made a little tougher for the new probationer than it needed to be. Mary didn't yet realize that she'd entered the hospital under an even greater handicap than her lack of years and experience. Her reconnaissance visit had not gone unnoticed. Her airy summer frock, her chic chapeau, her flirty parasol, and the fact that she'd been squired around the wards by none other than S.M., younger half-brother of the Olympian C. C. Rinehart who was the hospital's head, had stamped her as a society girl come to patronize the hoi polloi. Cornelia's gold watch and those hand-embroidered linen aprons had clinched the mistaken impression.

However, the delicate aprons did not long survive the hospital laundry, and Mary worked hard enough to convince the rest that she was not just a debutante looking for a new thrill. She was efficient at changing the sputum cups, carrying out the soiled linen, sweeping the floors and washing the coal dust off the windowsills. She did run into trouble the first time she attempted to slide a bedpan under a patient, but the woman was fortunately conscious enough to explain that Mary was doing it the wrong way around. Soon she would be promoted to combing the nits and lice out of patients' heads, a much-needed task in those days when any woman lacking a mane of long hair was likely to be either a fever victim or a prostitute.

Late in the afternoon of Mary's second day on the wards, Miss Wright had a new thrill ready for her. Miss Roberts and another probationer whom she hadn't met before were assigned to clean the operating room. The other girl's greeting to Mary was "I hope I don't get sick."

The operating room was actually an amphitheater on the top floor, with seats in a semicircle above a tiled well that contained the operating table, glass-topped instrument tables, and glass-fronted white cabinets to contain the instruments when they were not in use. Clearly the trend toward modernization was beginning here; although the wards were still lighted with gas, the operating room was illuminated by a big electric dome light over the table. Though some of the older surgeons still considered the new fad for antisepsis a bundle of horsefeathers, everything was kept scrupulously clean.

There were sterilizers for the instruments, towels, and dressings. The younger surgeons wore white coats over their clothes, they scrubbed their hands for a long time and douched them in antiseptic before approaching the operating table. They even talked hopefully of rubber gloves and face masks. An older surgeon might forget to put on his white coat, wash his hands casually if at all, not unload his cud of chewing tobacco in one of the pails beside the table until just before he started to operate, not even bother to tie a strip of gauze around his bushy beard before he picked up his scalpel and leaned over the patient. Strangely enough, a fair number of his victims would survive regardless.

The Pittsburgh Homeopathic did many amputations, most of these resulting from accidents at the steel mill or from the railroads and cable cars. Anesthesia was by this time common practice, and chloroform saved lives by reducing the pain and shock of the operation. Once the limbs were off, the stumps were sprinkled with iodoform. What seems to have bothered Mary most was not the blood or the sound of bones being sawed, but the all-pervading smell of antiseptic that got into her clothes and hair and never went away.

However skillful the surgery, operating was a messy business. It was done then by the now long-obsolete wet method. Glass bottles filled with antiseptic solution hung above the table with rubber tubes descending from them to irrigate the wound and keep washing away the gore so that the surgeon could see what he was doing. To clamp off a blood vessel, he must watch to find out just where the blood was spurting from. Heavy black rubber sheets were spread to catch the assorted liquids and direct them into pails set on the floor beside the table.

By the end of the day the operating room looked like an abattoir. On that first day, Mary was told to carry out a bucket. She didn't notice at first that there was a human foot in it. She disposed of the foot and went back, then she and her sister probationer started washing blood off those rubber sheets with a strong carbolic acid solution. The other girl became queasy and had to stand by the open window. She claimed it was the chloroform that upset her. Mary kept on washing.

She survived her three-month probation. By now she'd got the feel of the hospital, she'd become accustomed to the arduous routine, she was ready to stay the course. From here on, however, there seems to have been no further thought about going to medical school. Perhaps it was glory enough to realize that she, Mary Ella Roberts, student nurse, was now on an equal footing with all but one of her coworkers.

It is something of a stunner to realize that in this well-equipped, well-managed city hospital, Miss Wright and the assistant supervisor were the only two bona fide registered nurses. Out of the thirty on the wards, twenty-nine were still enrolled in the recently instituted training program. Their graduation would raise the number of fully accredited nurses in the entire United States of America to 500.

Thus Mary Roberts, the youngest in her class, was in the

vanguard of a movement that had already begun to change the entire concept of medical patient care. She probably wasn't thinking much about that, her main concern would have been how to budget her new salary. No charge was made for tuition and lessons were given in the evenings, after the student had put in her ten hours on the wards.

As a probationer, Mary had received only her room and board. Having been officially accepted as a student nurse, she was entitled to a monthly wage of eight dollars. Out of this, Nurse Roberts must furnish herself with official blue-and-white-striped hospital uniforms, white Eton collars, some of the white lawn neckties worn by both nurses and doctors, and heavy, wide-belted white aprons. By now she recognized the need to get sturdy material that would stand up to the ferocious hospital launderings. She must own a thermometer in a case, a pair of curved bandage scissors, and dressing forceps, as well as a little black chatelaine bag in which to hang these instruments from her apron belt. Smack on top of her head she must wear a cap the size of a muffin, made of stiff tulle that had to be pleated just so into a band. These caps were a dreadful nuisance to make, so Mary gladly paid one of the more experienced nurses fifteen cents to do the job for her.

It was the rule for first-year students to gain experience by working successively in every part of the hospital, alternating day and night duty. Nurse Roberts was also now eligible to be called to the operating room at any time; she learned to keep her clothes laid out, ready to be donned in a hurry if the night watchman came thumping at the door. In time, she became a junior ward nurse, with a new probationer under her who cried a lot. During night duty, she might be in charge of two or even three wards all by herself, with the gas jets turned down to eerie blue points. Should an emergency arise, she must handle it as best she could. One night on the obstetric ward, Mary couldn't get hold of an intern in time to deliver a baby so she delivered it all by herself, and managed just fine.

There were lots of babies, some of them legitimate, some

not. They all got the same care, as did their mothers. The hospital at that time was in the red-light district, so many of the female patients were prostitutes, inmates of the nearby bawdy houses. Most were ignorant and none too clean. A few had come from higher walks of life; one had taken morphine in a suicide attempt and had to be walked up and down for hours on end to save her life. Some had been slashed with knives or razors in jealous drunken brawls, more often they were being treated for venereal diseases. During her second year on the wards, Mary developed a coppery rash and feared the worst, but it turned out not to be syphilis. Whatever it was, it went away and Mary kept on working.

One cold winter night a policeman came in crying, carrying in his arms a little newsboy terribly burned from a fire he'd lit trying to get warm. Another boy had lost his hand in a printing press, he begged Mary to save it. Still another had fallen under a train and had his whole arm and shoulder sliced off. He came out of the anesthetic singing "After the Ball Is Over" again and again and again. An old woman insisted on giving the young nurse a quarter for being so kind. Mary went out on her break and spent the quarter on oranges for her patient—oranges were one of the things the old lady was allowed on her diet. A man was brought in who'd been through a flywheel. Every bone in his body was broken, he seemed to be made of jelly. There was nothing the staff could do but give him opiates and hope for his sake that the end would come soon.

Mary was in charge of the emergency ward the night six policemen carried in a man who had killed his wife with an ax, then cut his own throat so deeply that he was drawing what breath he could get through an exposed larynx. She wondered why they couldn't just let him die.

"You'll have to save him to be hanged," said the policeman.

Once his neck was healed, the noose went around it and justice was served.

Being a nurse was somewhat like being a Mother Confessor. Mary became accustomed to having patients grab her by the arm

and pour out their troubles: tales of unfaithful husbands, of un-
grateful children, of villainies and depravities beyond anything
she could ever have dreamed. Despite the attempts of kind lady
visitors to steer them on to the paths of righteousness, every single
one of the prostitutes was planning to go back to her old job as
soon as she got well. A few even tried to persuade Mary to go
with them. She found herself having to be extremely selective in
choosing topics for conversation when she went back to visit her
family.

Even though the Robertses lived only a thirty-minute trolley
ride away from the hospital and Mary got her half-day every
week, visits home didn't happen often. Inevitably, the gulf was
widening. Olive was entering her teens, totally involved with her
school and her friends. Tom was seldom around, Cornelia didn't
even want to hear the word *hospital*. Mary tried to enter into the
family gossip, but her mind kept drifting back to the new world
of which she was now a part. The others sensed this and resented
it. She wasn't their little Mamie any longer, she'd broken out of
the pattern.

And she was too tired to care. Better to spend her free time
right here at the hospital, catching up on a little of the sleep
she'd lost during the past week, studying for her examinations or
darning her stockings while she soaked her swollen feet. She saw
her old friends' names in the papers. They were going away to
school or college, staying home and giving parties. Once Mary
was invited, and went. She danced till three o'clock in the morning, got back to the hospital at four, was immediately tagged for
an emergency in the operating room, and went from there to
her regular daytime duty. Thirty-six hours without rest or sleep
convinced Nurse Roberts that the old life was indeed a thing of
the past.

Mary lost her childhood habit of spinning romantic fantasies.
She no longer had that recurrent dream of walking down the aisle
all by herself in a magnificent wedding gown, with every eye on
her and no bridegroom to clutter up the scenario. From now on,
such dream castles as Mary might build would have full basements

and modern plumbing. She was maturing, and she had come to realize that the real sins are those not of the flesh but of the spirit, that she was somehow akin to everyone whose life touched hers in any way. Henceforth, she would never be able to hate anybody.

Despite the long shifts, the indifferent hospital food, her perennially sore feet, and her inability to sleep during the day while she was on night duty, Mary was managing well enough. There were only two things that really got to her. One was having the night watchman rouse her out of a sound sleep in the middle of the night to assist at an emergency in the operating room. The other was having to lay out a body.

No matter at what hour of the day or night a patient died, the nurse who'd been on the case was expected to perform that final service. It meant going to the mortuary, a small room at the top of the building that could be reached only by the elevator and a short flight of stairs. In keeping with the Victorian emphasis on showing respect for the dead, the room had stained-glass windows. It held little else except a table in the center where the body would have been carried by male attendants and left for the nurse to cope with.

This was not the ideal job for a young woman still in her teens, but Mary got stuck with it just like the rest. Usually the nurse in charge would be allowed a helper. The two women would try to make sure they had everything they needed with them, otherwise one would have to go off after the missing item, leaving her partner in that isolated mortuary with a stiffening corpse and a severe case of cold feet.

The laying-out process consisted of washing the body, plugging all the orifices with wads of cotton, tying up the jaw with a strip of bandage, veiling the naked cadaver in a cheap cotton hospital shroud, and raising the head enough to keep the blood from congesting the face. From then on, it was up to the undertaker. A nurse had no time to waste in grieving for a dead patient—there were too many live ones needing her back on the wards.

Emergency duty at night was less spooky but potentially more harrowing. There was, to begin with, the agony of getting up, dressing in a rush, and hurrying to the operating room. No matter what the hour, Miss Wright would be there first, calm and in control as always. She would know which of the staff surgeons was operating and exactly what he would want in the way of solutions, catgut, needles, and other small particulars. Nurses would be flying around following her orders, filling the irrigators, getting the sterilizers working, adjusting the black rubber sheets and the buckets. The surgical intern would be laying out the instruments, the anesthetist would be hovering in the anteroom next to the blanket-covered cause of all the bustle. One or two outsiders would be hovering too, like as not. These would be the friends who'd brought in the patient, embarrassed and nervous about what might be going to happen.

Sometimes, after everything had been got ready at top speed, the whole crew would have to stand around until the surgeon could get to the hospital, maybe by streetcar, maybe driving his own buggy at top speed, rattling into the courtyard with his horse in a foam. As a staff member, the doctor would collect no overtime for the job ahead of him. Nobody would call him a hero except possibly those few in the operating room who'd witnessed what skill, what strength, what courage he might have displayed in carrying out some remarkable feat of surgery.

One night when Mary reported for duty she found that Dr. Stanley Marshall Rinehart would be operating. During her probation, she'd barely laid eyes on the man who was responsible for her being on the staff, but she'd had many an earful about him from the older nurses. S.M. was a good surgeon, everyone granted him that, but he was a hellion to work for. If the least little thing was not exactly the way he wanted it, he'd blow the roof off. Mary was in a swivet lest she trigger any fireworks, but she managed not to make a mistake and S.M. was so engrossed in his work that he didn't even notice she was there.

Later, during a daytime operation, Mary got a firsthand experience of the Rinehart temper. Another nurse had bungled the sponge count. This time S.M. had every right to wax wroth. Not keeping an accurate count of those sterile gauze pads used to clean the cavity during an operation opened the dread possibility that one might get left inside when the incision was sewn up. S.M.'s virtuoso performance that day sent the peccant nurse out of the operating room in a state of hysteria. Mary's trusty subconscious took careful note of the incident for future reference.

CHAPTER 8

Love Among the Ruins

Mary did have some notion of trying to put her hospital experiences on paper. A few times, after going off duty, she went back to her room, picked up a pencil, and wrote a sentence or two; but the subject was so overwhelmingly complex and she was always so desperately tired. Being shifted around from ward to ward, from day duty to night and back again, made it impossible to get into a manageable routine. One of the biggest disruptions occurred when smallpox broke out in the men's surgical ward while she was on duty there.

The hospital had to be quarantined, and only those suffering from smallpox would remain. Any other patient well enough to travel was sent home, any sick one who could be moved was taken to the municipal hospital. Most of the Homeopathic's nurses went along with them, but Nurse Roberts got turned down for transfer as being too young. Instead, she got locked in with a few other staff members and the smallpox patients.

Since smallpox was terribly catching and often deadly, this lock-in was serious business. Policemen were set outside to guard the doors. Nobody could go anywhere except to the courtyard or the roof for an occasional badly needed breath of fresh air. The empty wards must all be fumigated. The nurses got stuck with that job. The procedure involved sealing every window with strips of paper soaked in flour-and-water paste, piling a small cairn of bricks in the middle of the ward, setting a large pan of formaldehyde in the middle, dumping in a red-hot brick, and running like mad for the door.

Even with the doors closed, the acrid fumes leaked into the corridors. Everybody developed a nasty cough, nobody showed much interest in food although the kitchen staff stayed bravely on the job. As far as the smallpox itself was concerned, the medical staff didn't worry much. They'd all been vaccinated. This smallpox was not the confluent type, and the cases still on the wards were mild ones. Their biggest enemy was boredom.

Used to being worked off their feet ten or twelve hours a day, nurses and orderlies didn't know what to do with all this enforced leisure. Their problems were not so much with the sick men as with the convalescents. The better they got, the worse they resented being kept in quarantine. They threatened to mutiny and march out of the hospital in their nightshirts, even if it was December. The men squabbled among themselves, they started a miniature riot or two. One day they relieved the monotony by smashing up the furniture.

Despite the quarantine, some of the staff doctors were allowed to come in. It was during this period that Mary really began to know Stanley Rinehart. In order to relieve some of the tension, the staff tried hard to arrange various diversions for the patients. At Christmas, somebody smuggled in a tree. Each patient got an orange and a pair of socks. They were taken to the hospital chapel. Mary played the piano and S.M. led the carol singing. She discovered that he had a splendid baritone voice. Refreshments were served, and the two musicians got to talking. S.M. told Mary that he'd been in the glee club at Adrian College before he'd gone on to study medicine at Hahnemann. She was duly impressed.

At long last the quarantine was lifted, the formaldehyde smell was replaced by the somewhat less repellent odor of iodoform, the wards filled up again. Mary was reassigned, this time to the pediatric ward. S.M. had some patients there, and Mary marveled at the way he'd march into the ward, cast a stern look around through his pince-nez, be suddenly engulfed by a flock of adoring children, and settle down to play with them.

How could a grown man get so much fun out of a bunch of sick youngsters? To Nurse Roberts, they were just small, wiggly objects that had to be washed, fed, medicated, and toileted. She was still too young herself to feel much empathy toward sick children. She was too tired to play. She was fed up with the hospital, bored with herself. What had happened to her brave aspirations toward higher education? When had she last picked up a book for pure pleasure? How could she dig herself out of this rut?

Just why a girl of Scotch-Irish extraction suddenly elected to study German is open to conjecture. Considering how high a percentage of the hospital's patients were of German origin, how many still spoke the language of their forebears, Nurse Roberts's interest seemed reasonable enough. Rinehart was a German name, and Mary had learned that S.M. wasn't the ogre some people thought he was. Maybe it wouldn't hurt to ask his advice.

It did not hurt a bit. S.M. thought Nurse Roberts's idea was just great. The following day he brought a little German book to the ward and suggested that the aspiring student might care to drop in at his office on her next afternoon off so that he could help her practice pronouncing her umlauts.

For a doctor at the Pittsburgh Homeopathic to display anything other than a professional interest in a nurse was verboten in any language. Furthermore, Stanley Rinehart was just starting his private practice. He had no time for dalliance, much less was he in any financial shape to take on the responsibility of a very young wife. But umlauts involved a good deal of lip-puckering and it did seem a pity to waste all that effort on a few paltry vowels with dots on top.

Mary made little headway with her German, but she did develop a knack for articulating umlauts. One pucker led to another, the balmy spring weather led to clandestine buggy rides, that old covered bridge over the river might have been built for lovers. It was only a matter of time before Dr. Rinehart stopped his horse halfway across and popped the question.

What was a dutiful student nurse to say? In the merry month of May, Nurse Roberts was engaged. Secretly, of course—once again she was wearing a ring on a ribbon around her neck. This time the stone was not an ugly sardonyx, this time the ring would not be given back.

As for keeping their troth a secret, Mary and Stanley hadn't a prayer. The other nurses, the orderlies, the doorman, the night watchman, the hospital officers, even the patients on the wards and possibly the babies in the nursery had all been taking a keen interest in the burgeoning romance. Mary and S.M. were under constant surveillance. One night the chief engineer from the boiler room sighted the lovebirds together at a restaurant and the cat was out of the bag. There was only one thing to do, and S.M. did it. He stomped into C.C.'s office and announced in stentorian tone that he intended to take Nurse Roberts out for a drive.

He might as well have requested permission to burn down the hospital. Dr. Rinehart was hauled before the entire board of directors, but they didn't scare him a whit. Upstairs, hanging over the banister, Mary could hear her feisty swain informing the board and probably the whole hospital that he intended to marry Nurse Roberts and was about to give her an airing in his buggy, come hell or high water.

Thoroughly cowed, the board saved face as best they could. The engagement was not to be announced until Nurse Roberts had finished her course. She must not wear her ring, she must conduct herself at all times with utmost propriety. They knew better than to try laying any caveats on young Dr. Rinehart; they dispersed in thoughtful silence. Mary crept downstairs with shaky knees and got into the buggy.

Whether or not she was as much in love with this human juggernaut as he was with her, Mary honestly did not know. She was elated because a member of the hospital staff had bestowed the honor of his affections upon her. This was romance straight out of a storybook. Here was the handsome young prince, whipping the glass slipper out of his pocket and sliding it on her throbbing little foot. But real love, the lifetime kind, what did Mary Ella Roberts know about that? Where was the surge of ecstasy she'd read about in novels? Why wasn't her heart singing like the lark ascending, the way a heroine's heart was supposed to?

The advice she was getting from some of the other nurses didn't help much. They told her she'd be crazy to tie herself to that human tornado. She was too young, too pretty, she could do better. (And besides, S.M. was the only bachelor on the staff, and they'd seen him first.)

Nevertheless, Mary went on keeping an ear cocked for the unmistakable sound of her sweetheart's tread on the bare wooden floors of the hallways. She saw that S.M.'s famous tantrums were reserved for incompetent staff, for interfering bureaucrats who tried to keep him from the woman of his choice, and most often for inanimate objects that conspired against him, as objects so often do to persons who run on short fuses.

Stanley Rinehart was never other than gentle with Mary. The better she came to know him, the more she was able to recognize the true quality of this man to whom she had pledged herself: his blazing integrity, his swift intelligence, his fund of knowledge, so much greater than hers. She'd already found out, of course, what fun he could be on a buggy ride even when he wasn't joking. One day as they were jogging along, Stanley reined in his horse and reached into his pocket.

"I've found a poem that I thought you might like." He pulled out a slim little volume, opened it, closed it, and stuck it back in his pocket.

Mary wanted to know why he hadn't read the poem. Stanley didn't want to tell her, and at last she fished the book out of his pocket. The title was "The Therapeutics of Diarrhoea." The world of the inanimate had struck again. She laughed so hard her ribs hurt.

By this time, Mary was needing all the laughs she could get. During their second year of training, it was the hospital's practice to send student nurses out on private cases. For home nursing, the hospital charged a set fee of ten dollars a week. This was paid either by the patient's family or by some local charitable organization, depending on the circumstances. The nurse didn't get a cent beyond her usual monthly stipend.

The hospital's rationale was that this one-on-one care would fit the nurse for private duty. For Mary it was sheer misery with no redeeming features whatsoever. None of the cases to which she was assigned could have prepared her for anything except a series of spectacular nightmares.

In those days, only the very rich would hire a live-in nurse if the case wasn't actually desperate. Most families waited until their loved ones were so far gone that Aesculapius himself couldn't have done them any good. Mary's first patient was a woman whose horses had bolted, throwing her in front of a cable car and severing both her legs. She was already dead when Mary got to the house. There was nothing for the nurse to do but sit with the body until morning, when the doctor came to sign the death certificate and the undertaker to take the poor mutilated body away.

Her next was a ten-year-old child. Mary stayed on duty for thirty-six hours without a break. Nobody came to relieve her, for nurses were supposed to be indefatigable. The young sufferer slipped away quietly during the second night while his exhausted nurse dozed beside the bed.

Third on her list was a rich and extremely prominent old man who entertained the pleasant fantasy that he'd robbed millions of dollars from one of the great steel companies. This patient didn't need a nurse, he needed a keeper. He'd been sent for therapy to a sanitarium in the mountains; his wife had summoned up just enough courage to go along with him but was no earthly good at keeping him under control. Presumably the sanitarium staff couldn't cope either, hence the need for an inexperienced student nurse whose chief qualification was that she did not have the option of refusing the case.

The aged tycoon's favorite diversion was to wait until the electric lights were turned off at night, then light an oil lamp and lean out the window, waving it back and forth, or else stroll down the halls with the lamp in his hand, a walking invitation to a bad fire. Why nobody managed to keep either lamps or matches away from the patient was never mentioned.

Mary didn't get much sleep on that job, either. It was finally decided that the old man's presence was not doing either him or the sanitarium any good. His private railway car was made ready, and he and his reluctant nurse traveled back to Pittsburgh locked inside its drawing room together, he pounding madly on the windows with the handle of his umbrella and screeching the whole way to be let out.

During her hectic tour of duty at the sanitarium, Mary had been further shaken to receive a startling letter from her father. Grandmother Roberts was dead, suddenly and violently. At Aunt Tillie's house, on the previous Sunday morning, she'd tripped over the hem of her long wrapper and plunged headlong down the cellar stairs, landing at the bottom with a broken neck. Tom had written beautifully of the useful life his mother had lived, of her steadfast belief in a heaven where she had surely earned her place. He said nothing about his own lack of faith that such a reward would in fact be forthcoming.

Mary took the news badly. It seemed so unfair that the old lady had been robbed of her life just when things had grown easier for her, when she might still have had some years of quiet enjoyment. But there was no sense in going back to be with the family now—the funeral had already taken place. Mary might as well stay with her patient.

Then came another blow. Only a few days after Mrs. Roberts's death, darling Aunt Tillie's small daughter was run down by a train. The family seemed to be under some awful dark cloud.

The one ray of light was Mary's engagement. She was nineteen by now, she would be graduated in the spring, then she and Stanley Rinehart would be married. In the meantime, she must finish her course. Surely her next case would be less harrowing than the ones before it, surely no further tragedy could strike the Robertses. Mary was wrong on both counts.

Her fourth case, a woman suffering from typhoid, was a situation beyond any horror she could have imagined. Mary arrived at the small, dingy four-room house at night, astonished to find the downstairs front room floor covered with barefoot men, all asleep or drunk or both. She picked her way among the recumbent bodies and went upstairs. The sickroom was crowded with women. Mary had a hard time shooing them out so that she could get to the bed. Her patient was delirious with fever, flailing and raving; Nurse Roberts got no sleep that night. In the morning there was nowhere to eat but a filthy kitchen. She had to drink her coffee from a tin cup and fight a swarm of cockroaches for what food there was to be had.

A younger sister was out on the porch washing fouled bedsheets. Mary wanted to help the wretched girl but the sick woman kept trying to get out of bed. She had to run back upstairs and stay there while her patient raved on and on, through the day and late into the evening. Then suddenly, just at midnight, the woman died. Mary went to notify the husband but he wasn't interested. He went back to sleep on the floor and she followed the procedure she'd been trained to in the hospital mortuary.

She bathed the dead woman and laid her out according to protocol. She tied up the jaw with a bandage and set the body semi-upright on pillows to drain the blood from the congested face. Finally, exhausted by her twenty-four-hour waking nightmare, Nurse Roberts sat down in the rocking chair beside the bed and let herself doze off.

Sometime in the small hours, stiffening with rigor mortis and lying a little too close to the edge, the pathetic corpse pitched off the bed and landed across the rockers of Mary's chair. To be catapulted backward on top of an ice-cold cadaver was a particularly rude awakening.

That Nurse Roberts agreed to accept a fifth assignment says a good deal for her fortitude. This would be Mary's last and, in a bizarre way, her most tragic case. The patient was an elderly woman dying painfully from cancer of the stomach after a lifetime of tragedy. Born into a family so socially prominent that Mary refused to write down the name even in her private memoirs more than half a century later, the patient had borne a child out of wedlock and perversely refused to give it up for adoption. More concerned with their reputations than with their daughter's welfare, the haughty parents had cast off the ex-heiress with a pittance, settling her in a tiny house downriver where she and her nameless brat would not contaminate their rarified atmosphere.

This had happened some thirty years previously. The family were still adamant, their daughter was still an outcast, still existing on the same tiny pension that was by now barely adequate to provide the necessities. Her illegitimate child had been staunch. She'd stayed with her mother, tending her lovingly through this final episode in a drab and pain-ridden life. By now, the younger woman could go on no longer without a respite; the doctor, who seemed to be their only friend, had got in touch with the hospital's nursing service. Again Mary found herself on round-the-clock duty.

As too often happened, the patient had reached a stage where there was little a nurse could do except change the sheets and administer the opiates. The house was cold, the food was meager. Mary broke out in hives. On the third night she was sitting half asleep beside the sickbed when a Western Union messenger rang the doorbell with a telegram for Miss Mary Roberts. Her father was dead, she must go home at once.

Despite her own burden of woe, the dying woman's daughter showed kindness and sympathy. She helped Mary get ready to catch the early morning train. Her aid was not unneeded. Mary was completely bowled over. What could possibly have struck down a robust man, not yet out of his forties, who'd never been sick a day in his life?

Once on the train, she found out. She had bought the morning papers hoping to find some explanation. Sure enough, Tom Roberts had made the news. PITTSBURGH MAN SHOOTS SELF IN BUFFALO HOTEL ROOM.

What was her father doing in Buffalo? She hadn't even known he was there. Coming on top of physical exhaustion and the string of horrors to which she'd recently been subjected, having it broken to her in so outlandish a fashion, this dreadful news was more than Mary could handle. When the conductor came to ask for her ticket, she was crying so hard she could barely see him through her tears.

"My father," she sobbed. "He's dead."

The conductor didn't give a toot of his whistle. He didn't want somebody else's hard luck story, he just wanted this young woman's ticket. She'd bought one, but where had it got to? Mary rummaged frantically in her bag, the conductor simmered. At last she found the errant pasteboard on the floor. The conductor took it and passed on. She was left to grieve alone.

CHAPTER 9

A Funeral and a Wedding

Nobody met Mary at the station. She must have forgotten to wire back what train she'd be taking. Somehow or other she got herself home. Her father was there before her, laid out in an open coffin beside his wife's cherished plush parlor set. Uncle Joe Moffatt was with him, keeping vigil. Shivering with grief and shock, Mary went over to the coffin.

Her trained eye at once picked up a mark on the forehead that the undertaker had tried to cover. Tom Roberts had made a neat job of the shooting. He'd left no message for his family, perhaps he hadn't thought it necessary. The inventions on which he'd counted to make him rich and famous had brought nothing but frustration; his hopes had been dashed, one after another. For some time now, Tom had been drinking too much and too often. Alcohol is a depressant, and it must have been particularly so for a man who had failed at everything he'd tried, whose wife had been reduced to taking in boarders, and whose mother, the strong prop and mainstay of his early years whom he'd repaid by repudiating her most deeply cherished principles, had just met with a violent death.

As a former local merchant and younger brother of the highly respected John Roberts, Tom had been well known in the Pittsburgh area. His tragic end was local news. Reporters besieged the house wanting to know more. Of course they were not let in. Mary finally went out and begged them to go away.

They left, but the family could not escape unwanted publicity. One way or another, the press had managed to get hold of a letter that Tom had been carrying with him, one that Mary herself had written two or three weeks previously. To her horror, it was published in full. She'd told her father that he mustn't worry, that she and Dr. Rinehart would be married soon and would take care of things until the times got better. An editorial comment that Miss Roberts's letter was "a model of penmanship and construction" did nothing to ease the hurt and humiliation. Mary never forgave this tasteless intrusion into the privacy of her family in their sorrow.

The *Pittsburgh Chronicle Telegraph* of November 15, 1895, stated that "Despondency Drove T. B. Roberts to Suicide in Buffalo," and was probably right in that statement. The rest of the obituary reads rather strangely when compared with the facts as Mary gave them. According to the reportage, Tom had been well known for years in local insurance circles, had been in his youth one of the best salesmen in the city, and had been in the dry-goods business (*sic*) for some time. "During the oil excitement" he had allegedly speculated with his usual degree of success and "lost a fortune in one day." More recently he was said to have been involved in building-and-loan associations, and then traveled for the Nux-Phospho Company of Pittsburgh.

He had not been in good health, said the obituary. On the previous day, he had received a letter from the cash-register company notifying him of his dismissal. Thirty-seven cents was all the money found in his pockets. He had shot himself through the heart (this presumably accounted for the bullet wound in his forehead), covering himself with two quilts to muffle the sound of the shot. The body had not been discovered for some time.

The late Mr. Roberts had left a wife and two daughters. A

brother held a high position under the wallpaper trust in Cincinnati. A brother-in-law lived at Edgewood. Sisters evidently didn't count. The family had been visiting friends in the country since Monday and nothing could be learned about funeral arrangements (which in fact were clearly stated on another page of that same paper; it would be held at his late residence, 27 Poplar Street, Allegheny, and interment would be private).

The gun was a surprise to the family. The fact that Tom had owned one suggested that his suicide was no spur-of-the-moment decision. He had left a little insurance; Cornelia had her boarders and her dressmaking for added income; there was always Uncle John to fall back on in a pinch. Olive would be able to finish her schooling and be trained as a teacher. Mary stayed home for a week, helping out as best she could, then went back to work.

Having a job to do is always the most effective therapy at a time of mourning, and Mary found it a relief to be on the wards again. The soap opera that had been entertaining the entire hospital was just about played out by now. The hospital bigwigs were no longer insisting that Nurse Roberts's engagement be kept secret. S.M.'s fiancée was free to wear her ring, enjoy her buggy rides, and get ready for her wedding.

Uncle John offered not only to give the bride away but to pay for the wedding dress. His niece was marrying into an influential family. Her husband-to-be was descended from one of Pittsburgh's earliest settlers. Stanley's father, William Rinehart, had been a cofounder of W. D. Rinehart, a highly successful wholesale tobacco business. William was also a cofounder and director of the Pittsburgh Insurance Company and had even been nominated in 1854 for mayor of Pittsburgh.

William's first wife had borne him ten children. Five of them had lived and prospered. Edward, the eldest, was professor of music for all the Pittsburgh schools. It was he whom Mary would be startled to recognize at the wedding as her former music teacher. Dr. Clarence, second in line, was at least as well known as his illustrious father. Since 1884, C.C., as Mary knew him, had been on the staff of the Pittsburgh Homeopathic Hospital and on the faculty of the nurses' training school. Frank, another brother, was secretary and treasurer of the Standard Underground Cable Company.

Four years after his first wife's death in 1860, William had married a widow, Louise Gillespie Hancock. Stanley, much younger than his half-brothers, was the sole fruit of that union. Being the man he was, Stanley refused to be put off by Tom Roberts's sensational demise. He was determined to get married as soon as Mary finished her course. They set the date for April 21, 1896, four days after her graduation, just two months and nine days before her twentieth birthday.

The Robertses would still be in mourning, but a decent interval would have passed since Tom's funeral. Now, of all times, John Roberts argued, Mary must do the family credit. He gave his niece $100 and sent her to a professional dressmaker. This would be the first gown she'd ever owned that had not been made by her mother, her grandmother, or herself; it was going be a knockout.

Only the richest white satin would do. The impressive train was lined with row upon row of lace ruffles. The veil was of filmy white tulle, gathered into a satin bandeau that was pinned with an aigrette of white ostrich tips, called in the fashionable parlance of the day a bird of paradise. Mary's figure was far too slight to do justice to so much opulence; both the hips and the bosom had to be heavily padded.

Cornelia was sewing up a storm, turning out exquisite lingerie for Mary's trousseau, hemming table linens with all-but-invisible stitches, thanking the Lord that her wayward elder daughter was soon to be redeemed by a respectable marriage. She was pathetically grateful to Stanley Rinehart for rescuing her Mamie from the ignominy of hospital nursing. She rejoiced that hospital regulations forbade married women to keep on with their jobs. Anyway, Mary would have plenty to do keeping house. And she had so very much to learn.

Wedding presents came pouring in: silver, cut glass, gold-bowled coffee spoons, no fewer than seven tippy, impractical onyx-topped occasional tables—all the appurtenances of gracious living for a young couple who'd be lucky to afford a single hired girl at two-fifty a week until Stanley was more firmly established in his practice.

Stanley wanted to take his bride to Bermuda for their honeymoon. Mary didn't like to ask him where Bermuda was, so she sneaked over to the library and looked it up on a map. Six of Stanley's young doctor friends would serve as ushers. He'd have to give them a stag party, and boutonnieres. Olive was elected to be Mary's maid of honor, in her first long skirt. There would be no bridesmaids. This was still a time of mourning, and the Robertses hoped to keep the wedding as small and simple as possible.

That wasn't going to work. Besides Uncle John, Aunt Sade, Aunt Maggie, Aunt Tish, Aunt Tillie and Joe and their burgeoning family, there were assorted Gilleland connections and scads of Rinehart half-brothers, wives, nieces, and nephews, many of these considerably older than their aunt-to-be. They'd be coming back to the house after the ceremony to see the wedding presents—what if some of the Rineharts should wander back to the kitchen? On the fateful day, the Mrs. Klotz of the moment failed to show up. Mary spent a good part of the morning on her hands and knees with a brush and a bucket, scrubbing the kitchen floor.

The ceremony was set for early evening. Late in the afternoon, Mary performed her ablutions, spread a sheet on the bedroom floor, dusted her face lightly with powder, pulled her glossy dark tresses back into their accustomed simple knot, and got down to serious business. First, one assumes, came the underdrawers, of finest cotton, hand-stitched with a mother's loving care, probably flounced and lace-trimmed in contrast to the scalloped and embroidered short flannel petticoat that was to go over them. Stockings of white silk were carefully smoothed on. Perhaps these were a gift that Aunt Maggie had brought from the department store—did Mary spare a fleeting thought for the manager who'd attempted to catch her with his silken lure? How long ago that would have seemed, how fervently might the blushing bride have hoped that Stanley would never get wind of the incident.

But on to the corset, scarcely needed by one so slender as Mary but inconceivable for a young lady to go without; thence to the beruffled corset cover, to the flannel petticoat, to the other petticoats, each a masterpiece of Cornelia Roberts's art. And now came the moment of truth, when she had to draw the dressmaker's *chef d'oeuvre* over her many underlayers, to wrestle its many hooks into their appropriate eyes, to smooth its shimmering folds over all those pads and petticoats.

Finally Mary adjusted her satin bandeau, fluffed out the many yards of tulle, gave a final twitch to the birds of paradise, and donned her long white kid gloves, making sure that a seam in the fourth finger left hand had been slit open sufficiently for the wedding ring to be slipped on but not far enough to look tacky. Somebody, probably Olive, hollered up the stairs that the carriage had arrived. Mary gathered up her train as best she could and went to meet her fate.

Protocol decrees that the groom must not see the bride in her wedding gown until she sails forward to meet him at the altar. Whoever wrote the etiquette book did not reckon with absent-minded best men. Mary and Stanley had to cool their heels down-stairs in the shabby old Sabbath schoolroom until the forgetful one rushed back, red-faced and panting, with the ring. Then the organ began to play. Cornelia rustled up the aisle on an usher's arm in her black taffeta gown and long widow's veil. Olive straightened her sister's heavy satin train. Uncle John, in a new frock coat bought for the occasion, offered his left arm to the dithering bride. The two clergymen who were to perform the ceremony entered right and left. But where was the bride-groom?

The chancel of the church was set up on a high platform with stairs leading up to it, the front of the platform had been so lavishly banked with potted palms and Easter lilies that the stairs were not readily visible. Stanley, in his new frock coat and an advanced case of the jitters, thought he knew where they were. He was wrong. As he stepped forth to claim his bride, he dropped six feet and emerged from a sea of greenery like Tarzan hunting for Jane. Once again the world of the inanimate had shown how implacably it was out to get him.

The church was full of relatives, of friends, of Mary's comrades from the nursing school turned out en masse; and maybe with a few curious outsiders who'd just dropped in to see the show. This was a wedding like other weddings. Probably there were wedding cake and nonalcoholic fruit punch in the vestry afterward. No doubt Cornelia had more substantial viands prepared for those invited back to the house. Whether any of the visiting in-laws noticed the clean kitchen linoleum is not recorded in the annals.

Dr. and Mrs. Rinehart sailed off to Bermuda. Mary got seasick but gallantly maintained that she had a lovely time. They came home, relieved that the people who'd been living in the house where Stanley rented his office had moved out to make way for the newlyweds; their housekeeping had not been up to Cornelia's standards. Mary washed windows and woodwork, ripped up carpets to give them a sound thrashing and laid them back with her own hands. She and Stanley bought what furniture they could afford, which wasn't a great deal. All those onyx-topped tables helped to fill in the blank spaces.

Used to wearing a uniform, Mary created for herself some new ones; brightly printed washable housedresses, delicate lawn aprons like the ones that the hospital laundry had ruined, and gauzy kerchiefs to fold around her shoulders. She was enormously proud of her new status as a wife, of her husband the doctor, of their clean house, enhanced by so many elegant wedding gifts. She was delighted to be cherished and cared for; she was still a little short on ecstasy.

With regard to the sexual aspects of marriage, Mary was in a far less precarious position than many young brides of that late Victorian era who had gone to the bridal bed with no inkling of what was about to happen. The prostitutes she'd nursed during those long night shifts had given her many an earful about the facts of life on the seamy side, her work in the obstetric ward had shown her precisely how babies were born, she'd seen the labor pangs, she'd heard the cries of anguish, she'd personally steered a slimy, blood-smeared infant out of its mother's womb.

She'd had plenty of training at doing her duty, and she knew that a wife must accommodate herself to her husband's masculine appetites. Stanley and she had practiced enough umlauts together during their courtship for her to anticipate that this duty would not be an arduous one. She had repudiated her grandmother's doctrine that all sex was wicked, that the curse of Eve was that babies were conceived in sin and that the agony of childbirth was the penance a woman had to pay for her sinning. Nor was Mary locked into the then still current supposition that no decent woman could possibly receive any pleasure from the sex act except perhaps some mild satisfaction at having conscientiously performed a distasteful task.

Nevertheless, Mary had had hellfire and brimstone dinned into her from her earliest days. Her grandmother had seen the devil under every bed and behind every cribbage board, finding work for idle hands to do. She'd managed to instill in her children and grandchildren the notion that, regardless of how good you tried to be, you were never quite good enough. Considering the brainwashing to which she'd been subjected, Mary hadn't done badly so far. During her nurse's training she had faithfully performed far too many arduous tasks. She had seen the kinds of trouble that sent young girls into brothels or cemeteries, and stayed well clear of them. Within the past year she had lost her grandmother, her young niece, and her father, all under harrowing circumstances. She'd borne up under blow after blow; she'd had no leisure in which to prepare herself for marriage.

As a doctor's wife, Mary had taken on an awesome responsibility. If she wasn't hearing heavenly chimes as she ironed Stanley's shirts and darned his socks, she was finding far more to enjoy than to deplore in her new life. During those twilight years when the doctor's widow looked back over her marriage through the experienced eyes of a romantic writer, Mary recalled that none of the elusive aura called ecstasy had been hovering about her during that fateful moment when Stanley Marshall Rinehart had fought his way through the potted palms to claim her as his own. She didn't seem to have missed it much.

CHAPTER 10

The Doctor's Wife at Home

Although Stanley Marshall Rinehart came of a well-to-do family and Mary's Uncle John was by this time a minor mogul in the wallpaper business, nobody was showering largesse on the newlyweds. "Doctor Rinehart," as Mary would thenceforth refer to him in public and in print, was not getting rich on the standard fees then charged by general practitioners. One dollar was the standard rate for an office visit, two for a house call, no matter how long the distance or how late the hour.

The cost of delivering a baby depended to a great extent on what the parents could afford. Usually it averaged out to about twenty-five dollars. One of Mary's new responsibilities was to make out the quarterly bills, Stanley's part was to make sure they got paid. Every so often she'd hear him downstairs in his office, sounding off to a delinquent patient in his familiar, forthright operating-room style. Since the parents-to-be had known for nine months that the baby was on its way, why hadn't they had brains enough to set aside money to pay their bill?

Such was the life of a newlywed GP. Stanley had to put in many hours of hard labor and sometimes a lot of yelling to keep the rent paid and his wife provided with housekeeping money. Mary got fifty dollars a month with which to buy the groceries and other household necessities, including coal for the furnace in wintertime and two dollars and fifty cents a week for a hired girl, when they could afford one. There would be no "Tell that bill collector I'm not home" in Dr. Rinehart's house. Mary budgeted her allowance down to the penny and saved wherever she could. She baked her own bread, she put up her own jams, jellies, and pickles. She washed the lace curtains herself and trusted no hands but her own to perform the fussy job of pinning them on stretchers to dry.

One thing Mary Rinehart did not do was to lay out Stanley's clothes every morning as Cornelia Roberts had done for Tom. Perhaps she saw this not very arduous task as somehow de-meaning. More likely it was just that Stanley often had to get dressed at such odd times. Many a night, he'd be sleeping the sleep of the exhausted while Mary, awakened by a shrill whistle through the speaking tube that led up from the front doorway to the bedroom, would be listening to a desperate voice from below, pleading for the doctor. There'd been an accident, or somebody's old grandfather had been taken bad, or the baby was on the way; Doctor had better come quick. In those days, the doctor went, no matter what. Mary's job was to roust Stanley out of bed, which wasn't always an easy thing to do, and make sure that he was decently covered before he dashed off to the rescue.

These calls must have been almost as hard on her as they were on her husband. During the early months of her marriage, Mary herself was often unwell. This was not surprising. Ever since she'd enrolled herself in the student nursing program, she'd been stretching herself to the limit, and beyond. Now that she was out from under the too-demanding hospital discipline, she had time to collapse, as people who have undergone long periods of stress are apt to do once the pressure is lifted.

Mary Rinehart could have headed for the sofa and remained there as Aunt Sade had done, thus avoiding these new demands that went with being a doctor's wife. According to her autobiogra-phy she'd been a robust, athletic child; but accounts of later years are peppered with references to her ailments, including hospital visits and occasional surgery. Now that we know words like *neurasthenia* and *psychosomatic*, it would be easy to pin these tags on both Sade and Mary.

But Sade, though she didn't yet realize what was going on inside her, would die of cancer within the next few years. Mary, by hurling herself into that arduous training program while her teenaged body was still not fully developed, may well have done herself permanent damage in ways that the medical knowledge of the time was inadequate to diagnose, much less treat properly. She could have carried too many foot-filled buckets, inhaled too much hot formaldehyde, caught an insidious bacterial infection from cockroach-tainted food in that noisome kitchen where she'd been sent on private duty, overstrained some vital organ lifting the corpse that had spilled her out of her rocking chair back onto the bed from which it had fallen.

Whatever might ail her, Mary carried on, determined to be a perfect wife whether or not Stanley really wanted quite that much perfection from his zealous young bride. She ironed her husband's shirts and kept his trousers pressed. She prepared the hot lunches for which he was supposed to be home in time, since his office hours were from two to four and then from seven until he ran out of patients. In practice, their routine didn't work out that smoothly. Mary always had dinner ready on the dot of six but there was no way of telling when or whether Stanley would find time to eat. His irregular hours must often have exasperated her, but only once did she turn violent.

The Metropolitan Opera was coming to Pittsburgh. Mary and Stanley were both music lovers, and somebody had given them a pair of tickets. They hadn't had an evening out in ages, so this was going to be a rare treat. For weeks, Mary looked forward to the opera. Came the big night, she dressed early in her best evening gown and, for once, laid out her husband's dress clothes and his high silk hat. That done, she waited. And waited. And waited. When Stanley showed up at half-past nine, with only a brief apology, Mary went up in smoke. He could at least have telephoned.

No, he couldn't have. He suggested they drop the subject.

Had Mary been Eliza Doolittle, she'd have known what to say. Not bloody likely! She snatched the high silk hat and hurled it clear across the room. Being a sensible man, he picked up his topper and kept his mouth shut.

Several days passed. Finally Stanley got up his nerve to tell Mary why they'd missed the opera. He'd gone by streetcar to make a house call, leaving himself plenty of time to get home and dress. Stanley had caught the return car all right, but made the mistake of shutting his eyes once he'd sat down. Overworked, always tired, he'd fallen sound asleep. By the time he woke up, he was far out in the suburbs. There wasn't a thing he could do but stand and wait for the next car back, foiled once again by the world of the inanimate.

Generally speaking, Mary knew better than to resent being left alone while her husband was out on call, but for a while she found the evening hours hanging heavy. Once word got around the neighborhood that Dr. Rinehart's new wife was herself a trained nurse, however, she became the most sought-after woman on the block. She comforted expectant mothers who were having panic attacks. She greased a boy who'd got his head stuck in a wrought-iron fence and popped him out, to the admiration of all beholders. A woman fell downstairs and hurt herself. Mary strapped up her ribs with adhesive tape. A man rushed into the office with his finger all but cut off. Mary could see nothing to do but finish the amputation, which she did in a thoroughly professional manner, and put a surgical dressing on the stump. She collected no fees for these impromptu services, but they must have generated lots of goodwill for her husband's practice.

Not that Stanley couldn't generate enough goodwill on his own. Back at the hospital, Mary had often been amused to notice a general straightening of caps and smoothing of hair among her fellow nurses when S.M. showed up on his rounds. Now she was noticing those identical symptoms among some of Dr. Rinehart's female patients.

Allegheny at that time was a wealthy community. Among its residents were a number of affluent matrons with nothing much to do and even less to think about. Some of these women were finding a visit to Dr. Rinehart's office the ideal treatment for their nervous ailments, real or fancied. Mary didn't resent her husband's being cloistered with these well-heeled ornaments of the social set—she was too well aware what a serious handicap a jealous wife could be to a doctor on his way up. What really got to the doctor's young wife was having to open the door for all these beautifully gowned and coiffed ladies of leisure while she herself, in the midst of her household chores, had barely time to snatch off her kitchen apron and take a quick poke at her hair.

As any reader of romantic novels about doctors might predict, there was one not-too-attractive woman who let her crush get out of hand. She took to showing up every day during office hours, even telephoning for no good reason. Stanley Rinehart's temper was beginning to simmer, and his wife's was close to the boil. One day Mary took the call; the enamored lady had enough grace left to sound a wee bit embarrassed. It wasn't anything important, she'd only wanted to ask Dr. Rinehart the meaning of a curious word she'd run across.

What, Mary demanded with no excess of civility, was the word?

The word was *ultramontane.*

This meant simply "across the mountain." Mary told her so pretty sharply and slammed down the earphone. A patient who couldn't tell the difference between a doctor and a dictionary was not worth humoring, even if she did pay her bills on time.

Those first months in her new life taught Mary a great deal, but an even more vital learning opportunity was about to occur. Eight months or so after the wedding, it became clear that she was in an interesting condition. This was good news, for Stanley was eager to start a family and Mary herself had never been one to shrink from a new experience. Unfortunately her rosy dreams of motherhood soon took on a bilious hue. All during her pregnancy, she had a hard time keeping food down; as a result, she would sometimes wake up in the middle of the night absolutely ravenous. In her memoirs, Mary drew a touching word picture of her devoted husband in his nightshirt, grilling her a lamb chop over the coal fire in the bedroom grate.

It was Stanley's half-brother, whom Mary had known in the hospital only as the awesome Dr. C.C., who got her squared away. One evening while her errant digestive tract was giving her a particularly rough time, Brother Tal, as she had by now learned to call him, dropped in with a cardboard box in his hand.

"Here's something you will keep down," he told her in a voice of quiet authority. "It's a hot broiled lobster."

For as long as she could remember, Mary had loathed the mere sight of a lobster. She'd never so much as touched one of the crawly creatures and she'd never wanted to. As her stomach began the too-familiar churning, she clenched her teeth and shook her head. Brother Tal wasn't standing for that sort of nonsense. He sat down by her bedside, pried open her locked jaws, and kindly but firmly began feeding her the lobster, one tiny bite at a time.

Even a churning stomach knew better than to try any funny stuff with the great C.C. That lobster went down and stayed down. With some hot food lying peacefully inside her, Mary began to feel better, and to develop a positive attitude toward lobster that she retained for the rest of her life. Even Dr. Tal couldn't manage to fatten his new sister-in-law up, though. When her first child was born, she weighed only ninety-six pounds.

On January 25, 1897, Stanley Marshall Rinehart turned thirty. Stanley Marshall Rinehart, Jr., was born August 17, just five days after his mother's twenty-first birthday. At that time, doctors were all in favor of big babies. This one tipped the scale at nine pounds, which was fine for Junior but made delivery a nightmare for the slender young mother. Mary's labor pains went on and on, and it wasn't until she was close to delivering that somebody thought to drip a little chloroform on a towel and hold it under her nose. The agonies of childbirth were taken for granted as part of a woman's natural function. The ancient doctrine that her travail was to be offered up as an expiation for the sin of Eve still lingered at the back of even the most enlightened minds.

Three years later, in Freiburg, Germany, a preparation of

morphine and scopolamine to become known as twilight sleep would be developed to ease the agony of childbirth. This great boon to parturient mothers did not, however, reach Pittsburgh in time to do Mary Rinehart any good. Alan came along in November of 1900 and Frederick, or Ted as he would always be known to the family, came two years after Alan. Ted didn't come easily. Mary suffered a postpartum hemorrhage and had to be packed with ice for a wretchedly long time. There would be no more babies for her, nor any life insurance for some years because of her somewhat spectacular medical record.

That she wouldn't be able to bear any more children could not have been a source of deep mourning for Mary. What with her housekeeping, her husband's medical practice, and three little boys already in the family, she had more than enough to keep boredom at bay. Ted in particular was not an easy child to rear. He developed a terrible case of whooping cough during his first year and ran up a record number of 110 spasms. This didn't prevent him from developing at a faster rate than many boy babies do; by the time Ted had passed his second birthday he was walking well enough to escape his baby-sitter, invade the forbidden territory of his father's office, and treat himself to a gulp from a bowl of 95 percent carbolic acid solution.

His father was off on a house call, there was no time to fetch another doctor. Providentially, Mary remembered one of the few lectures for which she'd managed to stay awake during her nurses' training. She thrust Ted into the kitchen sink and poured cider vinegar down his burning throat. The vinegar neutralized the carbolic acid and saved the child's life. For weeks, however, an intubation set was kept on the table beside his crib in case his windpipe might threaten to close up and stop his breath forever.

Even with a doctor and a nurse for parents, the Rinehart boys managed to catch all the popular childhood diseases of the time, plus a few of the more exotic ones. These temporary setbacks didn't slow them down much. They played, they ran, they jumped, they fell, they skinned their knees. Mary spent many an evening darning the holes in their long black stockings. Sliding down the stair rail, Stanley Junior fell off and broke his arm. Ted threw a baseball bat and broke Alan's nose. Alan got into his mother's button box. The following day, Stanley Junior regaled a waiting room full of patients with the story of how Alan had swallowed some shoe buttons and how his mother had got them back.

Young Stanley caught diphtheria and gave it to his mother; Dr. Rinehart had to hire a nurse for her. While Mary was convalescing, the nurse mentioned that *Munsey's* magazine was asking for original poems. Why didn't Mrs. Rinehart try writing one? Remembering her early ambitions and not being up to much else just then, Mary wrote two, fumigated them in the oven, and mailed them off. She was thunderstruck to receive not only a letter of acceptance but a check for twenty-two dollars. It might be fun to try again sometime, she thought. Once she was up and back on the job though, Mary found her muse less amenable to being wooed.

In 1898, the Rineharts had moved from their undistinguished honeymoon home on Western Avenue to a larger dwelling in the same neighborhood, three stories high with a center entrance. Having the doctor's office on one side of the hall, separate from the family quarters, was a major improvement because Stanley's practice was thriving. Since 1894 he had also been medical inspector for Allegheny County, which brought in a little extra money. He and Mary were learning to refer to their hired girl as a maid, which didn't make the housekeeping any easier but did add a touch of class.

At least Mary had been relieved of the task of making out the quarterly bills. The doctor's accountant, by an interesting coincidence, turned out to be the son of a patient whom Mary had nursed at the hospital. Despite having fallen ten stories, the father had vowed he was going to survive, and he did. By now, though, ten stories didn't seem so much to Mary. The nursery and the master bedroom were on the third floor, the only telephone was on the first; between tending the children and taking Stanley's calls, she climbed that far and often a good deal farther every day.

Mary also helped in the office when her husband needed an

extra pair of hands to assist in a minor surgical operation or just to hold the patient steady. One of these involved a big sailor who wore the name Nellie tattooed over his heart even though that fickle organ had by now been passed along to a new sweetheart. Having Nellie removed from his chest nearly cost the not-so-brave Jack Tar a fainting spell, but Mary and her trusty ammonia bottle pulled him through the crisis.

By then, the Rineharts might possibly have been able to afford a nanny for the children but Mary wouldn't hear of that. While she'd never felt much enthusiasm for other people's off-spring, she absolutely doted on her own. Caring for the boys was sheer delight, at least part of the time. Dr. Rinehart was a great believer in fresh air and exercise, and the park where Mary had learned to ride her bicycle underwater was not far away. Even on cold days, she got her three little boys into their hats, coats, mittens, and long buttoned leggings and took them to see the iron deer in the grass and the swans in the lake. The one-armed policeman was no longer around to warn them off the grass, but Mary was too well trained not to keep her sons on the macadam paths.

Mary was also strict about the children's meals. They ate in the nursery, early and punctually. She carried up the trays herself. Perhaps this was her antidote for having to play guessing games with Stanley's dinners. Many a lovingly prepared meal dried up in the oven while one of those well-dressed patients from the expensive side of town lingered in the doctor's office, dawdling over her symptoms. There was one young woman who came to the office in a blue tailor-made suit that fairly tore at the heart-strings. Mary vowed that if she ever got her hands on enough spare money, she would buy one like it. With her first significant earnings, she did precisely that.

Diamond Jim Brady is said to have remarked of a certain opulent-appearing Floradora Girl, "There's deception behind that bust." So it was with Mary Roberts Rinehart's new suit. She'd made the tailor stiffen the bodice with crinoline in the right places and proportions, even if this did mean losing her figure when she took it off. Under the suit she wore the mandatory boned corset and rustling taffeta petticoat. Attached to her skirt band was a chatelaine to which she hooked her purse, her watch, her door key, and various other odds and ends. Also included was a contrivance to hold up the wearer's train at such times as she might need both hands free for some other purpose, such as snatching a too-fearless little boy out of a puddle or away from a threatening swan.

What with all their regular chores, plus medical emergencies and bedtime stories, Mary and Stanley didn't get out much by themselves. They'd been married for six years or so before they at last managed to see a play. Mary still had to face too many evenings alone, but she'd found a more diverting and profitable way to spend the time than sewing on buttons and darning black stockings.

CHAPTER 11

A Full Life Gets Fuller

Counting those three short stories she'd sold for a dollar each when she was fifteen, plus the two oven-baked poems she'd composed on her sickbed (one of these taking the mickey out of medicine all the way from Allopathy to the Water Cure and the other, of all things, spoofing the detective story), Mary had already earned twenty-five dollars by her writing. This was an amount not to be sneezed at; it was the equivalent of five office visits and ten house calls, or one bouncing baby! A young wife with lonesome hours on her hands and a penchant for blue tailor-mades might do well to try her luck again.

On the evidence thus far, verse seemed the way to go. Mary rattled out rhymes by the ream, made a few more sales, earned a few more dollars. She put together a small book of verses for children, took the tedious train journey to New York, wasted a day trudging from one publisher to another, came home, and tried a short story. According to Jan Cohn's meticulously researched chronology in *An Improbable Fiction*, Mary Roberts Rinehart sold nine poems, two short stories, and an article on housekeeping during 1904. Altogether, she earned something like $100 that year.

Between the practice and the children, it was hard to get out in the evenings, but Mary and the doctor were not entirely without a social life. They were learning to play an odd new card game that was gaining in popularity among the smart set. It was called bridge; two of Stanley's friends, another doctor and a lawyer, made up a weekly foursome with him and Mary.

An article that appeared in the *Pittsburgh Bulletin* November 27, 1909, described how Mary, when she was still an embryo writer, had tried to read her work in progress to the men. According to the reporter, the men had all stood up on their chairs and chattered at the tops of their voices to drown her out.

That a young gentlewoman, a cherished wife and without doubt a gracious hostess, could actually have been thus rudely treated by a loving husband and two guests of the professional class seems hardly credible. If it was true, the charitable conclusion is that they'd each had a beer too many.

Of course they all had to pretend that the evening's episode was just a jolly jape, but neither Stanley nor Mary could have enjoyed it. He must have felt embarrassed and somehow demeaned. For Mary, having found her métier and seeing her early effort ridiculed in this manner would have been tantamount to hearing her adored babies derided as ugly brats. But she was not about to quit, and she gained a sweet revenge some weeks later when she showed her erstwhile hecklers a publisher's check for thirty-four dollars, equal to nine office visits and a second bouncing baby, or a tasteful assortment of wills, deeds, title searches, and perhaps even a very minor lawsuit.

Despite Mary's small triumphs in the literary field, life went on as usual. Perhaps she'd picked up a signal from that too-revealing episode at the bridge table. Anyway, she made it a strict policy never to work at her writing while her husband was at home. Mary decided that her time then had better be his time; she maintained this dotingly uxorious attitude for as long as Stanley Rinehart lived. At least she said she did, and perhaps she believed it. Certainly in the early 1900s, her writing was still regarded as just a sometime hobby. Mrs. Rinehart the doctor's wife had many other things to take up her time. For instance, Olive was getting married, at a high-noon wedding in the same church where Mary had been a bride. As the organist began the wedding march and an expectant hush fell over the assembled guests, young Stanley piped up, wondering at the top of his voice when they'd be serving the ice cream.

These were prosperous times, and lots of people were speculating in the stock market. The Rineharts tried their luck and did quite well. The household now boasted two maids and a "Buttons," a young boy in a spruce, many-buttoned uniform whose main function it was to open the door for incoming patients and let them out again after they'd seen the doctor. There were other small luxuries. One day Mary came down to dinner and found a miniature velvet-covered box at her place. In it was a sunburst brooch, very small but exquisitely designed and set with genuine diamonds. She was ecstatic.

To put the frosting on the cake, Mary and Stanley were going to New York on a pleasure trip. With Olive married and gone, Cornelia Roberts had moved into a flat by herself, and was quite willing to look after her grandchildren while her daughter and son-in-law were on the town. The young couple had a marvelous two days. On the third, they stood aghast in the gallery of the New York Stock Exchange, watching a crowd of speculators go into total panic as stock prices plummeted. By closing time, the Rineharts, who must have committed the folly of buying on margin, were not only wiped out of the market but were also $12,000 in the hole.

They went back to Pittsburgh broke and worried. How could they possibly pay off such a debt? Mary was already scheduled for a minor gynecological operation. As soon as she was able to leave the hospital, she dismissed the "Buttons" and the less powerful of her two housemaids and went back to being a woman of all work. Besides the children and the telephone, she took care of the two top floors. On Mondays and Tuesdays, when the sturdy maid was totally occupied with the washing and ironing, Mary had to manage the entire house.

Stanley had by now become Allegheny's city physician as well as county health inspector. His practice had grown to the limit of his capacity. He couldn't raise his fees, so there was just no way to increase his income beyond its already high level. Economizing seemed their only recourse. Despite his evening house calls and frequent emergencies, Stanley offered to tend the children on alternate nights so that Mary would stand a chance of getting a good night's sleep now and then. Ted was recovering well from his acid burns but adequate nourishment was still a problem. They were giving him warm milk every two hours throughout the night; he was very punctual about letting the parent on duty know when it was time to heat up another bottle. Mary retained a tender memory of her husband standing straight and valiant in his pajamas with a squalling baby on one arm, warming a saucepan of milk over a gas bracket.

Mary did think of trying to earn a little extra money by writing but fatigue overcame the urge until one night her husband came home with a weird tale. He'd been to see a patient, a family man suffering from incipient tuberculosis. During the previous evening, one of the patient's children had knocked a lighted oil lamp off the table. Trying to grab the lamp before it smashed and started a fire, the man had hit his head and knocked himself unconscious. The blow must have reactivated an old injury. By the time he came to, the man had regressed to his youth, when he'd been struck on the head in a railroad accident.

The man didn't recognize his wife—he thought she was merely a strange woman who'd been kind enough to help him. He laughed at her for claiming the children were his own. When she handed him a mirror, he was thunderstruck by the visage it reflected. Later, when he was brought to Dr. Rinehart's office on a trolley car, he claimed he'd never seen one before. This true story had a sad conclusion. Eventually, unable to cope with what had happened, the man abandoned the family from whom he had become so pathetically alienated and vanished. Nobody ever found out what became of him.

For Mary, however, the outcome was far different. Here

was the spur she'd needed to get her started writing again, a gripping tale simply begging to be set down on paper. She dashed it off that same evening, changing names and details to make the protagonists unrecognizable and giving the story a happy ending. The next day, she hired a neighborhood girl to typewrite her handwritten draft, and sent off the typescript to *Munsey's* magazine.

As if her workload at home were not enough, Mary had taken on some volunteer nursing. One of her in-laws, a young woman who had just borne a child, was now desperately ill; Mary had gone to serve as relief so that the nurse on duty could get some sleep. She was busy in the darkened sickroom, with the ghastly stench of septicemia poisoning the air and the patient hovering on the edge of the Great Beyond, when Dr. Rinehart tiptoed in. He handed her a letter. Bob Davis, editor of *Munsey's*, would be happy to publish Mrs. Rinehart's story and sincerely hoped she would favor him with more of them. A check for thirty-four dollars was enclosed. Here was a doubly happy ending: The patient recovered and the Rinehart finances began to show a slight upturn.

Only a tiny percentage of published fiction writers have ever been able to support themselves solely by their output. Of those, an even smaller fraction have attained financial heights. The vast majority either live with a supportive wage earner or work for money at some other job and write when they can find the time. This is what Mary Rinehart was doing: running her house, answering the phone, nursing when needed, taking the boys for their afternoon walks, perhaps dashing off a sentence or two during such off moments as she could snatch during the day. Those evenings when Stanley was out seeing patients and the boys were abed became her real writing times. She was never at a loss for ideas. She worked plots out in her mind while she went about her daytime chores. Getting them down on paper was a race between her head and her hand.

Mary's voluminous and indiscriminate reading, particularly that chestful of dime novels she'd plowed her way through in

Cousin Maggie's kitchen back on the farm, served her in good stead now. Since she'd never been taught how to construct a story, she imitated what she'd read, snatching up oddments from the well of subconscious memory and weaving them into pastiches, dashing off wild yarns at a rate of speed quite as fantastic as their contents.

This could only be described as hack writing. It is significant that in years to come, when Mary Roberts Rinehart stood atop that seldom attained pinnacle of fame, the short stories she'd written for magazines after she became well known were collected into hardback volumes and resold at extra profits. Those early efforts, however, were left to moulder unwept, unsung, and no doubt quite justly unhonored.

But the stories sold. Some of them, anyway. At first they didn't bring in much money. In 1906, according to the Cohn chronology, Mary earned either a little more or a little less than $600. She was using a bankbook left over from before the crash to list her sales and payments, and was not always careful as to dates and amounts. Whatever Mary got was better than nothing, however, and she was learning her craft. Uncle John, shaking his head over one of his niece's early effusions, had remarked that there was enough plot in it for ten stories. Mary caught the hint and took more care to plan before she wrote.

Then Mary had another epiphany. Thus far, she had been sending out her stories just as they'd sprung from her pen in the first burst of often-misplaced enthusiasm, only bothering to correct whatever mistakes her young typewriting neighbor had made. But one day, after the postman had brought back a story about the Spanish War for the twelfth time, the discouraged writer read over what she'd written and realized why it hadn't sold. She did a complete rewrite and sent the revised version to *Scribner's*. Their payment was respectable, the lesson was invaluable.

The techniques of writing can be taught; many have learned them, applied them, and profited from them. This does not mean that people who write are necessarily writers. The genuine writer is a *lusus naturae*, an aberrant creature to whom getting words down on paper is not an occupation but a necessity. He may write well or ill or some of each. He will write for gain if he can. He will keep on writing when nobody will pay, even if he can't get anybody to read. The fact that Mary Roberts Rinehart was flying blind during those early years, churning out trash for little cash, did not make her any the less a writer. Though she was hitting too many wrong notes, she was gradually finding her voice.

Mary didn't realize it then, but she was somewhat handicapped by not knowing other writers who might have been able to give her helpful bits of information. So far, her only such encounter had been with Willa Cather, who had spent that one year teaching in Allegheny while Mary was doing her nurses' training. Miss Cather had told Mary that, after she had completed a story, she would lay it aside, sometimes for months on end. Eventually she would take it up again and rewrite the whole text from start to finish.

That was a valuable tip but Mary had either forgotten it during her arduous stint as a nursing student, bride, and mother, or else had brushed it aside in her fever to put down and send out the clamorous mob of plots and ideas that were rioting in her mind. Anyway, Miss Cather's method, while a good one, is not for everybody and Mary Roberts Rinehart certainly wasn't the type to sit around waiting for the muse to show up in its own sweet time. Whatever she wanted, she wanted it now.

However bright the fires of inspiration might burn, Mary's Covenanter conscience still wasn't allowing her to regard her writing as anything more than a spare-time diversion, and she had little time to spare. She was making all her children's clothes plus a few summer frocks for herself; a doctor's wife had to keep up appearances however little money she had to do it with. She was seeing new tragedies among her family. Olive's much-loved little daughter somehow got hold of poison and died. Olive herself was nearly dead from remorse, Cornelia was desolate at the loss of her only granddaughter, and Mary grieved for them all.

Aunt Sade sent for Mary, wanting professional reassurance that what ailed her was not cancer. She was lying in bed, still as a waxwork; she must not have spoken the dread word above a whisper. People didn't in those days, for it was too much like ringing the death knell. Mary told the lies that Sade wanted to hear, slipped out to weep in the hallway where her aunt couldn't see her, then dried her tears and tried to comfort Uncle John.

John was taking Sade's decline badly. Though she had been delicate all their married life, it never seemed to have occurred to him that his adored wife could actually die, and be buried, and leave him alone. John would sit by the bed, holding Sade's cold, slim, white hand as if warning the Grim Reaper to keep away. When he couldn't stand the silent anguish any longer, he would storm through the grandly furnished house like a desperate, trapped animal.

Sade died, of course. John brought her body back to Pittsburgh to be buried with the family. She lay in her casket in the Rineharts' parlor the night before the funeral. Mary must have felt what an inadequate way this was to requite Uncle John for his many kindnesses.

After Ted's near fatal experience with the carbolic acid, Mary and Stanley had taken a sitting at a Presbyterian church. This was not the church from which they had been married—here the doctrine was less rigid and the Sabbath was just Sunday. Dressed in the ruffled blouses and knee-length pants that their mother had sewn for them, the three boys walked to Sunday school holding their parents' hands. They behaved themselves as well as could be expected. They learned to say their prayers every night, kneeling in their nightgowns with mother or father looking on. As children do, the boys also learned to stretch out the number of names on their blessing lists, thus staving off getting into bed for a few minutes longer.

Alan added a small ritual of his own to the nightly orisons. Mary had noticed that her middle son's hair had the same fine texture as her late father's. Since Tom Roberts had gone bald quite early, she advised Alan to massage his scalp every day, for whatever good that might do. Alan was an obedient listener, and he was also something of an efficiency expert. Both parents were deeply touched by the sight of their little boy solemnly intoning his prayers while scrubbing his knuckles over his downy pate.

CHAPTER 12

A Toe in the Water;
A Foot in the Door

Mary's autobiography, when describing those early years, is rife with assurances that her family always came first. She was vehement in asserting that, no matter how brightly her creative fires might be burning, once she heard the slam of the street door and the pounding of footsteps on the stairs (the Rinehart males were all congenital bangers and stompers) she would immediately lay aside her work and become the consummate wife and mother. These protestations might have been thrown in as sops to the mores of the time during which she wrote, when a married woman's place was still considered to be in the home. Then again, Mary may have been telling the simple truth.

As any author can testify, creative writing is essentially a solitary profession, best carried on behind a drawn portcullis. Even the slightest interruption can smash one's concentration with the impact of a physical blow, scattering fragments of exploded imagery all over the room and making further efforts at getting a coherent sentence down on paper impossible until silence reigns again and wits can be regathered for a fresh start. Three little boys clamoring for their after-school milk and cookies, or a doctor husband shouting for his wife to come and hold her thumb on a spurting artery until he could get his needle threaded and his patient sewn back together, would have been powerful incentives for Mary to switch back into her housewife persona.

Nevertheless, Mary kept on writing. In the beginning she used a small mahogany desk that she'd brought with her from her mother's house. Finding this inadequate, she moved on to a card table. Once her earnings had topped $1,000, she felt justified in squandering $20 on a flat-topped desk at a secondhand furniture shop. She also acquired the use of a typewriter. This was a Blickendorfer, even then a dinosaur among typewriting machines, with a keyboard unlike that of any other on the market. It belonged to Stanley's cousin George.

Uncle George, as the children called him, was a regular Saturday evening visitor. He came for the weekly pillow fight. Between supper and bedtime, George, Stanley, and three wildly excited little boys would rampage through the bedrooms, up and down the stairs, snatching pillows off the beds and hurling them at each other in high and raucous glee. Work would surely have been impossible under such conditions, so Mary entertained herself by picking up pillow feathers and practicing on the Blickendorfer. She learned to peck out the letters with one finger of each hand, as many another writer was doing then and would continue to do long after her. She still wrote her original drafts in longhand, but now she could type the revisions for submission to her publishers instead of having to pay the typist down the street.

Mary never truly mastered the Blickendorfer, however. The master gremlin in her operation was Ted, who found it jolly fun to dash up and bang his wee fist down on three or four keys at once, jamming them together and making work impossible until they'd been patiently untangled. Persistent soul that she was, Mary did manage to poke out a number of short stories and her first book-length serial on that cantankerous old machine before total exasperation set in. She bade a relieved farewell to the Blickendorfer, mended relations with the typist down the street, and thenceforth stuck to her trusty fountain pen.

That first serial and the two that followed it were, though

Mary didn't realize it at the time, the catalysts that impelled her into the limelight. She'd done them at the urging of Bob Davis, *Munsey's* editor, for whom she had already written ten short pieces and with whom she and Stanley became quite friendly. In her autobiography, Mary told an amusing little anecdote about their going to New York and entertaining the Davises for dinner at the Waldorf Hotel. The Rineharts ordered quail for their guests because it seemed such an urbane thing to do. They hadn't realized what happened to a quail when you took off the feathers. Contrasting the miniature fowls with the stocky trencherman, Mary feared that Bob Davis must have gone away from his expensive meal still hungry. She herself had honored the occasion by wearing an orchid-colored evening gown and an enormous hat freighted with orchid plumes. She expressed a hope that the splendor of her attire had made up for the scantiness of the fare, but it probably hadn't.

Anyway, Mary took Bob's advice about the serial. She was diffident about her ability to sustain a long narrative, but was scheduled to have more gynecological surgery and was unable just then to do much else but sit, so she thought she might as well give it a try.

Now that they had some extra money coming in, the Rineharts decided to get the children out of the hot city for the summer. They rented a house in the suburbs fully equipped with a porch, a cherry tree, and a gardener named Jackson who was kind and quiet but apparently none too bright. Cornelia Roberts came to visit, and decided it would be fun to gather cherries for the grandchildren. Jackson fetched a ladder and held it for her while she picked.

Being Cornelia, Mary's mother was not satisfied to stay on the ladder. She ventured out on a limb. It broke under her by now not inconsiderable weight, she landed on her daughter, who'd been standing directly underneath. Jackson left Mary sprawled on the ground, struggling to get her breath back while he carried Cornelia into the house.

Neither of the women was badly hurt, it was Jackson who got into real trouble. A night or two after the cherry tree incident, he wandered downtown, got drunk, and shot a woman dead. He was given the death sentence but granted a reprieve; Dr. Rinehart managed to get him freed. Jackson came to thank the doctor afterward but seemed disoriented by what had happened. Mary said the traffic frightened him and he kept wanting to stop strangers on the street and talk to them.

Little things like a shooting and a squashing weren't about to stop Mary from working. She wrote most of her serial sitting on that rented porch with a notebook in her lap. She wondered later why she'd chosen to build her plot around a murder in a Pullman car, but the device worked well enough to bring in some real money. She called it *The Man in Lower Ten*, collected a hefty $400 for her work, and stuffed the carbon into a desk drawer.

Mary's serial ran in *All-Story* magazine from January to April 1906; by the end of its run she'd written some new short pieces and a play. Automobiles were quite the vogue by now; she based her play on an auto race. Her idea was to have a scenic panorama cranked rapidly back and forth across the stage to create the illusion that the cars were really moving. Her script was awful, her auto race a failure. Not until television became part of the American way of life would inane dialogue and mindless car chases capture the fancy of the American viewer. Mary chucked the worthless play aside and wrote another serial.

She'd hit her stride by now. She tossed off her second effort in a month or so. This time the locale was less exotic, merely a large country house reminiscent of those in which she'd attended a few dances before Allegheny became part of Pittsburgh and all the nabobs moved off to Sewickley. For *The Circular Staircase*, *All-Story* gave her $500 and scheduled the serial to run from November 1907 to March 1908. The carbon of her previous effort was already gathering coal dust in a drawer of her twenty-dollar desk, and she dumped this one in on top of the first.

Now that she'd learned how much better serials paid than short pieces, she batted out a third, *The Mystery of 1122. Live Wire* magazine paid her $500 and would start running it in February 1908.

As serials, the three that she'd dashed off in the midst of

having her operation, tending her children, running her household, and writing a variety of short pieces brought in some welcome cash but made no great stir. But late in 1907, Uncle John, lonely in Cincinnati, still missing his beloved Sade, came to visit his favorite niece. He'd heard on the family grapevine that Mary had been doing fairly well lately with her little stories. How about showing him something she'd published?

John Roberts was no gentle critic. Mary didn't want to risk his censure but how could she refuse? She fished in her desk drawer, took out the by now rather dilapidated carbon of *The Circular Staircase*, which happened to be on top of the pile, and handed it over. Uncle John sat down to read. He kept on reading until lunchtime, he hurried through his meal and went back to read some more. He finished in the late afternoon, and gave his verdict.

"That's a book, Mary. You ought to have it published."

Mary didn't think her story was good enough for a book. John said nonsense, he'd read lots worse. Stanley found the notion of approaching a book publisher quaint and amusing, but supposed it wouldn't do any harm to try. So the next morning Mary took the bedraggled carbon to a local bindery and asked if it could be made presentable. No problem, said the binder. He trimmed the ragged edges, bound the pages inside a limp cover, stamped the title in gilt letters on the front, and charged her three dollars. Seeing her humble effort in such elegant guise, Mary felt a little more confident about sending it off. But where?

That problem was also quickly solved. Mary took an Anna Katharine Green mystery novel out of the bookcase, noted the publisher's name, and addressed her package to Bobbs–Merrill in Indianapolis. She had no great expectation of getting a return on the three dollars she'd paid to the bookbinder. She'd begun to realize how bad most of her work so far had been, how little she actually knew about writing. She had started to study the techniques of authors whom she respected, she reviewed her high school grammar, she wore out one copy of *Roget's Thesaurus* and bought another. As to her reckless facility at getting words on paper, that was something Mary couldn't help. She wrote as swiftly as she thought, darting her fountain pen into the inkwell when the ink in the cartridge wouldn't flow fast enough to keep up with her hand.

And this was just in her spare time. There were still the housekeeping, the medical practice, and the family. Even with servants in the house, a conscientious wife and mother had to oversee every task and do her own food shopping. Mary was at the meat market some days after John's visit, meditating between the relative merits of steaks and chops, when the butcher's telephone rang. Surprisingly, this call was for Mrs. Rinehart; her husband was on the line. No, none of the boys had had an accident, it was just that Stanley thought she might like to know she'd had a letter from a Mr. Hewitt Howland at Bobbs-Merrill. Should he read what Mr. Howland had written?

Of course he should. Mary braced herself against the gory chopping block and listened.

"My dear Mrs. Rinehart," the letter began. "I have read *The Circular Staircase* not only with pleasure, but with thrills and shivers."

Thrills and shivers, indeed! Mary was having them too, had Mr. Hewitt Howland but known. Howland not only wanted to publish her book, he even offered to pay for the right to do so. And he wanted to come to her house, and talk to her about writing more books!

There was only one thing to do, and Mary did it. She dashed to the telegraph office and wired Mr. Howland to come right ahead. She dashed back to buy steak and ice cream, dashed home, and baked a cake.

When mother baked a cake, the Rinehart children knew it was a party. But whom was this party for? Mary wasn't quite sure herself.

"It's not really a party," she told them, "just a special sort of day."

"What's a special sort of day?"

A day when they had cake and ice cream for dessert, naturally. This was hardly the way to start a serious literary career, but Mary had no time to play author. Those guest room curtains had done well enough for her and Stanley's visiting relatives, but here was a big, important editor coming all the way from Indianapolis just to see Mary Roberts Rinehart. And that brass bed needed a valance, and what if Mr. Howland showed up tomorrow?

First on the next day's agenda was a quick trip to the dry-goods store. Mary bought fresh material, lugged it home, and began to sew. She kept on sewing until late the night before Howland was due to arrive, and the final curtain got hung in the nick of time. What her new editor thought of the bedroom decor was beside the point—what he'd come to see were manuscripts. Had Mrs. Rinehart anything else to show him?

She had. There was no time to take those other two ratty carbons to the bindery but Editor Howland didn't care. He read them both, sitting all day long in the living room with the Rinehart boys and the Rinehart dogs for company. He could not but have been impressed by the virtuosity of a young housewife who could spin off three diverse tales in such a fresh and often amusing style. He'd take them all and be glad he got them. He was already planning to publish *The Circular Staircase* in 1908, *The Man in Lower Ten* in 1909, and *The Mystery of 1122* in 1910. He didn't care much for that last title, so he and Mary wisely changed it to *The Window at the White Cat*.

Mary had scrupulously listed each one of the small sums she'd gotten for her short pieces and her serial rights in the old bankbook, but she didn't know what to put down for Bobbs-Merrill's three-book deal. That didn't matter. Her husband was by now making a goodly amount of money at his practice, and he naturally expected to be the family's major breadwinner for the rest of his life, but it was beginning to look as if there might be plenty of jam on the Rineharts' bread.

By now, Stanley must have managed to sublimate any atavistic qualms; he had begun taking an enthusiastic interest in his wife's burgeoning career as a writer. Knowing Mary as he'd had every opportunity to do since that fateful day when she'd tripped into his office with her flounced parasol and rose-bedecked hat, applied to join the nurses' training program, and proved throughout her arduous three years of training to have a backbone of good

Pittsburgh steel, he must have realized somewhere along the line that she'd never be content to spend the rest of her life sewing on buttons and ordering lamb chops. He'd taken her for better or worse. There'd been enough of the worse. Why play dog in the manger now that the good times were starting to roll?

Despite his ongoing war with the inanimate, the collar buttons that willfully leaped from his shirts, the matches that wouldn't light, the cussedness of things in general, Stanley Rinehart was clearly a man who would rather be happy than not. He showed himself a genial host to Mary's suddenly acquired editor. When they gathered around the piano after dinner, it was his fine baritone that led the singing. Mary played, the little boys sang, Hewitt Howland sang, even the family collie sang. This could hardly have been the kind of reception Howland was used to; he must have left the next day with a strong awareness that his newest author would turn out to be somebody altogether out of the ordinary.

CHAPTER 13

Stagestruck and Stricken

Mary Roberts Rinehart was her mother's daughter. As soon as she'd got hold of some extra cash, she'd begun splurging on ways to upgrade the Rineharts' standard of living. She'd hired more servants. Remembering the misery of her own grammar school days, she'd persuaded her husband to send the boys to a private school.

Mary had been uneasily aware of late that she'd been gradually boosting the family's lifestyle up to the thin edge of her husband's earning capacity. Of course she was easing the burden to some extent with her own sporadic earnings, but she still felt guilty. Mary was always ready to feel guilty. Grandmother Roberts had seen to that. Lately she'd been pushing herself harder and harder to earn more and more so that Stanley wouldn't feel overburdened. Now, with a substantial three-year contract tucked under her corset cover, she could let herself relax a little, get some rest, and indulge that unfulfilled hankering to write a successful play.

For no reason that Mary could put her finger on, she had been stagestruck ever since she was a little girl. Maybe this lust for the footlights had been triggered by her parents' daring escapade in going to see *The Black Crook*, even though it had apparently incited Grandma Roberts's implacable God to vent his displeasure by hurling Mary and Aunt Ella down from the balcony along with that overload of pianos. Maybe it stemmed from her being born under the sign of Leo. Anyway, throughout her childhood, Mary had played theater, staging little tableaux with her friends, making sure that she herself always got the starring part.

A couple of decades later, Alice Roosevelt Longworth would talk to Mary Roberts Rinehart about her father. If the redoubtable Teddy was at a wedding, he felt himself to be the groom; if at a funeral, he became for the moment both mourner and corpse. That was Mary all over, she had been playing one role or another for as long as she could remember. She always would, because this is something fiction writers do: feel their way into a character's persona then dart to the other side of the footlights to critique the plot and write the review. Mary had this ability to throw herself into a new situation, to play her role to the hilt but always to see past the tinsel, even while she was enjoying the glitter.

She knew what the theme of her play was to be. Amnesia was a trauma about which most people still didn't know much. That story of Stanley's about the amnesiac, the one that had already netted her thirty-four dollars from Bob Davis and would be used again on two future occasions, offered fascinating possibilities. Mary set about her work more systematically this time, cutting a stage out of an empty starch box, shuffling her sons' toy soldiers around on it to get the actors' movements right. Within a few days she had a one-act play down on paper. On Saturday morning of that same week she set off for New York to sell her magnum opus to David Belasco.

On this trip, the budding playwright was in much the same position as the pussycat going to London to visit the queen, although a cat might have shown a greater feeling of tolerance toward the personage she expected to meet. Along with her slender script, Mary carried a freight of ignorance and prejudice based on her early indoctrination, as well as the arrogance of a respectable young doctor's wife who'd just sold three novels to a prestigious publishing house. That a mere theatrical impresario, however renowned, might not care to see Mrs. Stanley Marshall Rinehart was simply out of the question. She left her script in the stage-door mailbox once she'd learned that stage-door mailboxes did exist and where to find one. She gave the doorman a dollar to make sure her masterpiece got into Mr. Belasco's hands at the earliest opportunity. She then went to sit in the room that she'd engaged at the Holland House and wait for the telephone to ring.

Having learned that Mary Rinehart was in town for the weekend, Mr. and Mrs. Bob Davis invited her to join them on a Sunday visit with famous cartoonist and writer Homer Davenport and his wife. Mary didn't want to go for fear of missing Mr. Belasco's call, but Bob was a hard man to resist. Mr. Davenport met them at the railway station with a team of white Arabian stallions out of the herd of twenty-seven that he'd obtained from the sultan of Turkey through the good offices of Theodore Roosevelt. Uncle John would have considered it an honor and a privilege to ride behind such magnificent steeds, but Mary was in fidgets. When she confessed the reason for her anxiety, she got the horselaugh; Bob told her that he knew playwrights who'd been waiting twenty years for Belasco to call them.

Nevertheless, Mary was relieved to get back to the Holland House and not a bit surprised to hear the telephone ringing as she opened the door to her room. David Belasco was on the line, as she'd known he would be. She was pleased to hear his voice but scandalized when he asked her to meet him Monday evening in Mr. Frank Keenan's dressing room.

What kind of soiled dove did Mr. Belasco think she was? Mrs. Rinehart was traveling without her spouse, she informed him stiffly; it was quite out of the question that she should enter a strange man's dressing room unchaperoned. Surely Mr. Belasco must understand.

Mr. Belasco quite understood, and he rose to the unexpected like a gentleman of the old school. Would Mrs. Rinehart come if he sent his private carriage for her, with Mrs. Keenan as duenna?

Mary was gracious enough to accept Belasco's offer and did not regret having done so, even when Mr. Keenan retired behind a screen to change his nether garments.

She would not have to wait twenty years to get her play read, for Mr. Belasco scanned it then and there. He liked her idea, he could see that Mrs. Rinehart had a sense of theater. What he wanted, however, was a three-act play. Why didn't she run along home, expand her script, and bring it back for further discussion? This might make an excellent new vehicle for Mr. Keenan after he'd finished playing the lovelorn outlaw in Belasco's own play, *The Girl of the Golden West.*

Mary kindly acquiesced. Mr. Belasco escorted her back to the Holland House, waited to see her safely inside, then probably went off to enjoy a quiet chuckle over his unexpected confrontation with a respectable housewife from Pittsburgh.

Quite a few years ago, a charming human-interest story appeared about Queen Elizabeth II. She'd spent a pleasant afternoon with members of a village Women's Institute. All of them, the queen included, chatted happily and informally about their families, their housekeeping, their needlework, subjects on which women have traditionally enjoyed sharing their views over the teacups. When the meeting ended, nice Mrs. Windsor thanked her new acquaintances with a friendly "This has been a change," and turned back into a queen.

That seems to have been much the way David Belasco reacted to Mary Roberts Rinehart. Here was a character quite outside his usual cast of acquaintances, this proper little doctor's wife who popped into New York for a day or two now and then in a homemade summer frock, gave him about the same amount of attention she allotted to selecting the Sunday roast, then scurried back to her waiting family. Because the theater was not a life-and-death matter to her, because she didn't take his every word as a threat or a promise, he found that he could talk with Mrs. Rinehart about anything he chose. It was indeed a change.

Belasco was happy to give what Mary didn't beg for. Sometimes he talked about her play, sometimes about the theater in general: what could be achieved with staging, what would never work. He sent her to watch other plays in rehearsal, to learn how they were put together. He let her see things about himself: he was superstitious, he was profligate with money, he was tactful. Toward her, at least, he was considerate. After they'd finished discussing the latest batch of changes to her play, he would take her somewhere for a bite of supper, then send her back to her hotel in his open victoria.

Belasco could also be vindictive. Once Mary had got her play finished to his satisfaction, he offered her a lump sum for the rights. Compared to her three-book contract, the money evidently wasn't much. Even so, she realized too late, she ought to have taken it. She'd already gained a great deal from Mr. Belasco in the way of technical advice. The prestige of having written the script for one of the great man's productions would have been invaluable to a novice.

But Mary had too good a memory. She recalled what her father had said when he'd been offered $10,000 for his revolving bobbin. If it was worth that much, it was worth far more. So she proceeded to make the same mistake Tom Roberts had made. One of her actor acquaintances intimated that Belasco was a sharp customer to deal with, suggesting that Mrs. Rinehart had better find herself an agent before she signed any contract. She did, and Belasco went up in smoke. It was years before he'd even speak to her again, much less have anything further to do with her play.

The agent who had roused Belasco's wrath by denouncing his contract as "infamous" was Mrs. Henry DeMille, widow of a playwright and mother of William and Cecil, both destined to become eminent figures in the motion picture industry. Beatrice DeMille not only found a new home for Mary's play, she also provided one for the playwright whenever Mary needed a place to stay in New York. This meant a significant drop in travel expenses. Mary became deeply attached to her new agent, although she occasionally found such an indomitably strong-minded personality somewhat hard to take. It's possible that

Mrs. DeMille might once or twice have felt the same about Mary.

A Double Life went into rehearsal in the fall under new management. Mary would waste far too many hours away from Stanley and the children, sitting in an empty theater, watching actors wander around a bare stage speaking lines she wished she'd never written. She would go back to Mrs. DeMille's apartment and spend all evening—sometimes all night—doing rewrites. Then she'd have to get up early and have the revisions typed in time for the new day's rehearsal.

Mary wouldn't have minded this hectic pace so much if she hadn't begun to suspect that it was lost labor. The management had cast a Dutch actor as the hero. This man, whom Mary tactfully refrained from naming in her autobiography, had a great reputation abroad but was totally miscast in his current role. He was too old, too fat, and too hell-bent on being the star of the show. He knew almost no English, he couldn't learn his lines, he demanded a prompter to feed them to him virtually word by word.

Prompters' boxes were standard equipment in Europe, Mary gathered, but not in America. When the show went on the road for a tryout, a young woman understudy had to be stuffed into a prop grandfather clock and hiss the right words out from behind the pendulum. Sometimes, Mary claimed, the clock delivered the dialogue more clearly than the star did.

Dr. Rinehart joined Mary for part of that very brief tour. He told her she looked ill; she was. That bumptious mass of vanity was wrecking the play, snatching away all the good lines for himself, making goulash of the plot and the cast's morale. Mary's one bright moment came when the self-aggrandizing star stepped forward to make a speech and got whacked on the head by the descending curtain.

Opening night in New York City was on Christmas Eve, the one time of year when even the stage-door Johnnies were nestled all snug in their own beds. Mary didn't even care. She washed her hands of the whole debacle and stayed home to trim the Christmas tree. Bob Davis did go to see the show, and telephoned Mary at midnight to complain about that awful leading man. Where the hell had she got him?

The reviews were less dire than Mary had expected. Nevertheless, with some vague hope of rescuing her play from the hands of the spoilers, she issued an injunction to stop the butchery and take *A Double Life* off the boards. She was, for the moment, all through with the theater.

CHAPTER 14

From Playtime to Paytime

When one door closes, another opens. The year 1908 brought Bobbs-Merrill's first Rinehart offering, *The Circular Staircase*. All of a sudden, Mary was getting rave reviews, being praised to the skies for injecting a new dimension into the detective novel.

So far, many of the mystery stories disdainfully classed by the literati as mere entertainment had, like the stage melodramas, been rigidly righteous outgrowths of the old morality plays. Authors of the Victorian era, dealing with gory plots that reeked of sin and shame, had felt duty-bound to maintain an atmosphere of drawn shades and festering lilies, with perhaps a deathbed repentance as a single touch of uplift. Take for instance this single sentence penned by Mary's famous predecessor, Anna Katharine Green, in *Hand and Ring* (first copyright 1883, republished by Dodd, Mead in 1926):

It was as if a veil had been rent before her eyes, disclosing to her a living soul writhing in secret struggle with its own worst passions; and horrified at the revelation, more than horrified at the remembrance that it was her

own action of the morning which had occasioned this
change in one she had long reverenced, if not loved, she
sank helplessly upon her knees and pressed her face to
the window in a prayer for courage to sustain this new
woe and latest, if not heaviest, disappointment.

Now here comes Rinehart's Miss Rachel Innes, a feisty
maiden lady with a large fortune and far more courage than she'd
ever expected to need. She squabbles with her somewhat faithful
maid, Liddy. She's duly shocked but by no means overwhelmed
at finding the slain body of a profligate young rogue sprawled out
in his dinner jacket and bloodstained white waistcoat on the floor
of the palatial but spooky house that she's rented for the summer,
out in the country where the crickets rub their legs together all
through the darksome hours.

Miss Innes doesn't much care about the crickets or the
corpse—she is too busy resuscitating her swoony young niece and
hiding clues to keep the police from arresting her beloved nephew.
She resists sudden, inexplicable pressures from sundry persons to
give up the house, partly because she's curious to see what happens
next and partly because her city house is being redecorated. She'd
much rather face an unknown murderer than a houseful of paint-
ers, as what sensible homeowner would not?

The chills and shivers that Hewitt Howland had mentioned
were present in abundance, but not the traditional fustian. True,
the beautiful niece did a good deal of hand-wringing and carrying
on, as beautiful nieces were prone to do when their lovers (this
word did not mean in 1908 what it means now) were threatened
with durance vile. The handsome nephew and the possibly even
handsomer lover combined, in correct proportions, nobility of
spirit with some foolhardiness in action, as young men of good
family were expected to do in novels written so soon after the
turn of the century. Through it all, there was Aunt Rachel, being
thoroughly real even while Liddy was pinning a false switch to
her mistress's back hair. And how the reading public adored them
both!

Hewitt Howland had shown excellent editorial sense in publishing *The Circular Staircase* before the other two novels. It was in this book that Mary Roberts Rinehart really found her voice: the indefinable, unmistakable, individual cadence that can be copied but never quite satisfactorily matched. She'd meant her brainchild to be no more than a mild satire on the pompously righteous mystery novels that certain other writers of the time were still turning out. There was nothing mild about Rachel Innes, however; she pulled the same trick on her creator that Tom Sawyer had practiced on Mark Twain in the year Mary Roberts was born. Each had set out to write a potboiler and wound up with a classic.

The Man in Lower Ten, written earlier but coming out the following year, shows some of the overplotting that Uncle John had complained about in one of Mary's early short stories. Undoubtedly the book got a boost from its predecessor's phenomenal success. It did have merit enough, though, not only to hit the best-seller list but also to have an unexpected effect on railway travel. Mary learned this fact in a surprising way. On her way home from a rest-cure establishment where she'd been trying to put on a little weight, she tried to get a Pullman berth. The clerk at the ticket office said they were all sold out, unless she'd be willing to take Lower Ten. Some fool woman had written a book in which somebody got murdered in Lower Ten, and now they couldn't get anybody to sleep there.

The Window at the White Cat apparently caused no such ruckus. As far as characterization went, the young lawyer who was both the narrator and the hero of the book could have been interchanged with the young lawyer who narrated and starred in *The Man in Lower Ten*. The plot here is less cluttered and the background of political chicanery provides an opportunity for some well-managed atmosphere. This book also sold well on the strength of Mary's earlier successes, but seems not to have raised any great furor on its own. *The White Cat* is again in print, however, and is still a good read for those interested in works from the Golden Age of mystery fiction that Mary Roberts Rinehart did so much to build and sustain.

While 1908 had begun auspiciously for Mary, things weren't so great for Stanley. An article that appeared in a learned magazine

during the 1980s solves the whole problem in a nutshell and offers
a diagnosis:

> Mary Roberts Rinehart has all of a sudden become
> rich and famous. Therefore, Doctor Stanley Rinehart has
> developed a mysterious, disabling condition in his hands.
> He will thus be kept from continuing to pursue a profes-
> sion that, while it pays pretty well and has made him a
> respected figure in his native city, will never yield him
> sufficient money and stature to keep up with his cele-
> brated wife.
>   This is known as a conversion phenomenon. It means
> that Stanley Rinehart's disability has automatically re-
> moved him from having to compete with her. Hence-
> forth the doctor can allow himself to enjoy a life of
> luxury at his wife's expense without having to suffer
> either public ignominy or private guilt feelings.

All this sounds very plausible, but there are some odd omis-
sions. By 1908, Stanley Marshall Rinehart was head of surgery
at Pittsburgh Homeopathic Hospital; he had already been doing
surgery there before Mary entered the nursing program in 1893.
Nothing is said in the article of the "wet" method that then required surgery to be performed under constantly dripping irrigation tubes at a time when viable rubber gloves were not to be
had, or that surgeons were on call night and day without extra
remuneration. Equally no mention is made of the grueling hours,
of the late-night house calls that were a standard part of Stanley's
general practice, of his chronic weariness during those early years
when he'd been the sole support of an often ailing wife and their
three little boys.

  Nor is it pointed out that such symptoms as Stanley Rinehart
was evincing do not, as a rule, come on suddenly. Who ever knew
precisely when he'd begun to notice pain and stiffness in his hands?
Typical behavior of the manly male is to make a great to-do about
a hangnail or a sniffle but to maintain a stoical silence about any
symptom that he suspects may indicate a serious problem. For

upward of twenty years, Dr. Rinehart had been recognized as a fine surgeon. Losing his finger dexterity would mean cutting off an important part of his career, not to mention of his income and prestige. It would have been in character for him to make light of his symptoms as long as he could.

As time went on, Stanley's suffering would increase. In later years, he was sometimes unable even to get out of his chair because the pain was so intense. At other times he might have normal use of his limbs. This was not at all remarkable, the "rheumatics" that so many of our forebears suffered from and passed on to succeeding generations is still a rather mysterious ailment.

Rheumatoid arthritis is the most common form. It can show up in a patient of any age, but is most likely to make itself felt in adults between thirty and forty. Stanley Rinehart had his forty-first birthday in January 1908. Pain and stiffness in the joints are the chief symptoms. These often show up first in the finger joints, tend to be worst on rising in the morning and may wear off to a greater or lesser degree in the course of the day. Sometimes they don't manifest themselves at all; a patient can be pain-free one day and in agony the next. This makes it easy for nonsufferers to suspect the aching one of hypochondria, malingering, or a conversion phenomenon whereas in truth he may be even sicker than he himself realizes.

Through Mary's autobiography and her travel books, we get a picture of Stanley as the direct antithesis of an idle sybarite. We see an overworked doctor coming home late and weary from his evening rounds, crawling into bed for a little sleep, getting up in the night to warm bottles for a sick baby so that his equally tuckered-out wife can get the sleep she desperately needs. We see a loving father romping with his young sons, then hearing their prayers and tucking them in for the night, hoping he won't get called out on an emergency but never refusing to go. We see a faithful husband refusing the blandishments of his rich female patients, keeping the home fires burning while the woman he's promised to love, honor, and cherish breaks free of the shibboleths against wives who work outside the home. Is it really credible that such a man could ever have appointed himself the family gigolo on any pretext, conscious or subconscious; much less at a time when Mary's writing career was still hovering on the brink?

Even today, laymen have many misconceptions about how much and how often writers get paid. The author of the article may surely be excused for not having known that, while *The Circular Staircase* was getting rave reviews, Mary still hadn't touched a penny of income from her surprising best-seller, and wouldn't for some time to come. Standard publishing practice at that time, particularly with a writer who had as yet no track record in hardcover sales, was to pay nothing on acceptance, nothing on publication. The author's recompense would come solely—and slowly—as a small royalty on each separate copy of the book *after* the purchase money had filtered back from the bookseller to the publisher. The reason Mary failed to record the payments she received from those early hardcover sales may well have been that it was just too much bother to keep track of the many fiddling sums that trickled in at unpredictable times. Since there was no income tax to worry about in those semihalcyon days, she would have been under no special compulsion to keep careful records.

During that exasperating hiatus before the gravy train rolled up to the door, Stanley's hands kept on hurting. Aspirin, which has been a standard panacea for arthritic pain as long as most of us now living can remember, would not be introduced in America until during World War I. There were a good many patent medicines on the drugstore shelves and many people dosed themselves just as recklessly as they do nowadays, but Stanley knew better than to fall for any quack nostrums. When the pain got too bad to be borne, he took a morphine tablet and carried on.

Morphine is still in the pharmacopoeia because it is still the most effective painkiller available. Nowadays it is a controlled substance available only by prescription; in the early 1900s, druggists would keep great jars of morphine pills sitting on their counters and scoop them out like jellybeans. Then, as now, most purchasers did not automatically become addicts. Using narcotics, except in moderation for therapeutic purposes, was considered a sign of a weak character. No respectable person, and respectability was important in those days, wanted to be tagged a hophead.

Stanley Rinehart's only problem, but a devasting one, was that the morphine made his hands shake.

This meant no more surgery. Stanley still had his general practice, of course. He also tried his now tremulous hand at writing some articles on nutrition and other medical subjects of interest to the lay reader. These pieces were accepted by the prestigious *Saturday Evening Post*, which Mary had thus far not succeeded in cracking. They must have provided some solace for the doctor's *amour propre* as well as extra cash for his pocket, since the *Post* paid quite well, but his writings did not lead to a change in his career.

Mary was not wasting any time waiting for those as yet hypothetical royalties from her first big seller. The sales she did record for 1908 and 1909 show that she was still churning out shorter pieces, meekly accepting whatever payment any publication chose to offer. In December 1908, Lippincott published a novella of hers called *Seven Days*. The following year, Dodd, Mead & Co. retitled the piece *When a Man Marries* and offered it as a full-length book in a handsome hardcover edition, eked out with a goodly number of peppy line drawings by Mayo Larkin and a couple of swoony full-color plates by the famous Harrison Fisher.

By a slight stretch of the publisher's imagination, this charming literary excursus of Mary's could have been marketed as a mystery. Mostly, it's pure fun. The narrator is a bright young butterfly of the social set. Her rejected suitor has recently married another, his wife has already walked out on him for reasons of boredom. His formidable old aunt is coming to visit and will expect to find a doting spouse in residence. Can't the girl he once loved please help him out for auld lang syne?

The once-loved says forget it, Freddy; but the rest of their mutual coterie pressure her to accept. Eventually she agrees, on condition that the whole gang come along to chaperon. No sooner are they all ensconced in the bereft bridegroom's house than his Japanese manservant comes down with smallpox and is carted away to the hospital. The entire houseparty, including the acerbic aunt, are put under quarantine with not a single lackey, serf, or esne to wait on them and hardly a clue about fending for themselves. A gaggle of reporters get wind of the story, they come to camp on the doorstep, and a mysterious presence starts riding up and down the dumbwaiter.

At the time of this writing, in 1993, the Rinehart mysteries are being reissued in paperback for the umpteenth time. Why no publisher has yet picked up this little bundle of delight is a puzzlement. The book sold very well at its debut and did even better as a play that Mary and Avery Hopwood later worked up together, going back to the original title. *Seven Days* ran for 397 performances on Broadway and eventually netted Mary $50,000.

Obviously the vow that Mary had sworn after her early fiasco never again to become involved with the theater had been made with her fingers crossed. She'd no sooner got back to Pittsburgh and licked her wounds when Beatrice DeMille, swamped with submissions from would-be playwrights that she had no time to read, began sending armloads of scripts for Mary's critical opinion. Most of these were awful. Mary took particular delight in rejecting the very worst of the bunch, which had been written by a well-known critic who'd given her play a merciless roasting.

Mrs. DeMille also coaxed Mary into taking on new assignments as a play doctor, calling her up every so often with a last-minute plea to come back to New York and turn some floundering turkey into a box-office smash. How could a stagestruck writer resist such a challenge? Mary would send her mother an SOS to come and mind the boys, throw a few things into a bag, and rush to catch the train. After a tedious commute and a hectic stint of nonstop writing, she'd stagger back, worn to a frazzle and too often depressed at her failure to pull off a miracle.

This chapter in the Rinehart saga was a short one. Stanley wanted a wife, not a whirligig, and was not shy about voicing his feelings. The smashing grand finale came when Mary was summoned to rescue *The Rejuvenation of Aunt Mary*, a play based on a book by the popular Anne Warner, in which May Robson was to star.

The trouble was easy enough to spot. Miss Robson, like Mary's late *bête noire* the Devouring Dutchman, wanted the whole show to herself. At this point the play was little more than a static monologue. Mary's attempt to introduce some lively dialogue turned it into a clawing catalog. Actress and playpatcher went for each other like two irate tabbies on a backyard fence. Beatrice DeMille, in a desperate attempt at fur-smoothing, met the two for lunch at the Astor wearing a blue-checkered kitchen apron that she'd been too flustered to take off before she left home. Probably nobody nowadays ever says, as our grandmothers were wont to do, "I'd like to take that she-devil over my checkered apron and give her a good spanking," but some such notion may have been floating around Mrs. DeMille's subconscious when she entered the fray so aptly attired. Anyway, she took it off; the waiter gallantly folded it up and presented it to her in a doggie bag.

Mary was finally talked into carrying on, and she got almost no sleep until the job was done. The play did well. Eventually and grudgingly, May Robson paid Mary $200 for saving her show. Even if this hadn't been the last straw, Mary would have had to quit running to New York. She'd lost her baby-sitter.

Cornelia Roberts had suffered a stroke. Temporarily paralyzed, permanently bereft of speech, Mary's and Olive's vigorous, capable, ever-resourceful mother had become, at fifty-five years of age, her daughters' baby. After a lengthy hospital stay, she was carried on a stretcher to the Rineharts' and Mary switched back from author to nurse.

The stricken woman never recovered fully, but she did regain some of her accustomed functions. Rehabilitating a stroke patient was, and is, a wearisome task. Cornelia had to be retaught even the most basic skills, such as how to feed herself gruel from a spoon. With good nursing and loving care, her strength and her memory began to come back. She could move her legs and her left arm. Although the right arm and hand would remain useless, she relearned certain hand skills, even the embroidery she'd always done so well. She never did get her voice back, however. For the next fourteen years she would remain, as Mary described her, "A silent, gentle, patient presence in the house."

Silent, gentle, and patient though she might be, Cornelia also became an ongoing problem. Once she'd got her legs back under her, she had to be watched like the child she'd become, to be kept away from the stairs, from the stove, from all the possible danger spots. She would lock herself in her bedroom and forget how to turn the key. As a result, the neighborhood locksmith became a frequent visitor. She developed a Jacksonian epilepsy. These sudden mild seizures were an additional worry.

Returning memory created new difficulties. Cornelia could hear and understand what others were saying, and though she wanted desperately to take her part in the conversation, the words would not come out. The family tried coaxing her to spell out words with the children's alphabet blocks, but this was more than she could manage. Finally they resorted to asking yes–or–no questions that she could answer with a nod or a shake of the head. The method was tedious and time–consuming, but it worked.

As time went on, Cornelia found herself able to read printed matter. Books and newspapers became a source of much satisfaction, but anything handwritten defeated her completely. Mary even had to read Olive's letters aloud. She must have been saddened to remember her mother's clandestine penmanship lessons and to realize that never again would she receive one of those exquisitely penned notes, with each separate character standing out proud and perfect for the recipient to see and to admire.

At least money was not lacking. Mary's mysteries and her play *Seven Days* were by now bringing in impressive royalties. The boys at school and Cornelia in the spare bedroom were doing as well as could be expected; the family's one big problem was Stanley's hands. By 1910, he and Mary had come to a decision. Doing general medicine without being able to practice surgery as well was not a viable course for a man who still regarded himself as the family provider. Sporadic payments from Mary's writing seemed too much like leprechauns' gold; who was to know whether all those serendipitous dollars might suddenly turn to dead leaves and blow away overnight?

As soon as Mary had begun earning, she'd insisted on adding whatever she got to the common pool. She had known women with money of their own that they felt free to use as they pleased while expecting their husbands to pay all the bills; this was not her idea of an honorable marriage. Stanley Rinehart was the head of their family, Mary was glad to be able to help her husband but had not thought of taking over his position. She was still distrustful, not so much these days of her ability to earn money as of life in general. She needed his strength to lean on, perhaps even more than she knew.

According to modern medical books, a type A personality is one whose life is "a chronic, incessant struggle to achieve more and more in less and less time." The "A type" tends to believe that he or she can win approval only through achievement, even though this may be far from the actual case.

Modern studies have revealed that hormonal responses to stressful situations tend to be higher in type A children. Mary Roberts Rinehart's life had been stressful from the day she was born. She never forgot those hellfire and brimstone sermons that had been standard Sabbath fare at grandmother's house, or the many senseless restrictions to which she'd routinely been subjected, or the trauma of that first day in school when she'd been chastised for not knowing that the hand which served her best was the one that she was somehow wrong and wicked to use.

Studies have also revealed that the parents of type A children often respond to their achievements not by praise but by pressing them to do more and more, better and better; whereas their laid-back type B siblings get approval for lesser achievements and no parental demands to try harder. This seems to have been the case with Mary and her sister. As Mary had outgrown that ever-ready switch, Cornelia had loaded her with errands, household chores, and extracurricular piano and dancing lessons, expecting her to keep up her grades at school but leaving her little time to study. Olive, on the other hand, was allowed to slide along at her own pace and to have her most unreasonable whims gratified without a murmur of protest from her mother.

Type A personalities basically enjoy being what they are and have no desire to moderate their breakneck careerings along the road of life. Mary had not balked at her mother's demands; she'd drawn satisfaction from being able to do more than her fair share. Her reaction to being freed from schoolday routine had been to subject herself to a far more arduous discipline, taking the nurses' training course over parental protests and sticking it out to the end even though the work was really far too arduous for a young girl of slender build and strong sensibilities.

Stanley Rinehart was himself an achiever, but he was also a cherisher. He'd taken time to show love as well as caring to the sick children back at the hospital. He must have seen pretty Mary Roberts as someone who needed what he had to offer, and he could not have been more right. He surely hadn't expected his wife just to sit on a cushion and sew a fine seam all her days; it was Mary who set herself the goal of being a perfect housekeeper and mother, slaving to keep up the high standards to which Cornelia had trained her, even though as a busy doctor's wife she had a far more complex household to run.

As parents, Cornelia and Tom Roberts had done as well as many and better than some, but that hadn't made them the world's greatest role models. Mary must have found her mother's instructions in lying to bill collectors a confusing paradox in one who professed such lofty religious tenets. Tom's rather cruel baiting of his half-blind mother, his absorption in his inventions, his increasingly excessive drinking, and finally his suicide just before his elder daughter was to marry a thoroughly eligible young man from a prominent local family suggest a neurotic self-involvement that might well have precluded any really deep attachment to anyone else.

It has been suggested nevertheless that Tom Roberts was the center of Mary's universe. For a child of her intelligence, disposition, and abilities, it seems more likely that Mary's universe would have fitted the metaphysical definition of a circle whose center is everywhere and whose circumference is nowhere. She had always found friends outside the family, at fifteen she'd been briefly engaged to a boy at school, at nineteen she'd been wearing Stanley Rinehart's ring tucked under her uniform tie. The grief that Mary showed over her father's suicide could have been compounded from one part affection, one part shock, one part exhaustion and depression generated by the hideous experiences she'd run into as a private nurse, and one part exasperation that he couldn't have waited till after the wedding.

All this is arguable. It is safe only to say that, whether influenced by heredity, habitat, or hormones, Mary Roberts Rinehart was what she was. That headlong plunge into the lake on her new bicycle can be taken as a symbol of her inborn penchant for leaping into fresh experiences without stopping to wonder whether she'd be able to put on the brakes.

Stanley knew his Mary perhaps better than she knew herself. He could not but have realized how greatly she needed his love and strength to keep her life in balance. Mary Roberts on her own could still have become an author and playwright, could still have raked in all the money and notice that she was getting now, and still have found herself socially unacceptable. Mrs. Stanley Rinehart the doctor's wife bore a cachet of respectability that could take her to places where a mere celebrity would never find entrée, except perhaps as some kind of amusing freak.

Mary was very aware of her position. Once she found herself being interviewed for the papers, she took care to present herself as a wife and mother who amused herself by scribbling a bit in her off moments. But this was a trivial concern. Her big worry was the state of her husband's hands. She loved Stanley Rinehart as a man, she honored him as a professional, she wanted him to be happy. Since he could no longer practice surgery, he must find something else to do. And, thanks to her sudden affluence, she could help.

A new trend had been sweeping the medical profession. At the beginning of a new century, the way for an American doctor to get ahead was to specialize, and the way to learn a specialty was to study in Vienna. Stanley came from German stock on his father's side, he spoke German well enough to get along, so to Vienna he would go. But not alone. For so devoted a family man to leave his wife and young sons for months on end would have been unthinkable even if that adventurous crew would have let him get away with it. There was money enough coming in from Mary's writing so that they all could go. Cornelia would stay at Olive's house, where there was a grandchild to pet and another on the way. Mary got out the steamer trunks and the boys' little suitcases and started to pack.

CHAPTER 15

The Rineharts Broaden Their Horizons

∽

Precisely why the Rineharts elected to drive from Pittsburgh
to New York instead of going by train is not recorded. It must
have seemed like a good idea at the time. A few months previously
they had bought their first motor car, a Premier, one of the more
splendid of the various models that were by this time being manufactured in small factories scattered around the country.

The question of whether a driver should sit on the right- or
the left-hand side of the car had still not been settled. The Premier's
steering wheel was on the right, with its gearshift and brake levers
outside on the running board. These were easy enough to get at
because the Premier, like other cars of the time, had no top. Nor
did its front seat have any doors, but the sides dipped lower in
front than in back. An agile male suitably attired in an ankle-
length dustcoat, a peaked cloth cap worn backwards and anchored
to the head by the strap of his driving goggles, and a formidable
pair of driving gauntlets could easily step in over the side.

A lady in a long skirt, a dustcoat like her husband's, kid
gloves, spatted boots, and an architectural marvel of a motoring
hat skewered to her hair with hatpins ten inches long would proba-

bly prefer to enter demurely via the rear door in the tonneau. She would not be wearing goggles, for she wouldn't have been able to put them on without messing her high-piled, side-puffed, and back-knotted coiffure, ruining the effect of her hat, and risking snags in its yard upon yard of filmy veiling.

It was not sexism that made driving primarily a man's job. A fair amount of muscle must have been required to keep a big touring car like the Premier on course, and considerably more to cope with the flat tires that were an inevitable part of the fun. By 1910, pneumatic tires had replaced the original hard rubber carriage tires; these gave a less jouncy ride but the air-filled inner tubes were subject to punctures and blowouts. No motorist in his right mind would travel without a jack, tire irons, a lug wrench, a repair kit, a hand pump, and a spare tire or two. It was by no means unusual to see a car with four or five spares strapped to the back or the running board.

Fixing a flat was in truth no job for a weakling. Those early tires carried fifty or sixty pounds' pressure. Aside from the jacking, unbolting, patching, and remounting, just pumping up the inner tube was a pretty good workout for even a sturdy male in rude health. Rude language may on occasion have assisted the process. We can picture Mary, mindful of Stanley's volcanic explosions in the operating room, tactfully suggesting to her boys that they all go and admire the beauties of nature somewhere out of earshot so that Daddy could have full freedom of expression while he practiced surgery on their fifteenth or twentieth blowout.

Roads in some of the cities that the Rineharts passed through might have been paved. Those in the rural areas, and they were far in the majority, almost certainly had not. This was late September, the dirt roads had had a long, hot summer in which to dry out, and the Premier's windshield could have done little or nothing to screen its passengers from the clouds of dust that were stirred up by every turn of the wheels.

The three boys perched in the high tonneau didn't seem to mind the dust. They amused themselves in various imaginative ways. One trick was to let their broad-brimmed straw hats fly off, always when some gullible soul was nearby to yell "Hey, boy, you've lost your hat!" The hatless one would then calmly reel in the long string to which the hat was attached and put his catch back on. Such were then the simple joys of childhood.

Their father and mother in the front seat, which was lower than the back, got the brunt of the dust. Driving goggles doubtless served Stanley well enough, but Mary's multiple veils could not have been all that effective at keeping the fine particles from sifting through their mesh. Her eyes became badly bloodshot. Somewhere along the way she read in a newspaper article that Mrs. Rinehart, the well-known novelist, was going blind and that this trip to Europe was being undertaken in the hope of saving her eyesight. Being Mary, she worried for weeks, even though bed rest and a milk diet easily cleared up the problem once she'd got away from the dust.

They boarded their steamship in New York and made a short stopover in England for sight-seeing.

Stanley Junior had been elected to keep a journal of the trip. According to his diary, they went to luncheon at "Ye Olde Cheshire Cheese," which had been a loafing place (*sic*) of Dr. Samuel Johnson. Father sat in Dr. Johnson's place at the table where the eminent lexicographer had gourmandized. Stanley didn't write "eminent lexicographer"; on the evidence he probably could not have spelled it. They visited Saint Paul's Cathedral, which was gloomy. They went to a curiosity shop. Stanley Junior bought a telescope. They took the subway to Madame Tussaud's; the boys must not have been allowed inside the Chamber of Horrors or Stanley's entry would surely have been longer.

Westminster Abbey was impressive, but the dancing at the Alhambra Theater was more to the young diarist's taste. They toured Old London in taxis, they had lunch at Pagani's. Stanley said the food was rotten and didn't eat any.

On October 22, they packed up and went to Folkestone, on the coast. The channel boat took them to Boulogne, and thence by train to Vienna.

In May 1910, Dr. Rinehart had spent a couple of weeks at his old college, Hahnemann in Philadelphia, ostensibly taking a refresher course, perhaps mainly trying to get his head together. Mary had missed her husband dreadfully, she'd been even less happy when he wrote that he'd decided to specialize in tuberculosis.

His was a brave decision, but a logical one. Doctors saw more tuberculosis cases than anything else. During the previous year, this highly contagious lung disease had still been the number one killer in the United States, with a death rate of one out of every nine patients. In some other countries, the rate was a good deal higher.

The great problem with tuberculosis was—and remains—that it is so dreadfully easy to catch. Just being on the same streetcar with an infected person who sneezed or coughed carelessly, spraying live bacilli into the air for fellow passengers to inhale, could hypothetically have wiped out every ninth rider. Even dust from dried sputum contains live bacteria, and there was far too much of that around in 1910, especially in cities where men chewed tobacco and spat on the sidewalks where well-dressed ladies strolled by, wearing skirts with trains that swept the pavement. Before pasteurization became mandatory, milk from cows infected with bovine tuberculosis was another serious threat. One bucketful mixed into a vat at a dairy where milk from various farms was collected could mean trouble for households all along the milkman's route.

In 1882, when Stanley Marshall Rinehart was fifteen, the tubercle bacillus had been discovered by a German, Dr. Robert Koch. With the cause of the disease established, progress could be made in controlling it on an international basis. Since 1904 there had been national tuberculosis associations in Canada, Great Britain, and the United States; but it was in Denmark that Einar Holbøll invented the Christmas Seal in 1903 as a device for funding research.

Studies were proving what doctors had surely suspected, that tuberculosis was more prevalent in crowded areas, particularly among people living in unsanitary conditions. However, nobody was immune. This was a full-scale war that would have to be fought on many fronts, with more knowledge, better medicines and techniques, and far more well-trained doctors than were then available. Dr. Rinehart's studies abroad, coupled with his already fine reputation, would qualify him for a high position. Still, Mary begged her husband to get himself an antiseptic spray before he faced those foreign germs.

Staying at a Viennese hotel would have been too expensive, so the Rineharts settled down in the Pension Columbia on the Dochgosse near the *Allgemeine Krankenhaus* (literally the "all-sorts-of-people-sick-house"; i.e. general hospital). Stanley Junior recorded the pension as a very homelike place. Dr. Rinehart got right down to hard work, taking German lessons on the side to supplement his imperfect knowledge of the language. Mary also began studying German, with a nearsighted fräulein who couldn't see the text unless she literally had her nose in the book; for a young woman to wear eyeglasses was not the done thing.

The boys acquired a governess. Her name was Reif, she was about twenty-five years old, and young Stanley liked her very much. She was supposed to teach the boys German. Instead, they did wonders for her English. After the turn of the year, Mary and the doctor decided to enroll their sons in school. The teachers didn't seem to care whether the boys showed up or not; it seems to have been their parents who were getting most of the education.

While Dr. Rinehart strove to fit himself for his new specialty, Mary went about broadening her horizons. She visited art galleries and studied the paintings and prints. She went to the opera and followed the libretto as the Viennese did. Wagner's operas, not yet well known in the States outside of New York, were all the rage here. Austrian patrons could go out between the acts and buy sausages; Parsifal might have been more palatable to then uninitiated Americans if they could have got their culture with a little bratwurst and sauerkraut on the side.

Another between-the-acts custom in Vienna was for men to

stand up and study the ladies through their opera glasses from only a few seats away. Whether this was machismo or myopia, Mary seems never to have found out, but she was gracious enough to be glad later that these pleasure-bent dandies had managed to enjoy themselves before the powder keg blew up.

The Rineharts' temporary home consisted of a suite of rooms on the third floor of a vast stone building. It had no lift and no lights in the hallways after 10 P.M., but Vienna was a night-owl city. Nobody went straight home from the opera. Some of the theaters and music halls didn't even open until midnight. On Saturday nights, when Dr. Rinehart borrowed time from his studies to take the family out to dinner and didn't bring them back until after curfew, the house would be dark and the front door locked. They'd have to ring the doorbell and wait.

Eventually a grumpy *Hausbesorger* (porter) would come down in his nightshirt, with his wide-spreading, formidably waxed mustache tied up in a contraption much like the whaleboned net collars that women were then wearing for no good reason that Mary could think of, even though she wore them too. The bandage went all around his head and tied at the back, and it had holes cut in the sides so that his ears could stick out and serve as anchors.

He would first collect the five hellers (one cent) per head that was his fixed rate for overtime, then he'd equip each member of the party with a lighted midget candle, the sort that the Rinehart boys associated with birthday cakes. The latecomers would then wind their little torchlight procession up those many stairs, take out the pads between the hermetically sealed double windows, and let in the perilous night air against which their landlady, Frau Gallitzenstein, repeatedly warned them.

Determined, like her husband, to squeeze every drop of juice from this once-in-a-lifetime experience, Mary took the boys and their governess to the Semmering (the Austrian Alps) for a before-Thanksgiving holiday. They had their first experience with skis, they went sledding. Young Stanley did not fail to record that Miss Reif fell off five times.

Candles were the only nighttime illumination at the inn.

Mary would light a dozen at a time in the living room and read by them after the children were in bed. She'd discovered a whole set of books by Lafcadio Hearn. Born in Ionia of half-Greek, half-Irish parentage, educated in France and England, a journalist in America, always writing but seldom successful in his earlier years, Hearn at last found his true home in Japan, married the daughter of a samurai family and became a respected university professor. He was a spinner of strangely intriguing stories, often with a thread of the supernatural winding through; just the candlelight fare for a compulsive reader's snowy winter evenings in a strange land.

Dr. Rinehart came up for the weekend, and then it was back to work for all hands. While the boys went through the motions of attending school, Mary began a novel. Her eyes no longer bothered her, but she found it necessary to light the candles by three o'clock in the afternoon when the gray twilight set in. Always, Vienna's misty air cast a chill over the room even though Mary crammed charcoal briquettes recklessly into the tall, handsome, but inefficient porcelain stove. Sometimes she wrapped the half-size goosefeather mattress from her bed around her legs, but it didn't help much.

Nor did Mary's study of German contribute anything useful to her writing style. When she got back to Pittsburgh and read over what she'd put down under the influence of all that braunschweiger and Sachertorte, she found her text so full of awkward semi-Germanic constructions that she had to junk it and rewrite the whole thing.

This book, based on an unproduced play of hers called *The Water Wooers*, is an almost totally American story of a health spa tottering on the brink of insolvency. A redheaded female Figaro narrates the story, and a number of other characters are involved in assorted dilemmas, which the engaging redhead has to sort out with a little help and a good deal of hindrance from her friends. It need hardly be said that two of the featured players are a beautiful American heiress and a suave European nobleman, complete with monocle and mustache, to whom she is betrothed. The heiress asks for the redhead's honest verdict on her princely spouse-to-be, the redhead comes up with a tactful answer.

"He looks all right. Perhaps you can coax him to shave."

Equally needless to say, it all comes out in the wash. *Where There's a Will* was published in 1912 by Bobbs-Merrill.

But didn't Mary do a novel set in Austria? Of course she did. How could she have resisted so beguiling a locale as the Siebensternengasse, the Little Street of the Seven Stars? She wasn't able to tackle this next project until after she'd got home; the book reads as if she was having withdrawal symptoms from all the *Schlag*-laden coffee she'd imbibed at the *Kaffeehaus* where she and the doctor had gone daily to read the newspapers. It's all about a poor but beautiful young violinist (female), a poor but noble young doctor (male), and a poor little orphan (boy) who is fading away in the *Krankenhaus*. *The Street of Seven Stars* was not enthusiastically received in the States, but Mary liked it. A writer can't help keeping a warm spot for even the sickliest of her brain-children.

Besides picking up ideas both good and otherwise, Mary was meeting some of the locals in Vienna. A lady professor from Berlin asked her how Americans were taxed. Mary said her husband had to pay a dollar a year poll tax and another dollar for a school tax.

And was that all? The *Professorin* was flabbergasted.

Actually Americans were taxed in a number of ways, such as on property, alcohol, and inheritance; but the Rineharts then owned no real estate, imbibed only modestly, and had no rich relatives leaving them money, so how was Mary to know? At least she gave the *Professorin* something new to think about.

New Year's Eve in Vienna was a night to remember. The city was one great festival with orchestras playing, dancers waltzing around and around to the heady strains of Strauss and Waldteufel, flowers being flung down from theater boxes and flung back again like confetti, a chimney sweep running around with a squealing piglet in his arms. To touch a sweep was lucky, to touch the pig was luckier still. Four years hence, the Austrians would be needing all the luck they could get; tonight the fun and feasting went on.

But then, feasting was always going on. A true Viennese

would have coffee and rolls upon rising, a hearty breakfast about nine o'clock, perhaps a little something around noontime to stay the stomach until the day's big meal at two, afternoon tea or coffee with *Schlagobers* at five, then an early evening dinner and maybe a midnight snack to make sure nobody went to bed hungry.

CHAPTER 16

Cities of Dreams and Nightmares

Nobody went hungry, that is, except the poor. Herr Doktor Rinehart was working in both the pulmonary and cardiac fields, at the *Allgemeine Krankenhaus* he found plenty of subjects for clinical study. This beautiful old city of Vienna was not all whipped cream and *Liebesfreud*. Too many dashing young soldiers were fathering illegitimate children on too-trusting girls and leaving them to shift for themselves however they might. Older women who had the misfortune to be neither pretty nor rich were held in low esteem, the Rineharts were aghast to see so many gray-haired matrons working on construction projects, climbing ladders, carrying hodfuls of brick, stone, and mortar up to the masons.

One of Dr. Rinehart's courses was in bronchoscopy. This included learning to remove foreign bodies from the bronchial tubes, a terribly painful process that involved having to give the patient heavy doses of cocaine. The numbers of poor volunteers who were willing to let untrained students like himself practice on them for a pitifully low fee shocked the American doctor to his depths.

What appalled Mary even more was finding out how many

of the foreign doctors who flitted in and out of the classrooms were staying in Vienna for only a couple of weeks, or a month at most. They would take a crash course or two, learn a few catch phrases and precious little else, then bustle off home surrounded by the glamorous aura of having studied abroad and hang up a diploma that was worth about as much in the way of credentials as a souvenir program from the opera.

The *Dozents* who signed these farcical diplomas knew what was going on, but what could they do? They were only there to teach; if these fly-by-night physicians were brash enough to go back to America and pass themselves off as specialists, was it any skin off the Austrians' noses? Nevertheless, honest instructors loathed being made parties to so blatant a fraud. After she got home, Mary wrote an article called "The Medical Quick Lunch Counter." It ran in the *Saturday Evening Post* July 26, 1913. Some American doctors took umbrage but one of the best-known Viennese lecturers sent her a letter of thanks.

Among the happier memories soon to be carried away by the Rineharts would be a ball given by the city of Vienna to the emperor. At the last minute, the aging Franz Joseph, who had by this time only about five more years to live, fell ill; his place was taken by his grandson, Prince Carl, then hardly more than a boy. Moral support was provided by an older archduchess wearing a diamond-studded crown tipped with enormous pear-shaped pearls on all its points. She looked frail, bored, and wearied by that glittering load of responsibility weighing down her head.

In 1917, Mary would poke gentle fun at Anthony Hope and George Barr McCutcheon with a Graustarkian romance in which the handsome prince is only ten years old. It's hard to believe that *Long Live the King* was not to some extent inspired by the memory of that night at the absent emperor's ball, dredged up from the subliminal ragbag that is so indispensable a part of any fiction writer's tool kit.

Romance was unavoidable in Vienna. It ran rife among all who could afford the luxury and no doubt a good many who couldn't. The Rineharts' Saturday night visits to the Bal Tabarin were given an extra touch of zest for Mary by a certain tall army officer. He never spoke to her, never begged to be introduced, but never failed to catch her eye, stand to attention, and raise his glass in a toast. Being an *anständige Frau* like the fair Valencienne in *The Merry Widow,* Mary had to pretend that she was unaware of the gallant officer's attention. Nevertheless, a woman in her midthirties, mother of three, could scarcely have come away without a smug little feeling that she still had what it took to please the troops.

Late in February, the family said good-bye to Frau Gallitzenstein, the mustachioed porter, and their neighbor the Serbian spy. Dr. Rinehart had dutifully done what he'd come for, and he'd earned a holiday before they hit the homeward trail. Their next stop was Munich. They arrived during the pre-Lenten celebration, in a rain of confetti that soon turned to hail and then to snow.

Considering what the Rineharts would be experiencing in a few years' time, it's hardly surprising that Mary, writing her autobiography a quarter of a century later, dismissed their visit to Germany in a few curt paragraphs. Stanley Junior's on-the-spot reporting paints a far livelier picture, starting with their first night in Munich, when his mother decided to take a picture of the three boys all huddled together under an enormous puff.

The 1911 equivalent of the flash bulb was a pinch of magnesium powder in a metal holder at the far end of Father's outstretched arm. When ignited on this night, the flash powder flared up for an instant in a strong white glare and incidentally set fire to a curtain that nobody had noticed in time. Dr. Rinehart, blinded by the flash, didn't react right away. Whether Mary remembered to snap the picture before putting out the fire, young Stanley forgot to say. Anyway, the curtain was only singed and the holiday went merrily on.

The Stanleys Senior and Junior went to cash an Austrian check. The easygoing Austrian bank clerk had assured Dr. Rinehart that he wouldn't need any notice, but the regulation-minded Teutons said he did, and furthermore that he'd have to wait several days for the notice to come from Vienna. The doctor had only seven dollars in his pocket, but he was not without his undaunted fighting spirit. By afternoon he'd got his money. One gets the impression that the boys spent it all on confetti. This was the first time they'd seen tiny bits of colored paper used as an offensive weapon. As young Stanley was ambling along with his mouth open, a prankster shouted "*Mahlzeit!*" (literally "mealtime," slang for "enjoy your meal") and shoved a handful down his gullet. Spectators on balconies tossed down balls of confetti wrapped in tissue paper, and children raced to get them, knocking other boys and girls and even grown-ups off their feet. Neatly dressed people trying to get through the crowd emerged looking like scarecrows. Stanley Junior recorded one man sitting on the sidewalk with a dent in his hat, and what surprised him most was that neither this victim nor any of the others seemed to mind getting mauled about.

The boys had a different fräulein now, a well-connected young lady named Hilda von Wagner von Florheim. She had a gentleman friend, a professor, who took them riding in his auto. According to Stanley Junior, the professor was short but cheerful and let the chauffeur drive fast. One object of their sight-seeing tour was the *Hofbrauhalle*, an enormous barn of a place starkly furnished with long wooden tables and benches. The wooden floor was soaked with spilled beer, and the boys estimated later that between two and three hundred gallons of beer got drunk every day. (And it was terrible, Stanley Junior added in a jocose parenthesis, when beer got drunk.)

The Munich pigeons were friendly, and Stanley Junior persuaded them to perch on his head by sprinkling bird seed in his hair. At the aquarium the boys met a seal who was clamoring loudly for fish. Alan went to buy him one—Stanley noted in his diary that they cost ten pfennig, or two and a half cents per fish. Once the seal had made sure Alan was really buying the fish, he stood up on his hind legs (*sic*) and waited with no more fuss. This was evidently standard procedure enjoyed by the feeder, the fishmonger, and most particularly by the seal.

The seal was not the only creature being fed. The boys saw the man in charge give a dead white mouse to a big lizard in a cage. They watched for five minutes while the lizard swallowed the mouse in a series of leisurely gulps. A water moccasin was offered a live mouse: It struck with its fangs, waited a few minutes, then grabbed the luckless creature in its mouth. Stanley Junior thought it did this to make the mouse jump and that the mouse did not enjoy the snake's attention, and about the latter he was probably right. After a while, the snake swallowed the mouse, still alive, at the same slow pace as the lizard had done. Stanley records that he and his brothers were horrified.

The Rineharts had got to Munich on the night of February 25, 1911. They left the night of March 4 for Berlin, and arrived at eight the next morning. The diarist gives high marks to the German sleeping cars but regrets having to leave fräulein's friend's motor car. Fräulein von Wagner von Florheim did take them walking down the famous Unter den Lindenstrasse. This bustling, shop-lined avenue reminded Stanley Junior of Broadway and made him homesick for New York; although, as he explained, he wasn't wishing to be there because he knew that once he'd got back to the States he'd be wishing he were still in Europe.

The doubly *von*ned young governess seemed to have friends everywhere. One of the Berlin contingent took the party out driving in an open carriage, and they went to a wonderful store that outshone most of the American stores Stanley Junior had seen.

Berlin was different from Munich and far, far different from Vienna. Berliners were organized, they were diligent, but they didn't seem to have much fun. The pension where the Rineharts were staying was literally too clean for comfort; every floor, every piece of furniture got polished every single day. The boys felt compelled to sneak around on tiptoe for fear of disturbing the *Hausfrau*'s impeccable appointments.

Here, the military motif was far too much in evidence. Queen Victoria's nephew, Kaiser Wilhelm II, had dreamed of expanding his empire; now it was beginning to look as though he and his generals might be on the way to converting their wishes for conquest into action. Berlin was full of soldiers, squads of them marching down the streets with a stiff-legged goose step that the Rinehart boys found amusing. Mary had to shush her irreverently snickering sons and tell them to wipe the smiles off their faces.

Those other faces under the peaked uniform caps were too set, too wooden, too dehumanized; she herself saw nothing funny about them.

King George V and Queen Mary of England had always liked their cousin the kaiser. In May 1912, they would attend the wedding of Wilhelm II's only daughter, Princess Victoria Louise, to their cousin Ernest Augustus, duke of Brunswick-Lüneburg, despite the growing tensions between their respective countries. Britain's king would make it clear to the Germans and particularly to his own somewhat jittery subjects that this was purely a family occasion and must in no way be interpreted as a state visit. George V did not then know that it would be the last visit ever paid between these two then reigning monarchs, or that, once the Armistice was signed, the monarchy in Germany would thenceforth cease to exist.

During the Rineharts' brief stay in Berlin, they had plenty of opportunities to observe that relations between Germany and Britain were already showing signs of strain. Americans were still tolerated but the English were anathema and it was not always easy for Berliners to discern the differences between people of two nationalities who spoke the same language. The Rineharts got sick of arriving at a restaurant, seeing plenty of empty tables, and then being kept standing around for an unconscionable length of time while the waiters fawned servilely over every *Oberleutnant* and *Unterleutnant* in the place.

Despite a good deal of rude treatment, the boys were enjoying themselves. They still had one day in the city, and they made the most of the time, collecting snapshots they'd taken to be developed, shopping for souvenirs. Stanley Junior bought his mother a calendar mounted on wood that was carved in the shape of a dachshund drinking beer. Fräulein's friend took them for another carriage ride, which Stanley thought was nice of the friend. And the cocoa was good.

On their last afternoon, the family took a sight-seeing tour by taxi. Going past some woods, Stanley Junior asked their driver if animals lived there. "Oh yes," the man replied, "there is a dog." The diarist commented sweetly on the German taxi drivers' penchant for humor, including their prankish way of driving strangers out into the countryside and giving them a choice of paying double fare or walking back to the city.

Then it was *auf wiedersehen* to Berlin and on to Cologne, another overnight journey. They changed trains for Brussels, where fräulein again proved her worth by being able to translate from English to German to French or Flemish, these last two being the only languages Belgian taxi drivers seemed able to speak.

Mary was not feeling well; even Stanley Junior was tired out. The next day they went on to Calais and straight to the channel steamer. The crossing to Dover was rough, but getting back to England felt good. Stanley was glad to be where everybody spoke English; still he referred to the hotel as a pension and remarked that the waiter was German.

Dr. Rinehart was still keeping his nose to the grindstone. He intended to finish his overseas studies with a two-week course at Guy's Hospital in London.

Having done their duty as sightseers on their earlier visit, Mary and the boys took the return trip more easily. They lounged around the hotel, they went shopping. They saw Maskelyne, the famous magician, who asked for a volunteer from the audience and got young Stanley. They went to the zoo in Hyde Park on Sunday and watched a baby camel gambol. Stanley Junior recorded in his diary that he supposed it was too young to know it shouldn't gambol (*sic*) on Sunday. They went to see an airship flight. There were three biplanes and a monoplane—this was a great thrill.

On March 25, 1911, the Rineharts said good-bye to fräulein at the station and went on to Liverpool, where they boarded the steamship that would take them home. The crossing was rough at times, but the fun went on. The best part of the voyage was docking in New York. On April 4, they were back in Pittsburgh, and content to be there.

CHAPTER 17

Be It Never So Humble

Nowadays we hear a fair amount about right-brain and left-brain characteristics. The general idea seems to be that the creative side of the brain feeds on honeydew and drinks the milk of paradise while the stodgy old other half is the dependable drudge that remembers to clean the cat box and pay the light bill. By now it must be clear to us that Mary Roberts Rinehart had a brain half that worked much like Mozart's, whizzing out new plots and dialogue even faster than her well-trained hand could write them down.

Unfortunately, her superdynamic creative half must often have forgotten to let the not-so-swift practical side know what it was up to. The faster Mary wrote, the more money poured in. The more money she earned, the more financial binds it got her into. That romantic imagination tricked her into buying a sixteenth of a gold mine that never got mined. In another burst of wishful thinking, she gave an ex-aviator a check for $10,000 to develop an oil well that existed only in *his* brain. Not long after the family got home, this mental communication gap of Mary's developed into the biggest case yet of "had she but known."

Dr. Rinehart's new career was going to make a tremendous difference in the way his family lived. He would no longer be on call night and day, his offices would not be in the house, the telephone wouldn't be ringing at all hours. Mary wouldn't be trying desperately to quiet the boys down so as not to disturb patients in the waiting room or frantically tracking down her husband and alerting him to the latest emergency. His business address would be an attractive suite in downtown Pittsburgh where he would hold no evening hours. Mary could invite friends to dinner with confidence that their host would be on hand to carve the roast with surgical skill and not fall asleep with his head in the soup. They could go to parties, to the theater, have a life of their own for a change.

And they would have a house of their own. All her life long, Mary had lived in rented dwellings. Other people bought houses, why shouldn't the Rineharts? She envisioned a haven of peace and security where the boys could grow up, a real home to which, in future years, her sons' sons and daughters could come and stay and be happy. She had money now, she could make her dream come true. She began to house hunt.

Here it came, the ultimate opportunity for Mary Roberts Rinehart to buy the Brooklyn Bridge. Twelve miles outside Pittsburgh, in the picturesque Sewickley Valley to which wealthy families had begun moving now that old Allegheny had been absorbed into the metropolis, beautifully situated on a high bluff overlooking the Ohio River, sat a magnificent ruin. Named Cassella, the mansion had been built half a century before for George W. Cass, one of the post–Civil War era's swashbuckling railroad barons. There remained in the gulley below the bluff a spur track to which the magnate's private railway car had often been shunted. Whether the Rineharts could ever make use of so particular an amenity was doubtful, but the track did add a certain cachet to the demesne.

Cassella had been nobly planned; in its heyday the house must have been magnificent. But any dwelling begins to decay if it sits too long untenanted; even the enthralled Mary could see that extensive repairs needed to be made before these rooms were again fit to live in. She was, as usual, undaunted. This was the house she wanted, this was the house she would have. And this was the house she would pay for, she vowed, every cent of it, all by herself. Dr. Rinehart had far more important things to do with his money than cater to the whims of his admittedly sometimes extravagant wife.

Stanley Marshall Rinehart had long been a person of note in the Pittsburgh area. His recent studies abroad and his decision to set up as a specialist were giving him added stature, and he was increasingly asked to write and lecture. He had already served for a number of years on Pittsburgh's Tuberculosis Commission; now, as well as conducting a private practice, he was in charge of the State Tuberculosis Dispensary. In 1914 he would be invited to serve on the planning committee to outfit the new city tuberculosis hospital. A longish biographical sketch of Dr. Stanley Marshall Rinehart in the 1922 *History of Pittsburgh and Environs* stated that "the fight for the prevention of tuberculosis has no more faithful proponent than he, his contribution that of exact medical knowledge and the enthusiasm of the true humanitarian."

The piece listed Dr. Rinehart as a member of the American and the Pennsylvania State Homeopathic Associations and of the Allegheny Homeopathic Society. His clubs were the Edgeworth and the Allegheny Country Club, his church Methodist Episcopal, his politics Republican. His sons' schools and colleges were listed in detail. His wife the authoress rated a courteous paragraph at the end.

While her husband was setting up his new offices, Mary was drawing every cent she had out of the bank and feeding it to her badly injured white elephant. Not until the die had been irrevocably cast did she quite realize what she'd taken on. Cassella was truly enormous—its walls seemed to have spread farther every time she went there. A room that none of the family could recall ever having noticed before suddenly manifested itself behind the kitchen. No doubt this room showed problems that must be dealt with, for there were problems everywhere else.

One of the minor dilemmas was what they should rename the house now that "Cassella" was no longer appropriate. Mary asked Stanley if he had any ideas. He suggested they call it the Bluff, since that was what they were putting up, and the Bluff it became.

Those workmen, however, weren't bluffing. They were there on the job, every week, swarms of them. Come payday, they expected to be paid cash on the barrelhead. Mary wrote like a perpetual motion machine, reeling off whatever words came into her head, hardly daring to lift her eyes from the page for fear of missing a payment. Her husband loathed seeing her in this state, but what could he do? Stanley Rinehart knew from experience that there was no use trying to stop his wife from knocking herself out with overwork until the gargantuan task that she'd so rashly set herself was done.

Nor was it all hack stuff that Mary was churning out. *The Case of Jennie Brice* was written in 1912 as an unassuming little mystery about a middle-aged widow who has seen better days and been reduced to running a boardinghouse down on the flats along the Allegheny River. It's flood time again. The widow takes up her carpets as she does every year, she moves her cooking stove upstairs, she rents a rowboat and keeps it tied to the staircase banister in her front hall for transportation until the flooding is over and the river flows back out of her door. Her second-floor front is giving her trouble—theatrical couples are always chancy tenants.

Sometimes you have the good fortune to come upon a novel that's like a suit tailored in Bond Street or an understated little black frock by a top designer, so exquisitely put together that you don't quite realize you're seeing something extraspecial until you take a second look. Even if the flood scenes were its only attraction, *Jennie Brice* would be well worth a second look.

By the end of that year, Mary was flagging sadly. Another mystery novel, *The After House*, written in early 1913, is no masterpiece. This one takes place on an old schooner that's been tarted up as a rich man's yacht. One of its lesser but more infuriating flaws is that Mary kept referring to the schooner as a ship. She'd lifted the plot from a true and grisly account of a triple ax murder aboard the lumber schooner *Henry Fuller* that had been told to her and Stanley by a fellow member one afternoon over drinks at the country club.

By the time the Rineharts heard the story, the first mate of the *Henry Fuller* had served nearly seventeen years of a life sentence for the triple murder. The case against him could not have been watertight or he would probably have been executed instead of incarcerated. Another member of the crew had been suspected but never indicted. The stir created by Mary Roberts Rinehart's new thriller caused the case to be reopened.

It was discovered that some years after the mate had been sent to jail, the other suspect, who was by then a patient in a Swedish hospital, had been seized with a sudden fit of homicidal mania and attacked his nurse with a knife. Once this fact was made public, the mate was exonerated and released. He wrote Mrs. Rinehart a heartfelt letter of thanks, swearing that he had been innocent of the crime for which he had spent seventeen years behind bars and letting her know that he was now running a night restaurant wagon in Atlanta.

So the stories went out and the money came in. The impossible was actually happening; in the spring of 1912, renovations at the Bluff were far enough along for the family to move in. By that time Mary had spent $50,000 on her dream house. She still owed $20,000, and she would have to shell out yet another $20,000 before work was complete down to the garage and the driveways and all seven acres had been brought under control by the landscapers.

Even after the job was done, expenses continued to be heavy. An estate the size of the Bluff required a staff of servants both indoors and out, and they had to be housed, fed, and paid. There were furnishings to be bought, there were the boys' school fees, there were endless duns for donations from the allegedly rich Rineharts to innumerable worthy causes. Mary told a touching tale of being hit up by the minister for a new church organ at a time when her bank balance totaled exactly $300. But no matter what it cost, the Bluff was worth every penny. Once again Mary could say, as she'd said on that long-ago night when her parents had at last moved into a place of their own, "This is my home."

She was at home here in more ways than one. She'd known the Sewickley Valley as a little girl, this was where she and Uncle John used to come riding. Now John was living out in Cincinnati with his second wife. The woods and fields that he and his niece had once roamed freely on horseback had given way to stately houses and rolling lawns. The country club was close by. The Rineharts were welcomed as new members and were making new friends. Here in this enclave of the privileged nobody bothered to lock doors in the daytime. Neighbors strolled in and out of each other's houses without ceremony, not even bothering to knock. Life was all marvelously free and easy after those frenetic years in the city.

Mary the workhorse was learning that much could be said for the leisured life of a well-to-do suburban matron. She played bridge, got invited to women's club meetings, shopped for wonderful hats, took her boys to the dancing classes taught by Miss Molly at the Edgeworth Club. When Miss Molly organized a costume dance for the children, Mary dressed Alan as a furry Robinson Crusoe and ripped the leather upholstery off an old chair to make him a real animal-skin umbrella. Ted played his brother's Man Friday in a costume that sounds a bit like Gunga Din's, with nothing much before and rather less than half of that behind.

All the Rineharts were animal lovers, and they began to accumulate pets: dogs, cats, pheasants, rabbits, a few sheep to nibble off the rank grass and weeds down in the ravine. One of the boys sent off somewhere for a pair of ferrets. These enterprising members of the polecat family came in a box, and sometime during the night they managed to chew their way out of it. William the gardener joined in the hunt. While he was on his knees searching under a radiator, a streak of whitish fur whizzed up his back and took a nip out of his neck.

This was a most disrespectful way for an old retainer to be treated. William wasn't actually old, but he had worked on the property before the Rineharts arrived and would stay at the Bluff until they were gone. In the springtime he planted, in summer he mowed the lawns and tended the flower beds, in autumn he raked leaves and mulched the roses. In winter he shoveled snow, on Christmas he played Santa Claus in a red velvet suit and a bushy white beard. Born in Germany, William had become wholly Americanized. A few years from now, his sons would fight on the Allied side. Nevertheless, William still shaved his head every spring with a razor because that was what his forebears had always done back home in Prussia.

Their other old retainer was Maggie, the cook. Mrs. Rinehart credited Maggie's good food for the fact that all three boys grew to be over six feet tall. Other servants came and went. One was a butler from Barbados who suspected Maggie of sneaking a love philter into his coffee. Another butler got drunk one night and decided to debag the village policeman. The butler removed the officer's trousers with aplomb and dispatch, as a good servant should, but Dr. Rinehart fired him anyway.

There were other minor vicissitudes. Mary had taken up horseback riding again. She got tossed once in a while but that was nothing to worry about. Somewhat more disturbing were Alan's chemistry experiments. Somehow or other, he found out how to make a railroad torpedo, obtained the necessary ingredients, put them together in the garage, then tested his creation by banging it with an iron weight. The explosion was impressive; Mary was aghast to see her young son stagger out of the garage in a cloud of smoke with his hair and eyebrows partly singed off and sit down in the middle of the driveway to ponder on what had gone wrong.

One the whole, however, life at the Bluff was going along happily. Mary had a real study to work in. Her desk sat in a bay window overlooking the garden, its walls were lined with bookcases, there was even a safe hidden behind a pair of glass doors camouflaged by painted-on books that could perhaps, she thought, have deceived a seriously myopic burglar. Mary never kept anything in the safe except a mess of odds and ends, mostly scribbled notes and early drafts of forgotten works, but no doubt a safe was a nice thing to have. Her plan was to work in the study each day until she heard the slamming and stomping that always meant her menfolk were home.

Like the other ladies in her set, Mary was still wearing her skirts brushing the ground, her choker collars up to her ears, her hair piled high on her head, her whaleboned corset pinched in at the waist. Her hats were enormous, her veils spotted with fluffy chenille polka dots the size of a dime. And, like her neighbors, she saw no reason to pass up the rich cream soups, the calorie-laden entrées, the lavish desserts that everybody's cook, including her own, knew so well how to concoct. Why should she? Dieting was a laughable concept; a fine figure of a woman was one with plenty of meat on her bones. Mary did gain some weight but she never got fat—she never had the time.

Whether she or her husband was the greater workaholic in those days would have been hard to judge. In addition to his private practice, Dr. Rinehart was building the State Tuberculosis Dispensary—*his* dispensary—into one of the biggest and best in the entire United States. As the facility grew, his staff increased. There was always more than enough work for the doctors and nurses to do but Stanley Marshall Rinehart never lost the personal touch. His poor patients were his children; he lectured them, scolded them, babied them into taking their medicine and working with him toward getting well. At Christmas he had no qualms about panhandling from the rich to give to the poor; there was to be a tree at the dispensary with presents for everybody. Perhaps Stanley himself led the carols, as he had done on that fateful Christmas years ago when Nurse Roberts had played the piano for those mutinous patients in the quarantine hospital.

And still the effort was not enough to keep up with the need. A young boy sick with tuberculosis, learning that he would have to wait weeks for a bed in the badly overcrowded state sanitarium, walked out of the dispensary, climbed to the top of a high building, and jumped off. Such tragedies must never happen again. Stanley went home and enlisted his wife in the fight. Mary willingly dropped her writing long enough to establish a women's organization dedicated to supporting and furthering the growth of the dispensary. Her fund-raising group succeeded, and kept on succeeding; Mary considered this one of her most important achievements.

It was also one more complication in an already overcrowded life. Mary reorganized her household on more businesslike lines, systematized the marketing and buying, and offloaded to her mother's hired companion the mending and darning on which she herself, from force of habit, had still been spending many of her evenings. She'd faced the fact that, while she might prefer not to think of herself as a career woman, she was indubitably and irrevocably a professional writer.

Every new success meant added stress: editors and agents begged to talk with her, lion-hunters showered her with invitations. Readers wrote scads of fan letters, and some of them tried to start an ongoing correspondence. All very flattering, of course, but also distracting and time-consuming. Mary spoke wistfully in her autobiography of "the creative writer's desperate search for freedom not only from interruption but from the fear of interruption."

Her fear was real. In this great, rambling house, with so many rooms that it was hard to keep track of which was where, the beleaguered mistress could find not one solitary corner where it was possible for her to write without being pestered. Her elegant new study was hopeless, so she fled to the boys' gymnasium and set up a card table behind the punching bag. Even there she was hunted down, by servants, by neighbors, by total strangers wanting to meet the famous author.

Mary's most implacable huntress was her mother. Cornelia Roberts had conceived the convenient notion that if she crept up ever so silently and gave her frantically toiling daughter just the slightest hint of a touch on the arm, it wouldn't count as an interruption. As any writer knows, the gentlest word, the smallest sound, anything that breaks the ferocious concentration necessary to get words that have formed in the mind down on paper before they dissolve into nothing can have the same impact as sticking a finger in a lamp socket. Greatly to Mary's credit, she refrained from matricide. Instead, patiently and lovingly, she would put down her pen and embark on the tedious round of question and signal.

"Is it something you want to do?"

Cornelia would shake her head. No.

"Something to eat?" No. "Someone you've seen?" No.

This could go on for hours, sometimes for the better part of a day, until both were exhausted and close to tears. Finally the magic word would be spoken, it would turn out that Cornelia wanted to know why one of her handkerchiefs was missing.

Stanley could not allow this silent hectoring to go on. There was a small room in his downtown suite that nobody was using, and he suggested that his wife had better come and work there. The only problem was that, thinking he might want to set up an X-ray machine, he'd had the walls and ceiling painted black. Should he have them repainted? Mary said no, she didn't mind a bit. By this time, a nice, dark, quiet cave was just the kind of place she needed.

CHAPTER 18

A Lot of Work, A Little Play,
A Gathering Storm

Back when they were newlyweds and too green to know any better, the Rineharts had bought themselves a consummately ugly golden oak dining table. This table, a matching chair, and a desk lamp went to the new office. Mary added a large blotter, a stack of the yellow paper that she found easier on her eyes than white, a bottle of ink, and her trusty fountain pen, and was ready for business.

With nobody creeping from behind to nudge her elbow, she was able to speed up production. For the next two years, this cozy cavern was where Mary cranked out a goodly number of the pieces that were sold to pay for the huge house in which she could find no place to work. Being just across the hall from one another, she and Stanley had no doubt envisioned commuting together, lunching together, coming home together. Sometimes they did, but far more often they didn't.

It was a twelve-mile commute by train. Because his afternoons must be given up to the dispensary, Stanley often had to schedule his private patients for early morning appointments. He usually left home before Mary had got herself bathed, corseted, tied, hooked, snapped, and buttoned into her multifarious garments, had seen the boys off to school, given her staff their orders for the day, telephoned the grocer and the butcher—daily deliveries were then a matter of course—made out her list of city errands that would have to be squeezed in somehow, and kissed her mother good-bye.

Perhaps Cornelia missed her daughter during the day, quite likely she didn't. Her ever-present companion was a kind woman, always ready to see to Mrs. Roberts's comfort, play questions and answers with her, thread needles for the exquisite handwork that Cornelia was by now able to turn out in volume. Mary had fixed a clamp that held an embroidery hoop to the arm of her mother's favorite chair. Inserting the needle with her one usable hand then reaching around and drawing it through the cloth took longer than when she'd lavished all that unseen decoration on Mary's wedding petticoats, but Cornelia Roberts had plenty of time.

As for those hoped-for tête-à-tête lunches with Stanley, Mary seldom found time to eat anything at all. By the spring of 1913, she was dangerously overtired from the never-ending pressure to keep ahead of the Bluff's constant demands for more money. Her mind wasn't working right, her hand would cramp up when she tried to grasp her pen. One day she mistook an express train for the local that she meant to take and stepped out in front of it, scaring the station master into fits and saving herself only by falling backwards away from the track.

She knew she was being unfair to her family, and Stanley thought she was being unfair to herself. Another short visit to Europe was what the doctor ordered—nobody could get at either one of them there. His prescription worked. They had a wonderful time and made a new acquaintance named Douglas Fairbanks. Adventurous off camera as well as on, the swashbuckling movie star wore them out playing a game he'd invented called "Follow the Man from Cook's." This was the beginning of a long and lively friendship; the Rineharts would be seeing Fairbanks later when their ongoing saga took yet another turn.

Mary returned to Sewickley filled with noble resolutions to

work less and play more, but there was no stemming the pressures. Early in the fall of that same year, she collapsed and went for some more surgery. The hospital seemed to be the only place she could get any rest, and even there she was not left in peace. Aunt Ella, Cornelia's sister, came one day to visit. Ella still limped from that long-ago near-tragedy at the exposition when she and her young niece had crashed down from the collapsed balcony with an overload of pianos; on this day she sat down beside the bed and told Mary that she was dying of cancer.

This was hardly the way to cheer up a hospital patient, but Mary comforted her aunt as best she could in the circumstances. Once out of bed, she added a new chore to her daily routine, getting off the train in Pittsburgh and climbing the hill to Ella's small house, which was situated not far from where Tom Roberts's office used to be. Mary would do what she could to make her aunt comfortable, then walk through familiar streets to her husband's office, enter her black-walled cavern, and get back to writing.

Mary offered to provide her aunt with a private nurse, but Ella wouldn't have one. She remained in her little house, alone most of each day except for the partially helpless, very old woman who lived upstairs. This woman was the mother of Ella's first husband, who had died of tuberculosis when his and Ella's only son was still a baby. Mary remembered her late uncle well. She could picture him bundled into an overcoat even on hot summer days, walking to the slaughterhouse where, under the doctor's orders, he would drink fresh blood still warm from the slain animals.

As Grandmother Roberts and later Cornelia had done, the widowed Ella had taken in sewing to support herself and the boy. After a while she'd married again and had a baby girl. Her second husband, also tubercular, had died within two years of their marriage; she'd kept on sewing. When she developed cataracts and lost the sight in one eye, she used the other as best she could. Mary was wracked with anguish to watch this gallant woman in such a state, and she hated to leave Ella alone. It was all right, her

aunt would reassure her, the children would be coming home
soon. The only complaint Ella ever made was that the morphia
made her mouth dry.

On the day Aunt Ella died, Mary was back in the hospital,
this time with diphtheria. She went into coma and almost made
it a double funeral. For two weeks after her aunt's death, once the
lights had been put out, she could feel Ella's presence in the room.
Then one night, Ella was gone. Why had she come? Where did
she go? What was life all about, anyway? Mary could find no
answers; she thought perhaps it was better not to ask.

Beatrice DeMille was still sending Mary plays to read, still
asking her now and then to serve as a play doctor. That fall, Mary
herself put on a farce called *Cheer Up.* Jesse Lasky and Samuel
Goldwyn were delighted to back a piece by the author of *Seven
Days.* Walter Hampden played the lead, Cecil DeMille produced,
his brother William assisted. But *Cheer Up* cheered nobody—the
play was pulled off in short order and Mary went back to her
regular job. She was finished (again) with the theater. She had no
interest in writing for the movies; that would have meant moving
her family to the West Coast, which was unthinkable.

She organized some more. Mondays became mail days, and
a secretary came in to help her get through the stacks of letters
that arrived every week. Sometimes Mary dictated all day long,
so at least her hand got a rest. As for the bookkeeping, that was
just a matter of jotting down in a notebook what publisher had
bought which piece, and how much she'd got paid for it. Often
as not, she didn't even bother to date her entries.

Mary was making a determined effort to live a quiet, orderly
life, to concentrate on her home, her family, and her religion.
She'd never quite forgotten those Sabbath-day sermons about a
God of wrath and vengeance, and she seems to have retained a
nervous feeling that he might still be out to get her. But there
were other ministers, she knew now, who preached of a merciful
All-Father, slow to judge and chary of blame. She knelt to be
confirmed in the Episcopal Church and arose with a new sense of
peace. After a while, her husband and sons were confirmed also;

at last Mary was able to believe that she and her loved ones were all of them safe.

They had reason enough to feel safe during the winter of 1913–14. Mary drew a cozy picture of Sunday night supper laid before a blazing wood fire in the den, the family gathered around their festive board, the dogs giving them hopeful nudges, scraps being slipped furtively under the table, sled tracks in the snow outside the windows; then, at dawn on Monday, the faithful William showing up to shovel a path so that they could get to the train and begin another week's work.

The one question that mystery novelists hear above all others is "Where do you get your ideas?" That's a hard one to answer. One modern-day writer always replies simply "Pittsburgh." It was in fact Pittsburgh that gave Mary the idea for a novel called, even more simply, *"K"*. More specifically, this was one of those vivid pictures that can flash into one's mind during the magical brief hiatus between sleep and awakening, and sometimes spark off the process of plot building.

Mary's flash was a memory of her husband as a young bachelor surgeon, throwing a fit because an incompetent nurse had miscounted the gauze sponges used to clean the open incision, almost causing him to sew up the patient with a sponge still inside. Such things had been known to happen during surgery. What might have been the result if Stanley hadn't been such a stickler for correct procedure in the operating room?

Mary began to develop her picture. She could see a quiet man neither old nor young, not well-dressed but not ill-kempt, walking alone down a quiet street lined with shabby dwellings and little shops. She envisioned two doctors, one middle-aged, the other younger, handsomer, more prosperous-looking. This was the street she'd grown up in. She moved a young girl into one of the houses, a girl just blossoming into womanhood, a good, helpful, hardworking girl who had begun to show the rare beauty of face and manner that too many men might covet. From here on, all Mary had to do was tag along after K and write his story as it came.

Halfway through the first draft, her hand gave out. Hot-water soaks and massage no longer helped, the fingers and palm were stiff and swollen, the wrist ached, the arm hurt all the way up to the shoulder. What did it matter? Mary had lost faith in K; she liked her story too much, therefore it couldn't possibly be any good. She foresaw that this would become another *The Street of Seven Stars*, perhaps not quite a flop but by no means a success. Still, now that she'd got this far, she might as well struggle along as best she could. Her tongue at least still worked. Mary called in her secretary and began to dictate.

Just telling a story to somebody who knows shorthand seems an easy way to get a book written. For some authors it's the perfect method; for others it offers a temptation to lose the thread of the plot, to ramble on about inconsequentialities, to become verbose and boring. Mary had 40,000 words on paper before she realized the book was a mess. Her hand was a little less painful by now, so she picked up her overworked fountain pen, went back to the beginning, and rewrote the entire text. She still couldn't make herself believe that "K" would come to anything. She was on the point of throwing it out, but she begged her husband to look over what she'd done and give her an honest opinion.

Stanley took her manuscript to read on the train. Mary stayed home and paced the floor. When his call came, she was in such a state that she could hardly pick up the phone. "Go ahead and finish it," he told her. "This is far and away the best thing you've ever done."

So it was not, after all, a mental aberration to like what she was doing. Mary wrote the last chapters of "K" in July 1914 and sent the typescript to Houghton Mifflin in Boston, her publisher at that time. Her editors were delighted, everybody was delighted. "K" would turn out to be another success, and it was time to give the author a treat. Since fishing and family were Mary's great delights, the Rineharts packed up their rods and reels and headed for French River, near the northern end of Georgian Bay in Ontario.

This would be Mary's first real experience of camping. Stanley loved the out-of-doors, he delighted in living rough. So did his sons. So, to her surprise, did Mary. So did their dog Jock, until he lost a fight with a porcupine and Dr. Rinehart had to operate. They made portages to inland lakes, the two Stanleys carrying the canoe overland from one body of water to the next; Mary, Alan, and young Ted tagging along behind with the provisions, the frying pan, and the coffeepot. They met Indians coming along in canoes who tried to sell them meat that was allegedly veal but was in fact venison.

Though Georgian Bay was already a favored vacationing area, amenities were primitive. Their bathtub was a sheltered cove. Mary got marooned there one day, until two strange men who had been casting their fishing lines across the mouth of the cove went away, little knowing that they'd kept a naked woman sitting up to her neck in chilly water with only a towel and a cake of soap for company.

That was nothing compared to the time young Stanley and another boy he'd met at the campground went canoeing, not realizing what a treacherous body of water French River could be. At five in the afternoon a violent summer storm came up. It passed over, darkness fell, the boys still weren't back. Dr. Rinehart rowed frantically over to Manitoulin Island to find help and a motorboat, Mary stood on a rocky point, fighting to keep from going crazy with terror. When the boys finally showed up, wet and tired but safe and sound, they couldn't understand why Mrs. Rinehart took a screaming fit.

A little steamboat plied Georgian Bay every day, bringing fresh provisions, boxes of fishing worms, and the Toronto newspapers, which told the vacationing Rineharts that Germany was at war. They were not at all surprised. They remembered far too well the smartly uniformed troops goose-stepping down the broad avenues of Berlin, their long waits in half-empty restaurants until the *Offizieren* had been seated, the dirty looks they'd got for speaking English among the patriotic Germans.

Everybody was predicting that the fighting would soon be over. The newspapers were full of grudging admiration for the superefficient Teutons and Kaiser Wilhelm's invincible war machine. As the United States shook its collective head and stayed neutral, the superefficient invaders blundered their way across Belgium, advancing in mass formation according to protocol and getting mowed down in rows, slaughtering innocent civilians in retaliation for their loss of face, mounting a campaign of terror among the overrun Belgians that would convert the West's reluctant admiration to wholehearted loathing and wrest defeat out of what might have been a fairly easy victory.

France and England immediately went in on the side of the Belgians. Canada, still a part of the British Empire, was consequently also at war with what would become the Axis. Canadian troops would enter the fray early in 1915 at Ypres in France, where some of them would get their first whiff of the foe's terrible new weapon, mustard gas. When the exhausted French troops broke, it would be the rookie Canadians who plugged the gap and prevented Kaiser Bill's alleged Invincibles from driving through to the channel ports and on to England.

From then on, as Britain's prime minister Lloyd George would avow, "whenever the Germans found the Canadian Corps coming into the line, they prepared for the worst." At Vimy Ridge in the spring of 1917, at Hill 70, in the bloody inch-by-inch slog at Passchendaele; on the "Black Day of the German Army," August 8, 1918, at Amiens, when it became apparent that the Allies were taking control of the war, it was the Canadians who spearheaded the attacks. Approximately 425,000 of them went overseas, and they would keep on fighting with great valor and often little credit until the war was won. By then their losses would have reached a staggering 60,661, roughly one-seventh of their entire strength.

All the Rineharts got to see of this valiant band were a few bewildered-looking young chaps in high-necked khaki tunics and clumsily wrapped puttees left over from the Boer War, standing guard over Canadian bridges. For now, the trouble in Europe was too new, too far away. The fishing at French River was almost too good. Mary and the boys kept reeling them in, Stanley Senior wielded the scaling knife. By the time they left Canada, he'd have grown to hate the mere sight of a fin.

While her menfolk slept in the pine-scented air and dreamed, perchance, of fish, Mary lay awake thinking about the war. Not about the horror, the brutality, the wanton destruction of property, the ghastly waste of human lives; those would impinge on her consciousness later. At the moment, she was focusing on how she could get overseas and what she'd find there to write about.

For the time being, however, she had nowhere to go but home. Word had gone out that any war correspondent found near the Allied front would be immediately arrested and thrown into jail. Mary put off her hopes of an active role in the war and sublimated her thirst for adventure with the help of her dream woman, Tish.

Here might be a reasonable place to draw a few parallels between Mary Roberts Rinehart and another writer of popular fiction who achieved international fame more or less by accident. Arthur Conan Doyle's first Sherlock Holmes story appeared in London in 1886, when Mary was ten years old. It did for him what *The Circular Staircase* would do for her a quarter of a century later.

Both of them had been trained for careers in medicine, both had begun writing simply in the hope of making a little extra money, both were astounded to find themselves getting rich and famous through the trifles they tossed off at breakneck speed. Both got caught up in wartime activities, using their medical training to get a foot in the door. Doyle had volunteered as a British army doctor in the Boer War, Mary would perform a valuable service inspecting Allied field hospitals for the Red Cross. Both wrote vividly of their wartime experiences, both would later skirmish with politics, both wrote long-running plays and straight novels. Both are now remembered almost exclusively for their mysteries.

And—perhaps not many of today's readers know this—both relieved the strain of being public figures leading admirable lives by writing outrageous farces. Fiction writers can hardly avoid putting bits of themselves into their characters. One can't help wondering just who ran rampant through their wilder tales, riding roughshod over everybody else, committing acts of pillage and vandalism with impunity, getting into impossible situations and, naturally, always coming out on top.

Doyle's rampageous alter ego was a bearded monster named Professor George Edward Challenger; Mary's was Miss Letitia Carberry, a spinster of uncertain years and infallibly certain opinions. Her two faithful satellites were Lizzie, the narrator, and Aggie, the one with hay fever. As was mentioned many pages ago, Mary's Aunt Tish (the one who made that disastrous marriage with the fickle floorwalker) liked to think that she was the model for the Tish who was to become for almost thirty years one of the brightest stars in the *Saturday Evening Post*'s galaxy, right up there with Tugboat Annie Brennan, Chief Engineer Colin Glencannon of the SS *Inchcliffe Castle*, and Alexander Bott, hotshot salesman for the Earthworm Tractor Company. In fact, Mary's muse had been nudged rather prosaically, sometime around 1910, by three nice ladies at a summer cottage who were trying by various ingenious but ineffectual methods to disencumber themselves of somebody else's dog.

At that time, *Harper's* magazine had asked Mary for a short story. Pleased to be solicited by so august a publication, Mary had dashed off a tale based on the three ladies' dilemma, titled it "Three Pirates of Penzance," and shot it along. *Harper's* had shot it right back with only a printed rejection slip enclosed. Once over the shock, she'd mailed her spurned brainchild off to the *Saturday Evening Post*. There Miss Letitia Carberry was greeted with delight; Mary vowed that Tish would be the *Post*'s for as long as they wanted her.

To get back to *Harper's*, though only in passing, once Tish had made her welcome debut in the *Post*, Mary got a plaintive letter from her erstwhile disdainers. They had not yet received the story she'd promised to send them. What *Harper's* would most particularly like to get from her was exactly the sort of tale that had so recently appeared in the *Saturday Evening Post*. Too bad, but nothing could be done about it now.

So Tish was a shelter in the time of storm, a way for Mary to work off her excess adrenaline during this holiday season of 1914. The Rineharts celebrated Christmas as usual, with William playing Santa Claus and presents all around. Underneath the gaiety, however, a new tension had arisen. The *Saturday Evening*

Post's Christmas gift to Mrs. Rinehart had been an agreement to finance her trip overseas.

While America was still neutral and hoping to stay that way, the Allies were being assisted with medical supplies, among other things. The Red Cross would be greatly relieved to have a representative in the field, finding out firsthand how field hospitals were being run and where the needs were greatest. After a long, serious talk, Stanley had agreed that Mary should go. His consent may have been predicated on a tacit assumption that his wife, like so many other hopeful American journalists, would get no farther than London. Had he but known!

CHAPTER 19

A Painful Good-bye,
A Dubious Welcome

When Mary sent Tish to war, her heroine took along Lizzie, Aggie, and a bottle of blackberry cordial. Mary herself would be traveling alone, but no less encumbered. Not having any idea what, if anything, she'd be getting herself into, she prepared for all contingencies. Her outfit for the trenches included a tan coat and skirt of sturdy fabric, high-laced boots, a long, dark military cape, a man's brown velour hat, a mackintosh, and an umbrella. She'd been told it rained a lot in the war zone. Along with her battle fatigues, Mary packed a few modish gowns, including one of white velvet, plus a set of ermine furs, a black velvet suit, and a tasteful assortment of jewelry. One never knew which foreign dignitary one might happen to meet; a member of the Sewickley Country Club in good standing could hardly go to visit a queen, much less a king, in high-laced boots and a mackintosh.

By the time Mary got through packing, her luggage consisted of a mammoth trunk, her hatboxes, her fitted dressing case, and one suitcase. At the last minute before boarding, she dashed into a New York store and snatched up a fur coat, which she casually charged off to the Curtis Publishing Company. This coat turned out to be the most practical thing she took with her. Next most useful, as it turned out, would be her umbrella. The white velvet gown remains an enigma.

Getting a cabin on the steamer *Franconia* had been no problem. Mary's biggest difficulty was in saying good-bye to her family. Maggie the cook presented her with a small religious medal to hang around her neck and never, never take off because she'd need all the divine protection she could get. Stanley Junior sent a telegram from school, demanding to be taken along as his mother's bodyguard. Stanley Senior came to stow his wife safely aboard, his stiff upper lip much in evidence. He hoped she'd stay out of trouble, but he had a dark foreboding that she wouldn't.

So prominent a figure as Mary Roberts Rinehart had naturally been getting a good deal of publicity about her projected visit to the war zone. Her stateroom was filled with the customary bon voyage telegrams, bouquets of flowers, baskets of fruit; she added to the accumulation a complete suit made of rubber that she'd bought herself. As soon as the ship got torpedoed, assuming that it did, she was supposed to put on the suit and inflate it by blowing into an attached rubber tube. Since the United States was at this time still a neutral country, its vessels were supposed to be inviolate, but Mary's innate distrust of things in general was still operating at full force.

As it happened, the old *Franconia* did get torpedoed and sunk, but at a later time on a different run when Mary was not aboard. This was a break for her; that rubber suit, had she ever managed to get it on, might have proven no more reliable than those fragile inner tubes in the Premier's tires. Later on, American ships would be convoyed; but the *Franconia* made this crossing without an escort, taking no more precautions against the German U-boats than to ban smoking or the lighting of matches on deck and to black out the cabin portholes with cardboard after dark.

As night came on, Mary began to feel shivery. She was traveling alone for the first time, she didn't know a soul on board, there was not a single other woman on the passenger list. She'd never left her family for more than a few days; she was already worrying about the boys and about her own willful need to plunge into whatever she elected to do, no matter what the cost to herself and her loved ones. She worried that her life insurance, which was all she had in assets except the Bluff, didn't cover mothers who went off to war. In London, she was to discover that Lloyd's were willing for £2,000 to sell her a war-protection policy. She took advantage of the offer and, again, let Curtis Publishing pay.

Fortunately the crossing was uneventful, though hardly enjoyable. Mary did have one great stroke of luck, which proved to be the "open, sesame" to her great experience. Herself a notable, she was assigned a seat at the same table as an eminent English barrister. Once the ice had been broken, she told her tablemate why she was going abroad and asked what her chances were of getting to see any action. The barrister's first reaction, like everybody else's, was negative. He did, however, mention that his wife was Belgian and might be able to give Mrs. Rinehart some helpful suggestions once they reached London, assuming they didn't get bombed or hopelessly snarled in red tape on the way.

The barrister's wife could not have been more helpful. She steered Mary to the Belgian Red Cross headquarters at the Savoy Hotel. The persons in charge were puzzled by this American lady but they listened, and what she said made sense. All the world knew in a general way how appallingly Belgium had suffered at the hands of the Germans, but what did other countries, especially America, know about the Belgians' daily life in wartime? What about those refugees who were keeping one jump ahead of the ruthless German war machine, trying to stay alive, to till the fields, to keep body and soul together however they could? What about the decimated Belgian army, still valiantly carrying on, ill-fed, ill-equipped, lacking hospitals, nurses, even dressings for their wounds?

The British and French were also fighting the Germans now, but what they were *not* doing was spreading the word abroad. How could Americans be expected to give all the help that was needed when they were not yet getting the whole, tragic story?

Telling the truth was the one way Mary Roberts Rinehart could further their cause, and this was what she'd come to do. Would they not help her to get started?

The Belgian officials took a good deal of convincing that this elegant little lady from Pittsburgh could really do them any good, but gradually they came to understand the force of Mrs. Rinehart's argument, her reputation, and her personality. She might go, and they would take care of her as best they could. They gave her a pink card. This was no hollow gesture. Only the king of the Belgians, his minister of war, and the premier held such cards. Hers would be the fourth, and the first ever issued to a non-Belgian.

Before she talked with the Belgians, Mary had already paid her duty call on Lord Northcliffe, as did every other U.S. correspondent. The famous newspaper tycoon was pleased enough to chat with an attractive, well-dressed American lady; he invited her back to tea more than once during her short stay in London. However, he either could not or would not lift a finger to help her across the channel.

Mary had no illusions about the famous publisher and political activist. She'd heard of his rapidly changing likes and dislikes, his violent reactions to being disagreed with about anything at all, but she did enjoy his sense of humor. When Northcliffe found out that, with no help from him, Mrs. Rinehart had managed to find a loophole to slither through and was really on her way, he sent young Valentine Williams, later to be known as a novelist, to escort her to the boat train with a quizzical (Mary's word) note and a big bunch of roses.

Mary had dressed for the crossing in a black taffeta dress, her fur coat, and a money belt hidden under her petticoat. That armload of roses was just the touch an embryo war correspondent needed to equip her for the next phase of her hegira. She'd left her trunk and hatboxes in London, she traveled with just the suitcase containing her battle fatigues, a large notebook, a tidy little leather case containing a knife, fork, and spoon, a good pair of field glasses, and a trench periscope.

Cornelia Gilleland Roberts at 23, the year her elder daughter was born.
(*Photo courtesy of Cornelia Rinehart Burton*)

Three lively young sons and a tired young mother, at Christmastime, 1904. Stanley Jr. was already the picture of his father.
(*Photo courtesy of Cornelia Rinehart Burton*)

At home in Pittsburgh, the doctor's wife and the chorus. LEFT TO RIGHT: Ted, Mary, Alan, and Stanley Jr. (*Photo courtesy of Library of Congress*)

Exploring the unknown. Mary never did learn to typewrite. (*Photo courtesy of Cornelia Rinehart Burton*)

Trout fishing in the mountains with Alan (standing) and Ted. Note the convertible skirt, rebelliously left unbuttoned. (*Photo courtesy of Cornelia Rinehart Burton*)

Is it a gun, a trick, or a silly joke? Mary could write melodrama and farce with equal facility.

A star must shine. The opulent fur turban must have been warm for evening wear, but the stole and muff were approved by Queen Mary's ladies-in-waiting in 1915. (*Photo courtesy of Library of Congress*)

An experienced horsewoman in an idyllic setting. Mary had ridden since she was six years old. (*Photo courtesy of Cornelia Rinehart Burton*)

Two fish that didn't get away. The Head claimed to have caught both on a single cast. Everyone, of course, believed him. (*Photo courtesy of Cornelia Rinehart Burton*)

Checking a simmering pot, watched by a simmering chef. (*Photo courtesy of Library of Congress*)

Out for a stroll in matching fur coats. Even Mary's pets had a sense of style. (*Photo courtesy of Library of Congress*)

The age of elegance. The Rineharts' chauffeur waits with a fur rug while the lady of the house enters her limousine bare-handed and flimsily shod. (*Photo courtesy of Library of Congress*)

Blackfeet Indians in Washington D.C., May 31, 1923. LEFT TO RIGHT: Chief Mad Plumes; adopted member Pi-ta-ma-kin (Running Eagle); Chief Two Gun White Calf. (*Photo courtesy of Library of Congress*)

A nurse again, ready for action. The impressive diamonds on the ring finger are not part of the uniform.
(*Photo courtesy of Cornelia Rinehart Burton*)

Mute and partly paralyzed after her stroke, Cornelia Roberts learned to embroider with one hand. The hoop fixed to her armchair was Mary's idea.
(*Photo courtesy of Library of Congress*)

The author at work. The office is a far cry from that black-painted cave in Pittsburgh.

A brave face and a worried wife. With only a short time to live, Dr. Rinehart still kept a straight back and a stiff upper lip. (*Photo courtesy of Cornelia Rinehart Burton*)

The Bar Harbor house was Mary's last and loveliest plaything. Only a few years later, it was destroyed by fire. (*Photo courtesy of Bar Harbor Historical Society*)

This last was a long, slender contraption of khaki-painted tin, something like a section of square drainpipe, with mirrors inside that reflected into a peephole at the bottom. The idea was to poke the top end up over the edge of the trench so that its holder could see what was happening across the battle lines without getting potted by a German. Judging from the numbers of these periscopes Mary had seen in London shop windows, they were *de rigueur* for every Tommy going to the front, but she never saw a single one of them being put to practical use. Hers was about as helpful as her inflatable rubber torpedo suit. Being a sensible woman, at least some of the time, she evidently mislaid them both somewhere. They were never mentioned again.

The full story of Mary Roberts Rinehart's experiences during those two months she spent covering the war would require a book to itself. As soon as she'd got home and fulfilled her contract for short pieces with the *Saturday Evening Post*, she wrote that book. *Kings, Queens, and Pawns*, published in 1915 by George H. Doran, was, like her *Post* articles, based on the copious notes that she'd made under conditions ranging from uncomfortable to impossible in the big notebook she'd toted all the way from Pittsburgh to the war zone and back again. It is a fascinating account of an all-but-dauntless woman's incredible journey. It is not a cozy read.

There is little in *Kings, Queens, and Pawns* of military strategy, of battles won and battles lost. Mary saw the enormities and iniquities of war through the eyes of a nurse and a mother. She wrote of the trainloads of wounded, dying, and dead soldiers she'd seen brought away from the front on stretchers, laid out like logs in ever-lengthening rows on bare station platforms when there was nowhere else to put them. She described their often ragged uniforms, stiffened to the texture of leather by dirt, sweat, and blood after weeks in the trenches without ever a chance to take them off, having to be cut away with surgeons' shears when the surgeons had any such tools to work with. The bare bodies underneath would be black with lice, the open wounds green with gangrene. She wrote of the many who died, not from lack of caring but from the shortage of hospitals, doctors, nurses, medical supplies, of bandages and soap, of blankets and cots and warmth and clean water.

She told of the still-unvanquished remnant of the Belgian army, of the cheerful faces on soldiers drilling in thin uniforms with no warm underwear beneath them. She described how decrepit their boots were, when they had any, how some were wearing wooden sabots insulated with wisps of straw and some had on carpet slippers for want of anything better.

She told of their dismal food. Mary wished some of those women back home who were helping the war effort by knitting miles and miles of khaki scarves would put down their needles for a while and start making jam to vary the bleak monotony of unsweetened coffee, of black bread with no cheese to put on it, of tasteless messes of minced meat and potatoes, of stews made from whatever came to hand.

What came to hand might better not have been examined too closely. Belgian dogs had traditionally been trained to work for their living. Mary saw plenty of the big, heavyset Bouviers des Flandres harnessed three abreast, pulling the *mitrailleuses*, the small, deadly, quick-firing field guns that the Germans so greatly disliked, but she saw no little dogs. When she asked why, she was told that the soldiers had eaten them. She prayed for some philanthropist to send the Belgian army a shipful of good American baked beans.

Mary waxed eloquent on the subject of canned beans. They could be carried in a knapsack, heated and eaten right out of the can, eaten cold if there wasn't any fire to warm them up. They were tasty, they were sustaining, they were the kind of food that fighting men needed. And the empty cans could be useful too. She thought it would be a good idea to put stones in them and hang them on the barbed wire entanglements so they could clank like cowbells and warn of approaching enemies. Food was so desperately important to health and morale. As the Belgians' greatest needs, Mary put portable kitchens right up at the top of her list along with hospital equipment, surgical supplies, jam, rubber boots, and, most definitely, canned beans.

On her way over, Mary had expected to dock at Calais. Instead, for some reason she was never to know, the ferry wound up at Boulogne. She'd heard stories of other journalists going to jail for straying outside their assigned itineraries, and she'd had unhappy visions of languishing on a bed of straw in a dank cell. Apparently, however, it had been assumed that a handsome woman in an elegant hat, a fur coat, and a black taffeta gown could be no other than the wife, widow, or (this being France) the mistress of somebody rich and influential. She had been politely ignored. She'd bought a ticket to Calais and hung around hoping she'd get a chance to use it.

That was how she happened to see her first hospital train, its cars filled with improvised racks that held row upon row of iron stretchers, three tiers of them, one above the other, all filled with men who just lay there, not making a sound. One by one, through an open window in the car, the stretchers had been passed down to orderlies who laid them out on the unsheltered platform, exposed to a cutting wind. Mary had been able to do nothing but stand there watching the line of stretchers get longer and longer. She'd been relieved when the Calais train came along and she'd been put aboard without any hitch, but the three hours the train took to make the twenty-mile trip did little to raise her spirits.

She'd stayed one night in Calais, just long enough to lose her field glasses and spend a cheerless morning visiting field hospitals, then she'd been driven to Dunkirk. Here she was well situated for what she hoped to achieve. Dunkirk was (and still is, despite the pounding it took in World War II) on the Strait of Dover, just across from England and only a short drive from the Belgian border. Her Belgian hosts were putting her up there at the Hotel des Arcades, along with about fifty officers of various nations and two Russian grand dukes.

By this time Mary was used to being the only woman among a crowd of strange men, but she was not happy about being unable to find a single bath amid so much faded elegance. She made her toilette as best she could and went in to dinner. Little did Mary know that this was the kaiser's son's birthday and that the Germans were going to honor the occasion by staging a bombing raid

on Dunkirk. She was seated next to the two grand dukes. She saw
no point in consulting a menu—the only food available was
stewed rabbit, which she detested but ate. It was just after the
demitasse was served that the airplanes droned overhead and the
bombs began to drop. Immediately every light in Dunkirk went
out.

Mary hadn't minded joining the upper classes in their villain-
ous demitasses, but at this juncture she did become deeply concerned as to whether heaven would in truth protect the working
girl. She could hear other diners making hasty exits, heading for
the cellar or the downstairs lobby. One of the two grand dukes
struck a match and Mary caught a glimpse of him and his companion nonchalantly picking up their coffee cups and sauntering toward the door.

What was good enough for a grand duke was good enough
for Mrs. Rinehart. Mary had not quite enough sangfroid to take
her coffee along; she left it on the table and followed the men.
Outside the dining room was an open area with chairs and sofas;
she settled herself there with the two dukes and a few others to
wait out the raid, scared stiff but trying to maintain an outward
appearance of calm in case the lights ever went on again. The
following morning, crossing the lobby, Mary was aghast to notice
that she and the grand dukes had been sitting directly beneath a
clear glass skylight.

Being attacked from the air during a war in which it was still
possible to get trampled underfoot by a cavalry charge must have
been a bizarre experience for those Russian grand dukes, who
would soon become as obsolete as the lancers. Hardly more than
a decade had passed since Wilbur and Orville Wright had demonstrated that a gasoline-powered heavier-than-air machine could be
a viable form of transportation, but World War I was already
proving the airplane's value as an engine of war. Aerial dogfights
between ace pilots of opposing sides would bring a splash of lurid
color to the gruesome monotony of war. The race to develop
faster, sturdier planes accelerated the growth of aviation as perhaps
no less grim set of circumstances could have done.

As yet, however, planes were hardly more than toys; tiny,

slow, flimsily built machines with open cockpits, unable to deliver missiles big enough to make much of an effect. The sixty-six bombs that night were all dropped by hand. They killed a few civilians, including an old woman who had been in the act of saying her prayers; they broke some windows, blasted a few more holes in the street, and gave an embryo war correspondent a very bad night.

Mary took off her black taffeta gown but kept on her undergarments. She'd manage to snatch a few winks, then she'd wake up, open her door, and peek out to make sure the sentry who had been assigned to guard the two grand dukes was still on the job. He would stand to attention and salute, she would venture a feeble smile and shut her door, feeling a degree less panicky. As time went on, she learned to shrug off the bombs and go on about her business.

CHAPTER 20

On Active Duty

Now that they'd accepted her, the Belgians were obviously determined to take full advantage of their volunteer public relations agent's proffered services. Mary's indoctrination began the following day, and for the next three weeks she became a steady visitor to the Belgian front. While other overseas journalists, most of them men, were cooling their heels and fuming, Mrs. Rinehart was trotting around in her Tish suit, her hiking boots, and the impulsively acquired fur coat that had already proved its worth as a garment, a lap robe, and a blanket.

During this period, and for her entire stay, Mary had no trouble getting wherever she chose to go. She was never sure whether this was due to a special dispensation from higher up or whether, because of the unorthodox way she'd wangled herself across the channel, she'd simply fallen through some bureaucratic chink and become an invisible woman.

There was, however, one man who did keep careful tabs on the ubiquitous American. Whether he was Secret Service or some kind of gentleman adventurer, Mary never knew. He could have been a cousin of Richard Hannay or King Alfred's long-lost uncle; she was pretty sure that the name he gave her was not his own.

Anyway, he seemed to go wherever he wanted to, driving a car which in no way resembled the sleek limousines that Richard Hannay kept stealing in *The Thirty-Nine Steps*, but showed the dents and scars of many parlous adventures. Stories about this mysterious figure abounded: He spoke flawless *Deutsch*, he could pass through the enemy barbed wire like a wraith, he'd once put on a German uniform and goose-stepped a squad of Belgian spies safely through the lines into occupied Brussels.

Maybe the stories were true. A woman, particularly a mystery writer, could get to believing almost anything after she'd spent a week or two being picked up night after night in a staff car with no lights showing, driven miles over shell-pocked roads to an undisclosed destination with an escort whose face she couldn't even see and a chauffeur who had to depend on luck as much as skill.

Once the going became too precarious, the driver would stop the car and her mysterious escort or an army officer would lead her forward toward the trenches. Often they would be within sight and sound of enemy shelling; sometimes the fusillade would brighten up the sky like sheet lightning. Startling as this was, it at least helped the walkers to dodge the many communication wires and the craters that had been dug by exploding shells and bombs. These potholes were often deep, always filled with icy, stagnant, horrible-smelling water, and hid things that Mary didn't want to know about. She would plod on, keeping up as best she could with her fast-striding escort.

Finding their way to the trenches was all too easy. The closer they got, the worse the stink. It wasn't only the dead bodies that fouled the air but the natural odors that resulted from many men being stuck for days and weeks in a muddy ditch with no way to get clean or even to deal with their bodily functions. These soldiers, the surviving third of the Belgian army, had gotten used to living under worse conditions than beasts in a filthy byre; Mary seethed with rage at the German military bigwigs who had brought decent human beings to such an inhuman pass.

If the shelling came too close, Mary's bodyguards would take her away from the danger zone. Sometimes, however, they cut it rather fine. She told of sitting in a staff car, watching the village that she and her escort had been on their way to visit being methodically knocked down by enemy bombardment. Another time they entered a shelled town just a blast too soon. One final shell dropped through the roof of the only house left on the street and killed the last inhabitant, an old woman who must have been either too slow or too war-weary to flee. Or perhaps she simply hadn't wanted to leave the warmth of her kitchen—she had been bending over the stove when she was hit. There wasn't enough of her left to bury.

As Mary and her escort approached the house, they could watch the stairs slowly collapsing. A wall was still standing. On it hung an ebony crucifix with an ivory Christ that had lost an arm, and somebody had painstakingly carved a replacement out of wood. The officer she was with took down the crucifix and presented it to Mary. Its former owner, he told her, would not be needing it any longer.

Wherever she went, Mary looked for corroboration of the gruesome reports about German atrocities against Belgian women and children that had been rife in American newspapers before she'd left Pittsburgh. One of these described a little girl who had lost both hands. The allegation was that, as she had held them over her head in a gesture of surrender, they had been wantonly slashed off by a saber-wielding uhlan. The child had been taken to England. When Mary got back there, she tracked down the woman who had taken care of the girl and learned that in fact the hands had been surgically amputated after being mutilated beyond saving by a shell that had fallen in a convent garden.

Mary never did find even a hint of corroborative evidence with regard to this sort of sensational propaganda. The realities were damnable enough, though, and it was the truth, the whole truth, that her inscrutable mentor wanted her to take back to America. After a few forays into trenches, ruined towns, and hamlets, once even into the blood-soaked morass called no-man's-land that divided the German barbed wire from the Belgian, where the shell-holes hid so many bodies of soldiers from both sides who had fallen under fire and couldn't be rescued, she would report to her inscrutable mentor. He would read Mary's notes, amplify and explain, help her to understand what in fact she had seen and how best to write it up for the American public without passing on any useful information to the Axis.

He made no bones of the fact that he was using Mrs. Rinehart as his messenger to the West only because he had nobody else available to carry the message as he wanted it carried. It was not until after Mary got home that an official liaison representative was accredited to the Allies and news began to get through on a regular basis.

Whoever had said it often rained on the battlefields had been right on the mark. Mary's umbrella served her well on these tours of inspection. She would be driven back to the Hotel des Arcades sometime before dawn, go up to her room, struggle out of her mud-caked boots and soggy trench suit, and write up her notes. Only then was she free to crawl into her clammy, chilly bed and grab what sleep she could before the traffic noises of rumbling lorries and dispatch riders on motorcycles made further rest impossible.

Gone were the amenities that had once made the Hotel des Arcades a luxurious haven for pleasure-seekers. The food was bearable but only just, and the harried staff had no time to cope with a foreign lady's laundry needs. Mary washed out her own stockings and lingerie in her basin, dried them as best she could, and shrugged off any hope of ironing her petticoats. Then came the ultimate blow. Through the medium of a fine-toothed comb, she became wretchedly aware that she was running what the flip young things of the pompadour period had been wont to refer to as a cootie garage.

Head lice among the long-haired women in a war zone were probably no great rarity. Nevertheless, though Mary Rinehart could stand a good deal in the way of tribulation, she found this particular indignity one too many. She was visiting Red Cross hospitals every day, and one of them managed to spare her enough disinfectant to cope with the situation. The stuff smelled to high heaven, as she faithfully reported, but at least she was no longer lousy.

These visits to field hospitals were as painful as Mary's battlefield experiences. Her trained nurse's eye could too easily pick out which of the sick and wounded would soon be dead, which were going to get better. But what did "better" mean? Better than what? How would they function as civilians, these soldiers who had lost feet, arms, legs, hands, had been deafened permanently by exploding bombs, blinded by flying shrapnel, had had their nerves ruined by shell shock, their constitutions undermined by disease, lack of treatment, lack of food? Where would they live, now that the Germans had wrought such devastation? How would they find work, if they were able to work? Who would have money left to pay them?

And what of the noncombatants? Civilians had suffered as well as the troops. Mary saw many of them in the hospitals, sick, maimed, stunned by the horrors of war. One was a tiny baby with both legs gone. What sort of life was in store for that baby, for all these unfortunates caught up willy-nilly in this hellish ongoing nightmare?

Mary wanted very much to be granted an audience with the king of the Belgians. She held no great hope of getting one, for King Albert had more important matters on his mind than chatting with foreign reporters. But she'd felt there was no harm in asking. Great was her surprise one morning when, standing by the dresser in deshabille, brushing her smelly but cootie-free hair, she got a visitor.

She assumed it was the boy with the hot water and told him to come in; she was jolted to see in her mirror a tall, lavishly bearded man in uniform bowing himself through the door. As she clutched her dressing gown about her and prepared to sell her virtue dearly, he bowed again and proffered an envelope. The king's chamberlain informed Mrs. Rinehart that His Majesty was expecting her in La Panne at three o'clock that same afternoon.

Here was a howdy-do! Mary searched frantically through her meager traveling wardrobe for the white gloves without which, somebody or other had assured her, she'd never get within curtsying distance of a royal personage. She combed Dunkirk for buttons to fill the gaps on her cloth-topped shoes. She experienced the miracle of finding a hairdresser and getting a proper shampoo; it was reassuring to know that her clean tresses would not offend His Majesty's nostrils.

By two o'clock, comparatively resplendent in her taffeta gown and white gloves, carrying her handbag and fur muff, wearing her one chic traveling hat with its veil adjusted to the acme of perfection, Mary descended. A general with a dreadful cold met her, and immediately commanded her to remove the veil. It was, she gathered, not the done thing to impose even a wisp of netting between the common visage and the regal gaze. Or perhaps the general feared she might be a spy.

Mary needed an authoritative report to give the American people through the *Saturday Evening Post*. She had inserted in her petition a hope that King Albert would allow her to take notes of their meeting. She would write them up and present them for his approval before sending them back to her publisher. Permission was granted. This turned out to be the only piece that Mary was actually able to write, send to the *Post*, and have published while she was still abroad.

Those interested in reading the official report will find it in *Kings, Queens, and Pawns*. The one in *My Story*, written long after she'd ceased to worry about censorship, draws a more intimate picture. The Belgian general's driver was a redheaded Flemish maniac (possibly an exaggeration—Mary was prone to them) with a ferocious mustache. He bounced her and the general over mended roads lined with earthen redoubts and barbed wire, alongside canals filled with barges. They passed a file of dark-skinned, bearded spahis in burnooses riding shaggy, tough-looking horses. These were Algerian cavalrymen, fighting bravely in the French army even as they cursed the chilly, rainy French climate. They passed a pig that had escaped from a slaughterhouse; it was being pursued by a small gang of soldiers clearly bent on an impromptu barbecue.

Between sneezes, the general made a brave stab at giving Mary a crash course in protocol. Madame Rinehart must not speak before His Majesty had spoken, nor sit down unless His Majesty invited her to. She must not get too close to the king, about two meters would be near enough. Mary wished to goodness the general would open the car window and let out some of his germs so she wouldn't infect the king.

King Albert and Queen Elisabeth were an attractive young couple. They had sent their two small children to England for safety's sake, and were living modestly in a villa not far from the hospital that the Bavarian-born queen had established in La Panne. Mary had already visited Queen Elisabeth's Hospital and found it by far the best-planned and -equipped she had seen, nor would she discover a better one during the entire tour of inspection.

At last the car stopped. So did Mary's heart. It was time to meet the king! A butler opened the door, the king's equerry came forward and shook the visitor's hand. The general, to Mary's surprise, stayed outside in the wind, still sneezing. The equerry opened an inside door and announced to a screen that was blocking Mary's view of the room ahead, "Mrs. Rinehart."

Then he stepped back and shut the door. Mary was alone. She took a deep breath and crept around the screen. A tall, blond man came toward her. While she was trying to remember how to curtsy, he held out his hand for her to shake. She waited for him to speak. He didn't. This was not the American way; Mary was horrified to hear her own voice admonishing the king.

"You know, Sire, you're supposed to speak first."

Obligingly, King Albert spoke, he suggested they sit down. She waited for him to sit first, instead he was holding a chair for her. Through the window Mary could see the general's military cape being blown up over his head. Obviously her mentor was in no position to put the king straight, so she might as well sit.

So this amiable young giant was the man who had turned down Kaiser Wilhelm's magnanimous offer to leave little Belgium unharmed on condition that the German army be allowed to march scatheless across her land on its way to conquer France and England. This was the man who had sat down beside his ministers and, with them, determined to buy no shameful immunity at the expense of Belgium's neighbors and allies. Albert's careworn face was testimony to the unimaginable strains to which he had already been subjected, to his awareness that there would be more and maybe even worse fighting to come. Yet here he was, being courteous to an American woman who'd been so flustered by the suddenness of his invitation that she'd forgotten to bring along her notebook and pen.

Albert wasn't much better equipped than Mary, but he rummaged around among some papers on a table and managed to come up with a pencil and an empty manila envelope addressed to *Son Majeste le Roi des Belges*. Mary turned it over to the blank side and began taking notes, using her lap for a desk, scattering her possessions one after the other: her handbag, her muff, the white gloves that she'd taken off as soon as she'd realized His Majesty wouldn't mind. Neither did he mind stooping to pick them up for her, even when she dropped them again. Mary herself was dreadfully embarrassed but not too flustered to keep on asking questions.

Inevitably, they talked about atrocities. The king was a fair-minded man, he tried to answer objectively. Not all the Germans had flaming red eyeballs and extralong eyeteeth, as some of the posters had shown them. But, yes, bad things had happened, mostly during the invasion when German resentment against the puny nation that had dared to defy their giant might was at its highest. The king and his brave ministers had been scrupulous not to credit stories that could not be verified. Madame Rinehart must understand that victims of torture did not often survive to testify against their persecutors; the most reliable sources of verification had been written journals kept by the German soldiers themselves. And yes, it was true that the invaders had protected their advance by driving Belgian civilians before them so that, when Belgian troops opened fire, they had perforce killed some of their own people.

There was more to tell, too much more. Mary and the king talked for an hour. Then he helped her reassemble her belongings one last time, walked her out to the car, and paused to chat with the sneezing general, heedless of the wind that was tousling his fair hair. Finally King Albert shut the car door and went back into the house. Mary was left to inhale some more cold germs and gloat over her coup.

She knew that every journalist in Europe would have given much to have been in her properly buttoned shoes this day. She hastened to write up her account of the interview, made three copies, and sent them by different routes to make sure at least one copy got through to America. The *Saturday Evening Post* did run Mary's interview with King Albert but turned down her cabled report that the Germans were using poison gas against Allied troops, for fear that the news would inflame public opinion enough to disrupt America's position of neutrality. The *New York Tribune* had no such scruples and Mary got scooped by their overseas reporter, Will Irwin. After she got home, Mary would be terribly disappointed to find out how small an impact her reportage made, how little her own countrymen cared about what was happening over here.

But she didn't know, and there were still many more hospitals to visit. Neither France nor Belgium had as yet developed the concept of training women to be professional nurses; their long-established custom had been for the Sisters of Charity, a Catholic religious order, to serve in the hospitals. Some of the sisters had been transferred out of the war zone; far too few were left to handle the workload and these, according to Mary's standards, were deplorably untrained, particularly in the importance of surgical cleanliness. This was dramatically evident at a hospital in Calais where French nuns in—and with—their medieval habits worked on one side of the building while well-trained, crisply uniformed British nurses practiced modern methods on the other.

However deficient some hospitals might be, at least their patients got care of a sort and usually a cot to sleep on. Too often, Mary saw a train stop at some little hamlet to drop off a load of casualties, perhaps with a few hours' advance notice, perhaps with no warning at all. Then the train would move on, leaving the wounded for the local authorities to cope with as best they could.

Usually the men were moved to some kind of shelter, a church, or a schoolhouse. Women of the village were willing to nurse them, but what did they have to work with? Food was none too plentiful, medicines were often limited to local folk remedies. Poor peasants could hardly be expected to supply spare mattresses, blankets, or even clean rags to be ripped up for dressings. Mary saw wounded men lying on straw for want of anything better, suffering agonies for lack of a single morphia pill to dull their pain. She saw convalescent patients on the bank of a stream, rinsing out their dressings to be dried and reused with no attempt at sterilization.

Now she knew about war. There was no glory in it, no romance. War was nothing but privation, discomfort, and boredom, punctuated by bursts of deadly fighting that brought only greater agony, worse shortages, more bodies to be wept over and buried. Nobody ever won. Whatever the generals might claim after the last gun had been fired and the smoke cleared away, wars could only be lost. Mary hated it all. She was getting closer and closer to a burnout.

CHAPTER 21

A Long, Long Trail A-winding

It was high time for a break, and Mary could hardly believe the one she got. She was going to London to visit the queen! She thought it must have been Lord Northcliffe who'd wangled the unexpected invitation for her, since she herself had made no move to do so. It seems not to have occurred to Mary Rinehart that an intelligent, energetic, well-informed royal personage with a highly developed bump of curiosity might herself have been curious to meet this nice American of whom she'd heard such remarkable things.

Being related to most of the crowned heads of Europe, Queen Mary could not but have heard through the family grapevine about Mrs. Rinehart's amusing audience with darling Albert, not to mention the sensible and informed interest Mrs. Rinehart had shown in dear Elisabeth's hospital. Born Princess Victoria Mary Augusta Louise Olga Pauline Claudine Agnes, Her Majesty was the only daughter of England's beloved, fun-loving Princess Mary Adelaide, affectionately known as Fat Alice and renowned not only for her ability to throw money around on beautiful objects and lavish entertainments, but also for her keen, well-furnished

mind and her diligence in helping the Crown's less fortunate subjects.

A direct descendant of George III, Mary Adelaide had married
Francis, Duke of Teck, son of the duke of Württemberg. Their
only daughter might too easily have wound up at one of the stuffy
little German courts, wasting a sharp mind and a near-genius for
doing good on the grand scale; the story of how young Princess
May got to be queen and empress of Britain is a romance in itself.

Princess Mary of Teck had originally been intended to marry
the eldest son of Edward VII, also named Edward. He died while
their wedding was being planned and Mary, so superbly qualified
to be queen, was passed on to the second son, George, Duke of
York. Oddly enough, and luckily for them both, their marriage
turned into a genuine, lifelong love match. As George V and
Queen Mary, this conscientious, dedicated couple did their duty
by their subjects at home and abroad to the limits of their abilities.
Now that their easily influenced Cousin Willy Hohenzollern had
allowed his own *folie de grandeur* and his ambitious generals to
push him into this dreadful war, they were sparing themselves no
labor, however distasteful or even dangerous, that might help to
win the war.

The Prince of Wales was in the British army. His younger
brother the duke of York was in the Royal Navy; King George
was touring the battlefields, boosting morale in the front-line
trenches heedless of enemy shellfire and falling bombs. Back in
England, the palace grounds had been opened to convalescent
soldiers. The queen was gathering relief supplies on a grand scale,
visiting hospitals, not letting her escorts get away with showing
her only the less harrowing casualties in their deluded attempts to
spare her feelings. When the German blockade of 1917 cut down
on supplies of food to the British Isles, Queen Mary picked up a
shovel and led the royal family in digging up a potato patch on
the palace grounds as an example to her people.

Had Mary Roberts Rinehart but known that she and the royal
Mary were sisters under the skin, she might have felt more relaxed
about the protocol she anticipated having to follow. As had happened with the Belgian king's audience, she'd been given very

little time to prepare for her English visit. She set off for Calais in such a rush that she forgot to obtain one all-important visa. Now here she was on the quay, her boat was preparing to sail. She mustn't keep the queen waiting, but she couldn't get aboard without the right papers. What was she to do?

A respectable-looking Englishman was standing nearby, also waiting to board. Mary rushed up to him waving her passport, poured out her problem and asked if he could give her any advice. He listened in silence, then walked away. She turned to another, this man wouldn't even stay to listen. She realized too late that both men probably had her pegged as a spy. Everybody had spies on the brain these days. Pretty women in fur coats, accosting perfect strangers at channel crossings with wild pleas to be saved from committing *lèse-majesté*, were particularly to be shunned by prudent males traveling alone.

Mary should have known better, considering that all during her stay in France she was never once allowed to sign the too-Teutonic name *Rinehart* to any of her cables home. Her husband's German ancestors had been among the earliest settlers in Pennsylvania, but Stanley Rinehart himself was of half-Scottish descent and American as apple pan dowdy. He must have been sadly puzzled by those overseas messages that told him only "Your wife is well and sends love" and were signed with assorted names that he'd never heard before.

Anyway, Mary rose above her panic, hunted up a station attendant who owned a bicycle, waved a golden sovereign under his nose, gave him her passport, the queen's cable, her Red Cross card, and a promise that he'd get the sovereign the second he came back to the quay with the missing document. He was off in a flash. She handed the man who was minding the gangplank another sovereign not to let the boat go until she was aboard, and stood dithering until the out-of-wind cyclist zoomed back down the quay with her papers all correct. He got his sovereign, she gasped out her thanks and rushed up the gangplank.

By now it was dark, the night was calm and clear. Mary spent most of the crossing on deck, standing all by herself at the rail. Once a crew member appeared out of the shadows and pointed out to her a white streak in the water diagonally astern of where they were standing. "Torpedo," he said, and returned to the shadows.

Mary didn't know whether or not the elusive seaman had told her the truth; but that one word of his was, for some reason, a balm to her tortured nerves. The enemy had tried and failed to blow them up, the danger was over, she might as well quit worrying. Not long after that calming incident, the searchlights of the port picked up the ferry and guided her in. Came the dawn, Mary was in London wondering how to get past those padlocked gates at Claridge's Hotel.

The gates opened, the red carpet began to roll out. Lord Cowdray, with whom Mary had had tea in Downing Street during her earlier visit, telephoned the hotel to let Her Majesty's distinguished visitor know that, since his wife was not in London at this time, Mrs. Rinehart was welcome to use Lady Cowdray's car. Mary had assumed that a chauffeur would come with the car, but she hadn't reckoned on a footman as well. Her prearranged visit to one of the queen's ladies-in-waiting that afternoon went off with more pomp and circumstance than she'd bargained for.

The lady-in-waiting was charming, as ladies-in-waiting are naturally expected to be. She poured tea for Mrs. Rinehart and chatted about the royal family, whose photographs were on display all over the room. The American Mary found the English woman's obvious devotion to the great lady whom she served rather touching, and her tactful way of dealing with a gauche American's faux pas an impressive lesson in diplomacy.

Mary had made the gaffe of intimating that Her Majesty seemed to be a humorless sort of person. She could not have been more wrong. The reason for those poker faces at public functions, she learned, was that Queen Mary's entourage knew from experience that, sometime during the event, something ludicrous was bound to happen. Whatever it was, the queen would notice, because she never missed a trick. If she happened to catch a sympathetic eye, she wouldn't be able to keep from laughing. Rather than risk upsetting the royal aplomb, her loving ladies-in-waiting had learned to keep looking straight ahead and thinking, one assumes, of the empire.

Now that she'd been briefed on the background, Mary got her orders. She would be received at Saint James's Palace. She would arrive punctually at the stated time, the queen would appear fifteen minutes later. When greeted, Mrs. Rinehart would curtsy and the queen would extend her hand. It was usual for the person being received to kiss the hand, but Mrs. Rinehart didn't have to if she would find the gesture awkward. Mary felt awkward just hearing about it, so they agreed on diplomatic grounds to scratch the kiss.

Mary must have been ineffably relieved to get out of that bedraggled black taffeta dress and change into some of the elegant clothes she'd left waiting for her in London. Her diary records the toilette she put together for her visit to Saint James's: a black velvet skirt, a white crepe blouse, a black brocaded coat trimmed with skunk fur, a black turban with black aigrettes, white-topped black boots, with all their buttons on, white ermine muff and stole, and the white gloves that she'd learned from her Belgian experience weren't really mandatory when visiting royalty but she took them anyway.

Mary's choice of skunk to wear before the queen may sound absurd to modern readers, but this rich, glossy, long-haired fur was all the rage then and for some time to come. Why it went out of fashion is anybody's guess. Those Lifebuoy soap ads sensitizing the public to the social consequences of BO may have been a factor, for skunk fur did tend to retain a certain faint but distinctive whiffiness that neither perfume nor mothballs could ever quite eradicate. But it was awfully pretty.

The ladies-in-waiting told her how smart she looked. Mary probably said pleasant things to them in return but later on, in *My Story*, she would wax a bit catty about the queen. Perhaps she'd been disappointed that day when Her Majesty showed up wearing a plain green broadcloth suit, a black hat with feathers, fox furs, and what Mary dismissed a bit contemptuously as "some diamond and emerald jewelry." She said the queen dressed badly, had too much hair, and wore her hats too high.

It would have been kinder and truer to have said that Queen Mary did not conform to the mode of the moment. According to James Pope-Hennessy's comprehensive biography as well as a multitude of portraits and photographs, both as princess of Wales and as queen, Her Majesty had always realized the importance of dressing as befitted a representative of the Crown. Her taste was excellent. She had the height, the figure, and the presence to carry off elaborate gowns and displays of court jewels that would have overwhelmed a lesser wearer.

Before the war, when foreign travel was possible, her elegance had charmed great crowds both at home and abroad. As for whether some people now considered her style passé, Queen Mary could not have cared less. She dressed for one person alone, and that one was her "own darling Georgie dear," that shy, gruff, inarticulate, often irascible ex-naval officer who hadn't wanted to be king and could never bring himself to speak aloud the tender words of love, devotion, and gratitude that he poured out in letter after letter to his "sweet Angel May." King George V was not a man to welcome change; he liked his wife the way she'd always been. Her job was not to look chic but to look regal, and she did.

In those parlous times, the royal wardrobe was the least of Queen Mary's concerns. Like Elisabeth of Belgium, she had rushed into the war effort almost before the first gun was fired, outlining plans to assist existing relief organizations in whatever ways were possible. Relief would have to be women's work; the men would be needed for sterner tasks. But what could women do? At the beginning, it appeared that the only ways for them to serve would be by collecting clothes and money for the many who were already destitute or being thrown out of work as a result of the sudden upheaval, or by knitting khaki socks and stomach belts (shades of Amelia Peabody Emerson!) or performing the service that would inspire a popular song titled "Sister Susie's Sewing Shirts for Soldiers."

As to sewing, Her Royal Highness had an organization already in existence. Queen Mary's Needlework Guild was quickly mobilized and greatly expanded, the enormous State Apartments at Saint James's were given over as workrooms. This was where

Mary Roberts Rinehart was shown upon her arrival; her visit turned out to be much less formal than she had anticipated. When she went in, she found the ladies of the guild hard at work. When the queen came along, they dropped the mandatory curtsy then talked shop with her in a manner more professional than courtly. It was business as usual until Her Majesty got to Mary Roberts Rinehart, who of course must be formally introduced.

Mary bowed over the queen's hand and waited for her to speak first. Her Majesty knew the protocol better than King Albert had, and she said kind things about the aid Americans were sending. She was even kinder about the Canadians, as well she ought to have been, considering how generously they had responded with both supplies and troops. She remarked that, while Londoners were by now taking the British troops as part of the scenery, they still burst into cheers when a Canadian regiment marched by.

This could have been meant as an oblique hint for the Americans to get further involved, but Queen Mary was too good a diplomat to pursue the matter. She asked whether Mrs. Rinehart had visited any of the English hospitals during her stay in France, and whether they were getting all the supplies they needed. Mary managed to respond intelligently, even though she was having to revise some preconceived notions in a hurry.

The queen must be the most unphotogenic woman alive, Mary thought, for even simply dressed for her work party with the wrong kind of hat and and with her hair dressed too high, she was very handsome. Her coloring was delicate, her complexion exquisite, her eyes a lovely blue. She was a bit stiff at first—Mary sensed that she was basically a shy person. Once the lady-in-waiting had prompted Mrs. Rinehart to tell the story of her sadly unorthodox audience with King Albert of Belgium, however, Queen Mary demonstrated most convincingly that she did indeed have a sense of humor.

When the queen showed signs of moving on, Mary stepped back but was motioned to go with her. She was talking freely now, showing her guest from overseas some of the countless articles that the guild was collecting and dispensing. She picked up a baby's sweater knitted in a hideous shade of yellow and expressed a tart opinion of anybody who would pick such a horrid color to put on a tiny baby. She waxed mildly prideful over a skillfully packed canvas roll, one of many thousands that had been sent to the army. Along with a towel, soap, toothbrush, nail brush, and tooth powder, the roll contained a change of flannels, extra socks, and abdominal belt, in case the men in the trenches ever found time to bathe, brush, and change their underwear.

Having got all this stuff out, the queen despaired of getting it back in again. One of the ladies took over, and the queen passed on, but not without a final word. As Mary took her extended hand and curtsied, she asked, "Were you not frightened the night you were in the Belgian trenches?"

"Not half so frightened as I was this afternoon, Your Majesty," Mary responded. The queen smiled, the audience was over.

Later, Mary Roberts Rinehart extolled the work of the Queen's Needlework Guild. She did not mention—perhaps she never knew—that at one point the needlework guild nearly sabotaged the queen's purpose by doing too good a job. Those mountains of socks and shirts that the volunteers turned out were threatening to take away the livelihood of other women who worked in garment factories or did piecework at home.

As soon as the situation was made clear to her, Queen Mary steered the needleworkers into less fiscally disastrous channels and launched the Queen's Work for Women Fund as a subsidiary of the National Relief Fund. This led to the Central Committee for Women's Training and Employment, which had the queen's patronage but not her personal involvement. Even a queen could do only so much, and there was always so much to do.

Mary Roberts Rinehart's London schedule was getting as tight as the queen's. She had to go to Buckingham Palace the following day for the sole purpose of signing her name in the guest book. Queen Mary, the Grand Acquisitor, collected signatures as well as works of art and many other things. One thing Her Majesty hadn't collected, Mary discovered, was a decent pen to sign with. After having debated with herself as to whether she was properly Mrs. Stanley or Mary Roberts in this instance and opted for the latter, Mary picked up the terrible pen and signed the book with a shaking hand. She made a poor job of it, but what could the Crown expect from a mere foreigner?

Her main purpose achieved, Mary kept a few social engagements that had risen out of her royal visit and even managed to spend a little time in her own milieu. Sir Charles Wyndham and Mary Moore were producing a British version of *Seven Days*. Mary Rinehart attended a few rehearsals and got the disturbing impression of a major culture gap. As has been explained earlier in this book, the entire plot hung on the fact that the house was under quarantine. Over here, where an Englishman's house was his castle, nobody was going to believe that a whole cast of characters would allow themselves to be held incommunicado by the health inspector just because a servant came down with smallpox. Mary tried to explain this to Miss Moore over a cup of tea. The coproducer seemed to understand what she was saying but failed to be convinced. The show went on, and soon came off. The playwright wasn't around to watch the final curtain descend; Mary was back in the war zone.

She had been startled to learn that, during her brief stay in London, civilian travel between England and the Continent had suddenly been made next to impossible. Visas were harder to get, travelers were being searched at railway stations and ports of embarkation. The Germans had announced that, as of February 18, all vessels leaving the coast of England would be sunk by their U-boats. Mary's agenda called for her to be met in Calais on the nineteenth and given a tour of the French and British fronts, a special privilege that no journalist could afford to miss. Lord Northcliffe told her she'd better wait a few days and see what developed, but Mary didn't want to wait. She'd been away too long. She was aching to finish what she'd come for and go home.

So she packed her suitcase, picked up her umbrella, and took her chances. At the railroad station a matron searched her from the tip of her umbrella to the linings of her shoes. That was the easy part. Around ten at night, Mary was shivering under her open umbrella in a cold rain on the quay at Folkestone. She must have caught the Belgian general's flu, she felt miserable. She'd had

to go through an examining board, her papers had got passed
from hand to hand, then back to her. There would be no boat
carrying passengers to Calais tonight, she was told, only the boat
to Boulogne.

Boulogne was no good to her, so she walked up to the Calais
boat and called out to a man on deck that she wanted to speak to
the captain. Some officer or other came out, she handed him her
papers, he looked them over, handed them back, escorted her off
the boat, and disappeared. She was alone on the quay again, and
she couldn't see a soul on board. Mary took a firmer grip on her
suitcase and umbrella and sneaked up the gangplank.

Nobody stopped her, nobody even saw her. She found an
empty cabin with the door ajar, felt her way in the dark to a wall
settee, and sat down, terrified at the prospect of being put in irons
or shot as a spy once she was discovered.

She was not discovered. Mary stretched out on the settee and
spread her fur coat over her. She was running a fever, having
chills. She slept by fits and starts, troubled by nightmares. She
woke to a gray, wet, silent dawn and peeked out from the cabin.
The boat was tied up to the quay in Calais and nobody was on
deck. Just across the way was the Hotel Terminus. She crossed
the wharf, not daring to look behind her, and woke up the desk
clerk.

When she dared to venture from her room, Mary found
security here even tighter. Calais had its own examining board.
It took a solid twenty-four hours of explaining before they'd let
her go on to Dunkirk. That they released her at all, Mary suspected, was due to their amusement over the way she'd tweaked
the tail of the British lion. Once back at the Hotel des Arcades,
she went to bed and nursed her flu.

But this was not the time to be ailing. As soon as she'd
got her legs back under her, Mary was off to Cassel to keep an
appointment with General Foch. He was not at his headquarters,
she found him by accident in a little Catholic church, kneeling at
the altar, saying his prayers. She tiptoed away and went back to
her cold, dank, inhospitable hotel room. At noon, a French officer
appeared to escort her to lunch with the general and his staff.

General Foch seated her himself, then took his own place and—
quelle horreur!—realized that, counting the staff and Mrs. Rinehart,
there would be thirteen at the table. With true military dispatch,
a colonel was ordered to go and sit at a small table by himself.
For the duration of Mary's short visit, the poor colonel had to eat
his meals alone.

General Foch was a martinet, an austere man who ate little
and drank water barely flavored with claret. He'd trained his staff
to speak only when they were spoken to, he had no time for social
graces, but he was tremendously kind and they loved him anyway.
The general was particularly solicitous of his guest and anxious
for Madame Rinehart to understand France's situation before he
sent her to the front. He told Mary that the Germans were in fact
already defeated but would not surrender. The war might drag
on a long time, perhaps for years. He amazed her by revealing
that the French troops were holding more than 400 miles of front.
Didn't America realize that?

Mary knew the drill by now. After her chat with the general,
she was sent off in a staff car with an officer in attendance; her
first view of the front left her with some strange impressions.
Paris buses and taxicabs were still being used to move troops. The
poilus were, by and large, a jolly lot; even those whose uniforms
were in rags could still cheer and smile when they caught sight of
a woman. Most of the men she saw en route were carrying huge,
round loaves of bread. Mary would see some of them in rest
billets, sleeping in barns on beds of straw, using the loaf of bread
as a pillow.

Her experiences at the French front were mostly undramatic.
Work was proceeding on a new system of trenches; these had
become a vital part of this new kind of warfare that had developed
into a double siege. Things didn't liven up until Mary visited the
salient beyond Ypres, and that was only inadvertently. Her French
escort had taken her to see a battery situated at a fair distance from
the German lines. The gunnery officer in charge was desolated—
here was a lady come to call and nothing to entertain her. It did
happen that a German battery had been located; was *Madame*
interested?

Madame found it necessary to maintain her neutrality. These gallant soldiers must not shell the Germans on an American woman's say-so. Of course, she insinuated gently, if they were planning to fire anyhow, that was no business of hers. This was all the gunners needed. They began ripping away the camouflage while their visitor walked closer to see the big guns shoot. On the way, an officer picked up a horseshoe and handed it to *Madame*, for luck. He showed her what they called their cyclone cellar, just in case the enemy failed to take the upcoming demonstration in good part. Since the hole was full of murky, stinking water, Mary decided she'd prefer to risk the barrage.

She was told to open her mouth in order to relieve the pressure on her eardrums. The gray throats of the great guns opened as well, the barrels recoiled one by one, then roared together. The noise was horrendous. That part of the entertainment over, the soldiers invited their unexpected guest to inaugurate a small bridge they had just finished building. As Mary began the impromptu ceremony, a German shell burst high overhead, then another, and another. Nobody else seemed to mind much. If the men could be calm, so could she. Mary walked firmly across, the first woman to set foot on that brand-new bridge and quite likely the last.

The Germans were still shelling. Perhaps it was time for *Madame* to depart. Unfortunately, *Madame*'s car got stuck in the mud. Mary had to sit in the back seat clutching her horseshoe until the soldiers had dug her free.

Next it was on to Saint-Omer and the British lines. Mary's hotel accommodations here were fully as wretched as those she'd had at Cassel, lacking adequate heat, toilet facilities, or comforts of any kind. She went to bed to keep warm, spreading her trusty fur coat over the inadequate covers. As she lay there wondering if she was going to get any sleep, somebody knocked at the door. Hoping it might be the chambermaid with a hot-water bottle, she said, "*Entrez.*"

In walked General Huguet, head of liaison between the French and British armies. Mary sat up, drew her fur coat up to hide her nightgown, and played the *grande dame* as well as the circumstances allowed. She suggested graciously that the general sit close to the small fire, he accepted the invitation with equal aplomb, they discussed Mary's coming itinerary with all the politesse and gentilesse available at the moment.

On the following day, General Huguet took Mrs. Rinehart to meet Field Marshal Sir John French at British headquarters. She would never imagine that her very brief and wholly chaste visit, added to that of a duchess who'd come to dedicate a hospital, would be used by some of Sir John's political enemies to spark an inquiry in Parliament. French must have known what was in the wind; he got rid of his attractive visitor as fast as he decently could, passing her along to young Lord Claude Hamilton, stuffing them both into a staff car, handing them packets of sandwiches prepared by the headquarters cook, and warning Mrs. Rinehart, as he must have been warning himself, to stay out of trouble.

Over the next few days Mary saw more of the British front than she was by now in any shape to assimilate. She was too tired even to go through her usual nightly routine of writing up her notes. She tried to get some sleep in the damp, uncomfortable bed, thinking how much worse off were the men in the muddy, filthy trenches.

There were a few bright moments. Once Lord Claude Hamilton and she lunched at the officers' mess at General Haldane's headquarters on the Scherpenberg Hill. A tall young officer with a quirky smile asked her to sign their visitors' book. They'd collected pathetically few signatures so far, only those of King George, the prince of Wales, Prince Alexander of Teck (a brother of Queen Mary), and Sir John French. At least Mary was in distinguished company.

The young man turned out to have been the son of a Lady Congreve from whom, fifteen years later, Mary got a card. Lady Congreve had read a book of Mrs. Rinehart's. Did the author know that Billy Congreve had mentioned her in his published diary?

Mary got hold of the book. She learned that the young writer had won many honors, including the Victoria Cross, and had been killed in action only a few months after their one and only meeting. He'd written in his diary on February 25, 1915:

We were just sitting down to lunch today when suddenly Hamilton turned up with a lovely lady, the first
woman other than natives I have seen out here. A simul-
taneous exclamation of "Good Lord!" broke from us.
She turned out to be Mrs. or Miss Mary Roberts Rinehart, an American who had come out to look around in
her capacity as journalist. She was very amusing, and we
gave her lunch. I don't think she very much appreciated
our sour wine of the country. "Reminds me of eating a
persimmon," she said. (Whatever that may be!)

Billy Congreve added that Mrs. Rinehart talked about twice
as fast as most people and with a strong "twang." She would be
leaving for America on the following day, if the submarines would
let her.

CHAPTER 22

Home Fires and Campfires

Afire to get back to her family, papers all in order, Mary boarded the steamer *Arabic* for New York. Her stateroom, with its private bath, was sheer luxury after those gloomy, dank French provincial hotels. Chubby Captain Finch was an affable man, the U-boats left them alone. The crossing could not have gone better. Soon afterward, Mary learned that the *Arabic* had been torpedoed and sunk. Captain Finch, true to the law of the sea, had gone down with his ship but, thanks to all that good cooking under his belt, he'd bounced right up again and got hauled into a lifeboat by members of his thankful crew. There were some casualties, but Mary mourned less for the drowned men than for her lovely tiled bathroom, now on the ocean floor and accessible only to mermaids.

It was a happy homecoming. Her men were all well. Alan and Ted were fascinated by the souvenirs she'd brought back: some shell casings, a Gurkha knife, her gas mask (really nothing more than a strip of chemically treated gauze), one of the needle-pointed steel darts that had been dropped in bundles from German airplanes at the very beginning of the war. Stanley Junior, on the other hand, hid his new wristwatch in a bureau drawer. While wristwatches were proving invaluable to soldiers overseas, they were still considered effeminate by Americans.

This was the least of the prejudices that Mary found herself running into. Many of her countrymen were still either pro-German or desperately neutral, still refusing to believe that the Germans were actually using poison gas against the Allies, ignoring her protests that she'd sat beside men in the field hospitals and watched them die from its effects.

Writing up her hastily taken and sometimes almost illegible notes helped Mary over the transition period but gave her some extra problems. She'd learned too much, and she was forced to become her own censor, making sure she didn't reveal any facts that might be helpful to the enemy. Her neighbors might not want to believe that there were spies and saboteurs in the United States, but Mary had plenty of cause to know better.

She had signed approval to write about her two official royal interviews but was not sure how to treat the informal visit she'd had at La Panne with Queen Elisabeth. Grieving for her Bavarian homeland, sickened by what the Germans had done to Belgium, Elisabeth had expressed herself all too freely about Kaiser Wilhelm and his ruthless myrmidons. Mary decided she'd better not quote any of this, and settled for writing an innocuous personal impression of this unaffected, friendly, dauntlessly merciful royal young personage.

In this piece, at least, she struck a chord to which readers feeling the stir of conscience could respond in a practical way. And respond they did; all of a sudden Mary found herself being forced to organize a clearinghouse for the avalanche of supplies and money being donated to Belgian war relief. Even more astonishing was the Medal of Queen Elisabeth that turned up in her personal mail. This was not the sort of decoration one put on to play bridge in Sewickley, but Mary did get asked once to wear it for a photograph. Never shy about seizing the chance of a little extra publicity, she sent a maid to get her medal. The picture was duly taken and published; too late, Mary noticed that the medal she was shown wearing was inscribed *Harvard Athletic Association.*

Another mixup occurred when Mary tried to straighten out her expense account with the *Post*. Even counting the fur coat and the suite at Claridge's, she'd come back with $1,200 of her traveling allowance left over. Her publishers didn't know how to handle the refund—none of their writers had ever returned any money before.

Mary was working at home because she couldn't bear to leave the family even for her downtown office. Two months away had been far too long; she needed her big, safe house and the peace of her garden. By putting in a full day, every day, she managed to finish all her articles in good time. Correcting the proofs was harder. She was exhausted from her labor and dispirited by the way her editors had emasculated her work. She complained that the writings she'd hoped would awaken America to the desperate situation abroad sounded in their final form like "the piping of small birds in a hurricane."

Summer brought a new, more personal tragedy. Uncle John Roberts, the family's rock of Gibraltar during those early years, was dead.

John had taken Sade's death hard but in due course he had married again and, to his great joy, begotten a son. Determined to provide handsomely for his boy, he'd got rid of his wallpaper business and set about making a fortune in the stock market. Perhaps John's Calvinist upbringing had worked against his efforts to get rich by gambling, for he'd thrown away money on one wrong guess after another. Common sense had asserted itself at last, though. He'd pulled out of the market and used what few assets he had left to buy a small farm.

This was what in truth John Roberts had always wanted, a place for his horses, some chickens, a few cows. He didn't know much about farming but he was happy in his new life. His wife was not. She took the boy and moved out. John was alone again. One morning, driving into the barn, he felt a terrible pain in his side. Mary went out to the farm. Seeing her beloved uncle stretched out on that same bed where Sade had lain with her delicate shawls around her was almost more than the bereft niece could handle.

John's death and her own frustration about her neighbors' willful blindness to the war, though not to the huge profits that they were making from armaments manufactured right there in Pittsburgh, were turning Mary increasingly morbid. Dr. Rinehart was worried about her unsuccessful attempts to pull herself out of her depression. Then one day a man named Howard Eaton strolled into the downtown office and the clouds began to lift.

As a big-game hunter and guide, Howard Eaton had become something of a legend. Back in the 1870s, he and his two brothers had taken up ranching in the Dakota Badlands, and made good at it. Eastern friends had flocked to enjoy the Eatons' hospitality. Howard had been happy to guide them where the grizzlies and bighorns could be found. After a while, the visitors had begun to insist on paying their way; and thus, as Mary observed, was established the first dude ranch in the American West.

Howard Eaton had come to Pittsburgh, the Rineharts soon learned, to talk them into joining a riding party that he was planning to lead through newly opened Glacier National Park. He was particularly eager for Mrs. Rinehart to come along, probably hoping that the famous writer would generate publicity for the park. Dr. Rinehart thought the trip might do her good. Mary wasn't so sure. She was still dreadfully tired, and she had her mother and the family to consider.

But Howard wasn't the man to take no for an answer. It was finally settled that Mary would go ahead. Stanley and the boys would meet her later at the Eaton ranch. The plan didn't go off quite the way it was intended; what it did do was give Mary a taste for western living and camping that would change the Rinehart family's vacationing habits for years to come.

It would also pave the way for a dramatic change in Mary's wardrobe. Her first long trek on horseback convinced her that there was much room for improvement in women's equestrian attire. Cowboys were prudes, it appeared; breeches on females would offend their delicate sensibilities. Mary bowed to convention and settled for a long, divided gray skirt with a matching coat over it. That skirt was a hateful thing, it made mounting and dismounting awkward and had a nasty habit of creeping up and wadding itself between the wearer and the saddle. In deference to the easily embarrassed cowhands, it also had elastic bands at the hem to be slipped over her boots lest some vagrant breeze sneak up from underneath and afford a shocking glimpse of a nether limb. The other women in Eaton's party were similarly accoutered; their first move on dismounting was to duck down behind their horses and do up the buttons that turned the splits back into skirts.

To eastern eyes, the West looks depressingly barren at first sight; then its austere hugeness begins to grow on the viewer. Stanley had prescribed the right medicine after all. Mary was feeling the lure of the wild country. Imagining herself surrounded by herds of buffalo and painted tepees, she'd nudge her pony into a lope and take another brisk trot around the old corral.

After a short break-in period at the ranch, the party—twenty or thirty, Mary estimated—was taken to Glacier Park. Their mounts were saddled for them, the camping gear strapped to the pack animals, and they hit the trail. Mary was more frightened by those mountain passes than she'd been by the big guns in France; she slid off her horse and led him along, wincing when he stepped on her feet, afraid to look down. But that was only the first day, and she soon learned to stick to her saddle and trust her mount. She also learned how hard and cold a mountain could feel at night when there was nothing between her and the bedrock except a ground sheet and a couple of blankets.

Howard Eaton was a no-nonsense guide. He'd roust out his far-from-dauntless band of Glacier pioneers at five every morning, rain or shine, feed them huge western-style breakfasts, and set them on the trail again, up and up till they could go no higher. The well-known western artist Charles Russell, another of the celebrities in Eaton's party, moaned that he was right tired of standing in a cloud up to his waist.

Lack of visibility might be tough on a painter, but it didn't stop Mary Rinehart. Wherever they went, she was quick on the draw with notebook and camera. Out of this first trip west would come a little travel book called *Through Glacier Park* that would bring the Eatons hordes of new visitors and be a catalyst in developing the concept of dude ranching into a major industry.

The West was calorie country, no question about that. Breakfast was strong black coffee, bacon, eggs, and flapjacks doused with molasses. Lunch was strong black coffee and sandwiches. Supper was fried beef, fried potatoes, and strong black coffee. Mary wolfed down whatever was put in front of her and throve on it; the cure was definitely working.

Never one to miss a trick, Howard Eaton had arranged a small extra attraction for his band of riders. A few Blackfoot Indians were brought into camp. They beat their drums and sang strange, almost eerie songs that somehow evoked the aura of this vast, lonely country. Once they learned that Mrs. Rinehart had been to the Great War, they made her a member of the Blackfoot tribe in a solemn rite, giving her the Indian name Pitamakin after a great woman warrior of their own tribe.

On a later occasion, the tribe presented their adopted heroine with a long pictograph that had Pitamakin's history. This was when Mary first realized that the original Pitamakin had won glory not in battle but through her consummate skill as a horsethief, and that her most celebrated geste had been the theft of a mule. The likelihood here is that the mule had belonged to the U.S. Army; the Blackfeet might well have considered it a noble deed for an Indian woman to put them one-up on the government for a change.

By the time Mary met them, this remnant of a once great tribe was in desperate straits. The Blackfeet had been Plains Indians, not farmers but hunters. The white men had slaughtered their buffalo, driven their people to a far northern reservation on a high plateau where the few crops they tried to raise were often killed by frost. Their chief told Mary through a translator how many of their children had died during a famine the previous winter.

They blamed the previous federal agent for making them drive their large herd of beef cattle to the eastern side of the reservation and leave them there to be run off by rustlers. A half-blood managed to find his way to Chicago and trace some of the hides by the tribal brand but, even with their case proved, the Blackfeet could get no redress. The culpable agent was still on the reservation, and he came to see Mary. They disliked each other on sight but he did write her a letter later, excoriating Cato Sells, who was then commissioner of Indian affairs. If he thought the Blackfeet's new recruit might be persuaded to help him get his job back, he thought wrong; but when it came to helping the people he'd betrayed, Mary was ready.

She gave the tribe her solemn promise to go to Washington and fight for their rights. She was surprised and greatly moved when they loaded her with gifts: beaded moccasins and belts, a wonderful painted parfleche made from buffalo hide, a medicine necklace of rare old Hudson's Bay brass trading beads and small bones from a buffalo's ankle. Most precious of all was the tribe's last war pipe, a cherished relic of the old days before they had been driven from their homeland.

This time, the promise would be honored. As soon as she got to Washington, Mary went straight to Franklin Lane, secretary of the interior, and poured out her rage. The Blackfeet had been viciously exploited, they were debilitated from neglect and lack of food, many were going blind from trachoma. Spurred by her vehemence, Lane acted at once. By the time she'd had lunch and gone back to her hotel room, he was on the phone, letting her know that supplies were already on the way and that a full-scale investigation would follow. From then on, Mary would serve as a friend and mentor to the tribe.

But her own husband must come first. While she was still on the trail with Howard Eaton, a ranger had galloped up to her with a telegram. Dr. Rinehart had been operated on for appendicitis. The abscess was draining nicely, but Mary knew too much about those draining abscesses: She galloped frantically down the mountain, caught the first possible train, and sat in agony through the long ride. She found Stanley gray in the face but over the hump. When he was well enough to travel, they went to a seaside resort where they were lucky enough to find another convalescent with whom he could exchange talk about his symptoms.

The man was Irvin S. Cobb, a newspaperman from Kentucky

who'd become widely known as a comic writer and speaker. A few years later, Mr. Cobb and Mary fought a duel of the sexes; *American* magazine, in October 1919, carried two articles. Mary's was titled "Isn't That Just Like a Man?"; Cobb's was "Oh Well, You Know How Women Are." Their modes of expression made an interesting contrast.

Cobb swung his broadsword like a true male chauvinist, taking wide swipes wherever he saw his chance to get a horselaugh at a woman's expense. At the end he wiggled out from under with some high-flown rhetoric about Mary Magdalene redeemed in the persons of those noble, self-sacrificing women who, however bitchy they might be as a general rule, were willing in times of crisis to work their heads off doing all the dirty jobs and expecting no thanks for their labors. As, he seemed to think, why should they?

Mary's was a subtler, more penetrating appraisal. She liked people in general and men in particular, but had few illusions about them; she had a lovely time exploding the popular misconception that women are cats, while men resemble dogs. To her, it appeared to work the other way around.

Cats, she pointed out, were night wanderers. They loved familiar places, but didn't allow their love of the hearthside to interfere with their nocturnal rovings. Cats could conceal under the suavest exterior principles that would make a kitten blush. And, heavens, how those whisker-frisking tomcats enjoyed being petted and praised. They liked love, but not as a steady diet. They preferred to select their own companions. They were predatory creatures . . . and showed a few other traits that Mary enumerated with reasonably ladylike restraint.

Women, on the other hand, were like dogs. They loved with doggy devotion and expected plenty of pats in return. They could be trained to fetch and carry and often had to. They were always ready to gnaw a bone of contention, they sometimes enjoyed a good growling match so long as it ended in (metaphorical) tail wagging and kisses. As to men resembling dogs, Mary finally concluded that the two species were alike only in the respect that both tended to have disproportionately big feet during their early puppyhood.

In 1917 Mary's and Cobb's articles were bound together into an attractive but unfortunately fragile little book by Doran. In browsing through it, the reader comes upon such delights as "Men . . . are curiously loyal. They are loyal to ancient hats and disreputable old friends and to some women. But they are always loyal to each other. This, I maintain, is the sole reason for alluding to them as the stronger and superior sex."

The *Saturday Evening Post* had been publishing Mary's war pieces in sequence from April through July. On July 17, they had varied this sometimes hard to digest diet with "Clara's Little Escapade." Now they wanted Tish to come along and liven up the menu. Mary obliged with "My Country Tish of Thee," a two-part story that would run the following April.

She also experimented with a new character. "*The Sub-Deb*," a word alleged to have been coined by the author but in fact supplied by Stanley Junior and meaning a girl almost but not quite old enough to make her debut in society, appeared March 4, 1916, featuring a semiliterate flibbertigibbet named Bab. Within the next three years, Mary wrote a total of six Bab stories. Those were quite enough; Bab is a joke that ceases to amuse. But she paid well. Mary got a total of $9,250 out of the stories from the *Post*, another $10,000 from Famous Players-Lasky for the film rights, and an unlisted but no doubt impressive sum from Doran for the hardcover collection.

In her autobiography, Mary mentioned that she hadn't been feeling well that fall. All the while she sat churning out comedy she'd been comparing herself to the family parrot, which startled visitors by emitting peals of raucous laughter without cracking a smile. Perhaps she was having belated sympathy pangs with Stanley, or maybe those huge meals of beans and bacon and strong black coffee she'd gobbled on the Eaton expedition had done her in. Whatever the cause, she too lost her appendix in January 1916.

When Mary was able to travel, Dr. Rinehart took her and Ted, then aged thirteen, the only one of their sons still living at

home, on a trip to Panama, Costa Rica, and Cuba. In Panama
they met Rex Beach and his wife. Beach, a highly successful
author of red-blooded he-man novels set in Alaska, married to an
actress-turned-innkeeper whom he'd met in Nome, was also an
ardent sportsman. Having lived in Florida during his boyhood,
he knew all about tarpon fishing; the two parties joined up on a
yacht on the Chagres River to catch some tarpon. Mary, the ardent
fisherwoman, had no luck until Rex Beach ripped off a strip of
his red flannel shirt and made her a lure. Thanks to Beach's shirt-
tail, she landed two good-sized fish and became, as far as she
knew, the first female member of the Tarpon Club of Panama.

In Costa Rica, Mary was presented with a baby ocelot but
had to return the scratchy little bundle of fur and fury to the donor
rather than face permanent mutilation. In Havana, nobody wanted
to give the Rineharts anything but a hard time. Maybe the Cubans
just didn't like the Americans; the islanders were rude to tourists
for no reason, and they expected too much money for extremely
poor service. Little did those insolent islanders reck the power of
the Rinehart pen. As soon as Mary got home, she sat down and
ripped off a piece of her mind. *The Pirates of the Caribbean* ran in
the *Post* on November 16, 1916, and the Spanish-American War
was on again. The Cuban government protested to the U.S. State
Department; Mary was deluged with nasty letters and hostile
editorials. They didn't faze her a whit. She'd got her facts straight.
She let the ravers rave without bothering to answer back, even to
the man who wrote furiously that he wouldn't marry her if she
were the last woman on earth.

Much as Americans tried to ignore the real war overseas, it
was obvious to Mary that the United States was going to be drawn
in before long. And her sons were growing up fast. Stanley Junior,
now at Harvard, was already older than many of the young soldiers she'd seen at the front. Alan, finishing up at prep school,
would be seventeen on his next birthday. How long would it be
before they were in uniform?

Nineteen sixteen was an election year. In June, the Philadelphia Public Ledger Syndicate importuned Mrs. Rinehart to cover
all three conventions—Republican, Democratic, and Progres-

sive—for them. Mary didn't want to do it, but eventually she capitulated; perhaps because this would be a new experience, perhaps because, being Mary, she wanted the money. Her first assignment was to interview the old Rough Rider, ex-President Theodore Roosevelt, the man for whom all the Teddy bears in the world are named.

Roosevelt had served as vice president under McKinley, had succeeded to office in 1901 when McKinley succumbed to an assassin's bullet, and had been enthusiastically reelected in 1904. At the end of his second term, he'd declined to run again and thrown his support to his then secretary of war, William Howard Taft. Once elected, however, Taft balked at carrying on some of the programs that Roosevelt had initiated; a schism opened between the conservative and progressive elements in the Republican party. The upshot was that, in 1912, Taft was dutifully renominated by the Republicans, Roosevelt ran as a Progressive, and both of them were defeated by Woodrow Wilson, the Democratic candidate.

Mary found the legendary Teddy a hard man to interview, not because he was unwilling to talk but because she had such a tough time getting a word in edgewise. Roosevelt was particularly outspoken about America's foot-dragging on the war. If he had stayed on for a third term, he said, he would have called in the German ambassador and let it be known in no uncertain terms that, if Germany threatened Belgium's neutrality, the United States would immediately mobilize to defend her. Teddy was vehement that America must forthwith drop its neutral position. These American pacifists were nothing but a pack of cowards; the reason he'd refused to enter the race this time was that he had no desire to preside over a country riddled with cravens.

In fact, Theodore Roosevelt must already have known that he wasn't going to be offered the Republican nomination; that was patent to Mary from her very first day at the convention. Nor would Roosevelt accept a nomination from the Progressives, he was too astute a politician to let himself in for another defeat. Instead, he backed Charles Evans Hughes for the Republican nomination. Hughes had not gone after the nomination but did not turn it down. The convention drafted him in November; Hughes wound up losing to Wilson by a fairly close vote.

All this politicking was confusing and worrisome to a novice reporter, particularly with the Republican and Progressive conventions both going on at the same time in the already superheated Windy City. Mary had brought her secretary to Chicago with her; the poor woman must have had a boring time of it, sitting behind a typewriter back in the hotel room, waiting for her day's work to begin. Mary herself had to divide her time between the two sweltering convention halls, trying to figure out what was going on. The Republican proceedings were decorous enough, and Charles Evans Hughes was nominated without a hitch. With Roosevelt out of the picture, however, the Progressives were going hog-wild. Speakers whom she dubbed their lunatic fringe were making all sorts of mad proposals. Much of this so-called lunacy, it may be noted, would have become law by the time Mary wrote her autobiography.

As her daily deadline drew near, Mary would race back to her waiting secretary, try to put her impressions into coherent form, correct the first typewritten draft, and have the secretary make several copies to be put on the wires by six o'clock. Then she'd eat a light supper and collapse into bed. Mary didn't mention a cool, cleansing bath as her evening treat, but it's unthinkable that she wouldn't have taken as many baths as time allowed in the hectic circumstances.

One rainy day, Mary joined a Suffrage parade. As she marched down Michigan Avenue, she asked herself pessimistically what she was doing there. Her innate skepticism dampened any great hope of change. She'd seen too much wheeling and dealing at the conventions. What good was it going to do for women to get the vote? There'd be that same old male cabal, still putting their heads together in some smoke-filled room, making up the American people's minds for them as to who would get to run their country next time around.

At the Democratic convention in St. Louis, the weather was even hotter than in Chicago. Politicians, delegates, and reporters sat in their shirtsleeves, trying in vain to cool off by waving palm-leaf fans while an impassioned orator cried, "Every mother whose son is today safe in his home may thank God for Woodrow Wilson, who has kept us out of war."

More experienced political correspondents than she were exchanging cynical smiles, Mary noticed. This was nothing but campaign rhetoric; a statement, not a promise.

Mary couldn't wait to get home, she wrote her final report sitting up in a lower berth on the overnight train to Pittsburgh. Hughes and Wilson would be pitted against each other in November, and she didn't give a hoot or a holler which of the two was going to win.

CHAPTER 23

A Lull Before the Storm

By the time the conventions were over, Mary's compatriots had begun to talk more positively about entering the war on the side of the Allies. Intelligent Americans had by now grasped the fact that, unless the United States stepped in, the carnage and ruination would drag on and on, just as General Foch had prophesied. Far too many others were romancing the war, calling it a great adventure, seeing it as a new thrill to relieve the drabness of everyday life. These dreamers pictured the brave boys marching off in their jaunty uniforms to cover themselves (and, by association, their stay-at-home friends and relations) with medals and glory. Of course every Johnny would then come marching home again with his eyes, limbs, and patriotic ideals all intact.

Mary doubted whether one citizen in ten thousand had any real idea of what these romantic notions were going to cost in money, material, and human suffering. Dr. Rinehart agreed with her absolutely; nevertheless, they decided to go ahead with the family expedition that had been abruptly terminated the previous summer by Stanley's turbulent appendix, and spend two whole months riding and camping in the Rockies. The Head (short for

"Head of the House," a term Mary would apply to her husband when describing this and subsequent trips) had been a happy camper all his life. Mary had got her basic training the previous year in Glacier Park. The boys were all novices but they took to the rough outdoor life like three ducks to water. It was a good thing they did, considering some of the hair-raising situations they would find themselves having to face.

Tenting Tonight, the book that inevitably developed from this trek, sold well when it came out and is highly readable today, alternating humorous incident with hair-raising episodes, carrying the reader back to a time when the Northwest was still pretty much virgin territory and it was possible, though sometimes foolhardy, to take a pack train into areas where no human had ever gone before. After the grim subject matter of *Kings, Queens, and Pawns*, the ersatz gaiety of those too utterly killing Bab stories, and the hectic reportage of three political conventions, Mary clearly reveled in the chance to get away from it all with her beloved menfolk.

Theirs was not, however, just a family party. The Rineharts went first to the Eaton ranch and spent a couple of weeks at Glacier Park, giving the boys their chance to adjust to life in the saddle before they went back to the ranch and began packing for their own expedition. By the time they'd got organized, they'd wound up with fifteen men, thirty-one horses, and the one small woman who was the driving force behind it all.

Mary mentioned some of the ranch hands by name. The head guide was called Pete, probably because he was really something like Emil or Fritz and the times were getting chancy for people with German names. The teamster was Bill Hossick, the cook was another Bill, their movie photographer was Joe. There was also a still photographer who didn't get called much of anything because he never talked to anybody. Somebody else named Joe, defined solely as an optimist, was the idea man, one of his inspirations being to bring along two sturdy boats in one of the wagons. Bills, Petes, Toms, Dicks, and Harrys were sprinkled throughout Mary's text; she had a habit exasperating to a biographer of dropping names without explanation. Perhaps, being the sociable soul that she was, she stuck them in just to give some of her cronies the fun of seeing themselves in print.

The Rineharts kept together on the trail. Mary rode at the head of the line, the three boys followed their mother. Dr. Rinehart brought up the rear to encourage the stragglers, make sure none of his sons fell off a cliff, and provide the smokers among the working crew with matches. The Head had an almost kleptomaniacal way of acquiring matches; Mary claimed her husband had so many boxes of them distributed about his person that if anybody were to whack him hard enough on any part of his body, he'd go up in smoke. Fortunately, nobody ever tested her claim.

Once Pete, the guide, had been assured that this expedition was not going to cross the border into Canada, where he, as a German, would have been an enemy alien and treated accordingly, he loosened up. Like a true cowpoke, he sang to his horse. Being German, he sang German songs. Dr. Rinehart happily joined in, but the only German song he knew the words to was "Die Lorelei." "*Ich weiss nicht was soll' es bedeuten dass ich so traurig bin*" is pretty at first hearing but can get monotonous in wholesale quantities. After a week or so of the same old tune, everybody else in the party knew perfectly well why the ballad of the fatally seductive Rhinemaiden made them so sad.

Despite her passion for camping, Mary liked her creature comforts. Sleeping on the ground was not her forte. Bough beds didn't work unless they were properly made, which they usually weren't. An air mattress was better than nothing, but not if it had a sharp rock under it. As the only woman in the party, Mary had to have a tent, even if the shelter was just big enough for her to crawl into and lie down. But where to pitch it? Come time to make camp, she took to flopping on the ground in likely spots. When she found one that felt right, she'd stay where she was and instruct the men to pound in the tent pegs around her.

Mary might have been the queen bee but the camp cook was, and always would be, the kingpin of every mountain trek. He had to be astir before anybody else, set up his makeshift stove, get the coffee water boiling, fetch supplies out of the chuck wagon, and start cooking gigantic amounts of food in too few pots and pans, crouching over an open fire, squinting through the smoke, dodging flying cinders, catering to everybody else's ravenous appetite before he got to satisfy his own. These chores done, he had to clean up, wash up, pack up, and jolt off in his wagon toward the next meal.

This was a job for a good-natured man. The Rineharts were dreadfully upset to realize after only a few days on the trail that their cook didn't like them. He didn't say so, and he did his work well enough, but cooks have ways of making their feelings known. They tried praising his cooking, they offered to help with the dishes. He hung on doggedly to his grouch.

Perhaps the cook resented the camera crew, perhaps he was sick of the "Lorelei." Whatever the reason, one day after a long, difficult trek the party stopped, took care of the animals, and waited for the chuck wagon to roll up. They were all starving, of course; they hailed its late appearance with joy. Then joy turned to dismay, for the cook wasn't there. According to the teamster, the cook had told him to pull up a few miles back, had picked up his bedroll, got out of the wagon, and started walking back over the trail.

But what had the cook said? they demanded.

He'd said "so long," the teamster replied.

Here indeed was a predicament. Mary was a good cook, but she wasn't crazy enough to take on the task of feeding all those hungry males in the wilds. Surrounded by clouds of gloom and foreboding, they scrambled together a lunch of sorts and got back on their horses. Great then was their surprise to come upon a man all alone, sitting beside the trail doing nothing and apparently quite content to be idle. The Head pulled up and, in desperation, asked whether the contented man had any idea where they might be able to locate a cook. He said they need look no further. His name was Norman Lee and he'd be glad to cook for them.

Mary took Lee's appearance as an act of Providence but apparently this was just something that happened along the trail. They would find another cook later in an even unlikelier spot; the new chap was friendly enough but had a terrible singing voice, so they left him and went on.

They were quite satisfied with their first find, and well they might be. Norman Lee was a soldier of fortune. He'd been in Cuba, in the Philippines, he'd fought in the Boxer Rebellion. Lately he'd taken to trapping marten and lynx, which presumably ranked with skunk as fashion furs. One of the packers had told Mary that there were just two kinds of camp cooks, those who made great biscuits but hated the people who ate them, and the jolly souls whose culinary skills stopped short at opening a can of beans. Fortunately for the success of the Rinehart expedition, Lee was both affable and able.

The farther they rode, the wilder became the terrain, as did their idea man's suggestions. In those early days of moving pictures, actors were expected to perform their own stunts. Joe thought it would make a nice sequence for the famous Mrs. Rinehart to shoot the rapids for a hundred miles or so in one of the boats they'd brought along.

"No way!" cried the outraged male Rineharts. If Mrs. Rinehart went, they all went. So they all did in fact go, taking turns riding with Mary and an experienced boatman, changing shifts when the first man got too exhausted from dodging rocks and trying to keep the boat right side up. Mary, who had to make the entire trip, did manage to get in some good fishing in the quieter parts and even to enjoy the rapids, some of the time.

A while later, Joe got a taste of his own medicine. He went mountain climbing with a couple of the other hired men, lost his footing on a snowfield, slid anywhere from a hundred yards to a mile and a half, depending on who was telling the story, and had to hang in midair over a crevasse until his companions managed to haul him back. Joe's face was whiter than the snow when they brought him back to camp. A full twenty-four hours elapsed before he began bewailing the fact that nobody had taken any movies of his slide.

The worst time for all hands came when they climbed to Doubtful Lake, 3,000 feet in the air, and found nothing there but rock and ice. A snowfall that shouldn't have happened made it impossible for the horses to find any grazing. After Stanley Senior's mount had gone hungry for almost two days in a freezing rain, the ever-compassionate doctor fed him a rain-soaked biscuit, an apple, two lumps of sugar, and a raw egg, all of which the horse accepted gratefully. Fortunately, sundown found them in a lush valley where the horses could eat their fill. For the Rineharts, this was the end of the trail. It was time to go home.

CHAPTER 24

Mary Goes Back to War

Strenuous as they'd been, those two months in the Rockies had put Mary back on her feet. As tensions about the war grew more intense throughout the country, she settled back to work, finishing *Tenting Tonight*, writing short stories for some quick cash. She started a play called *The Bat*. She'd meant this to be a dramatization of her first great success, *The Circular Staircase*, but got a better idea. When Mary asked Edgar Selwyn whether a mystery play that kept the audience in suspense until almost the final curtain would work, he told her it would be worth a million dollars.

A million dollars sounded fine, but the play would have to wait. Woodrow Wilson had spoken the fateful words, America was at war with Germany. Stanley Junior had taken ROTC training at Harvard but was only eighteen, too young to be given a commission; he telephoned his parents for permission to enlist as a private. What could they say but yes?

Almost the next day, Mary's editors at the *Saturday Evening Post* were begging her for a piece that would encourage other parents to release their sons for duty. Having learned the hideous truths of warfare, Mary was appalled by what they were asking. She wrote the piece, however, in one twelve-hour stint, crying all the time. She called it "The Altar of Freedom"; she had already made one sacrifice of her own, and knew there would be more to come.

Olive Roberts Barton's husband had enlisted. Mary's sister was going to teach school to support herself and their two small children until her husband came home. Mercifully, he did come back, one of the few survivors of a machine-gun company that had seen heavy action from the time they got overseas until the end of the war.

Dr. Rinehart applied for a commission in the Army Medical Corps. While waiting to hear from Washington, he was assigned by the state governor to serve on a three-man draft registration board. Immediately he closed his private practice, delegated the work of the dispensary to his associates, and joined in the gigantic task of helping to pull an army together at short notice.

Mary had tried to register as an army nurse. She was not accepted but soon got a government assignment of a far different nature. After the declaration of war, the U.S. Navy's Atlantic Fleet had been mobilized; Secretary of the Navy Josephus Daniels wanted Mrs. Rinehart to write up a story about it for propaganda purposes.

Daniels sounds from Mary's description rather like Sir Joseph from *H.M.S. Pinafore.* He'd stuck close to his desk and never gone to sea, which of course explained his being made the ruler of the U.S. Navy. Daniels would later become an effective administrator, but in these beginning stages, Mary said, he seemed to know nothing of navy protocol and was innocently wreaking terrible damage on tradition and morale. He even invited Mrs. Rinehart to sit in on one of the General Board of the Navy's sessions in Washington before he sent her to review the fleet.

Daniels evidently didn't realize what a gaffe he was committing, but Mary did. She ought not to have been allowed either at the session or on board the ships, she knew these upper-echelon officers resented her presence although they were gentlemen enough not to show their ire. Daniels must have caught on, but he could hardly back down. He sent his own carriage to pick Mrs. Rinehart up at the Shoreham Hotel and put her on the boat to Norfolk.

Mary's ignorance of battleships was total. She hadn't even known what clothes to bring; when she learned that she'd be expected to go clambering all over the ships, she had to borrow a pair of tennis shoes from an officer's wife. Unfortunately, the other woman's feet were quite a lot bigger than hers. Less unfortunately, she didn't have to wear the sneakers for her first meeting with the admiral of the Atlantic Fleet. Regardless of whatever personal feelings he entertained about females being allowed to infiltrate the fleet's all-male purlieus, Admiral Mayo had Mary piped aboard the flagship *Pennsylvania* with due pomp and circumstance, and greeted her in person. Almost his first question, however, was, "How long are you staying?"

Mary didn't know, she thought maybe a week. She further assumed she'd be billetted on the *Pennsylvania*, she could not have been more wrong. The admiral explained, no doubt with inner relief, that it would take an act of Congress to let her bunk aboard for even one night.

He did provide what hospitality was within his powers. Mary was Admiral Mayo's guest for lunch and dinner all during her five-day stay. He made sure Mrs. Rinehart got all the facts she needed, and no doubt some that she didn't. Mary walked, she climbed, she even crawled through narrow openings, praying that she wouldn't get stuck. As always, she made notes. One item she tried to decipher later claimed that "Every part is duplicated so that if one is shot away another takes up its function. If the after-end is shot away, the ship can still steam ahead." She sensed something not quite right here; it had been her impression that propellers were only on the after-parts.

Barring such glitches, Mary learned a good deal about the fleet's many components: battleships, destroyers, cruisers, mine-layers, colliers, oilers, supply ships, each with its own job to do. She watched an experiment in which an airplane was catapulted from the deck of a battleship and was astounded to see that it worked.

The grand finale came when the presidential yacht *Mayflower* sailed in bearing Mary's champion, Secretary Daniels of the navy, along with Secretary of War Newton D. Baker and their entire staffs. They were to spend a day with the fleet. All the admirals and high-ranking officers would be lunching together; Mary was quietly sent to inspect some onshore installations and keep out of sight. Daniels, however, noticed his protégée's absence and insisted that Mrs. Rinehart be among those present. For a fashion plate like Mary, given no time to change, having to flop aboard in those too-big tennis shoes must have been agony. She'd just got settled among the dignitaries when a gaggle of newspapermen were allowed to board and feast their eyes on so much assembled glory and one small woman with feet like a circus clown.

Daniels further invited Mrs. Rinehart to sail back to Washington on the *Mayflower*. Regrettably, after dinner Mary began to feel sick. As the only female aboard, she'd been given the cabin assigned to the president's wife; by midnight she was convinced that she would soon breathe her last in these exalted surroundings. Mary finally got a cabin boy to understand that he'd better assemble all the dignitaries to witness her death throes. He sensibly brought a doctor who took her diagnosis of food poisoning as a personal insult but gave her something to quiet her stomach.

By morning, Mary felt well enough to go in search of toast and tea. Mr. Daniels was in the dining room eating a boiled egg; she took one look at that egg and rushed for the deck. Before an august assemblage of rank and glitter and in full view of a crowd that had been waiting on the wharf to watch the dignitaries come in, Mary Roberts Rinehart doubled up over the rail and gave the Potomac all she had.

Secretary Baker was a true gentleman. He drove Mary back to the Shoreham, helped her up the stairs, and made sure she was properly looked after. Little did she know then that her upset stomach was about to get her a new job for the War Department.

All unaware, she went home and wrote up the article she'd come to research for Secretary Daniels. "The Gray Mailed Fist" ran in the *Saturday Evening Post* June 23, 1917. It explained to

American parents exactly what their sailor sons were doing, it excoriated the penny-pinchers who had forced the U.S. Navy to battle for its very existence and were now clamoring for its protection. By the time the piece she'd done for Secretary Daniels appeared in the *Post*, Mary was already starting to carry out her new assignment for Secretary Baker.

Although Newton D. Baker had been hand-picked by President Wilson, he was hardly the man in the street's notion of what a secretary of war ought to be. Baker made no pretense of being a fire-eater; he despised war and had no wish to become involved with the logistics of fighting. That was the generals' job. The secretary's position was that of a lawyer and an administrator.

Baker also realized that this new U.S. Army was going to be, for the first time, a true cross section of America. The draft was gathering up young boys and grown men of every social level, every sort of background, factory workers and college professors, bank clerks and cowhands. So heterogeneous a congeries of recruits would not all fit meekly into the rigid old army traditions of discipline and training.

What Secretary Baker wanted from Mary Roberts Rinehart was not just a quick overview of the new army but detailed observations, starting with the officers' training schools and working through to the cantonments where raw recruits took their first marching steps toward becoming soldiers. He wanted to know about conditions in the camps and in the towns nearby, the morale of the men, the kinds of meals they were getting—details that a woman would notice and a man might not catch. Mrs. Rinehart was to be in no sense considered a spy: the camp commanders would be told exactly what she was there for. Some of the officers in charge would soon find her a useful go-between with the War Department concerning problems that might not otherwise have got a hearing.

Baker had made it plain that his new emissary must not expect the same red-carpet treatment from him as she'd got from Secretary Daniels. He couldn't even give her any expense money. That was all right with Mary; the *Post* had paid its usual rate for her navy article, and she knew her editors would be glad enough to buy whatever might come of this new assignment. In the end, what came would turn out to be quite a lot.

During the summer of 1917, in the midst of her extensive travels, Mary finally got around to awarding herself a qualified encomium. She was, she said, a bad novelist but a good reporter, relying heavily on her knack for retaining clear visual memories and describing things as she'd seen them. Like Mark Twain, Mary had written some fairly wretched stuff to keep the home fires burning. All in all, though, she was *not* a bad novelist and knew perfectly well she wasn't. We have to assume this demurrer was a hangover from her early indoctrination. She still retained an uneasy feeling that it wasn't quite nice to write the kind of fiction readers could enjoy.

Long and arduous as it was, Mary's American tour of inspection offered certain advantages that her European investigations had lacked. Nobody was shooting at her, nor was she in any great danger of being torpedoed. She could take baths when she chose, she got enough to eat, she had no worries about not having the right visa. Better still, she was able to get home between trips. During June and July, Dr. Rinehart was still in Pittsburgh. The couple would manage to snatch a few evenings and weekends together after he'd processed his quota of recruits and she had made some progress in writing up her reports for Secretary Baker, plus another article for the *Post*. Then it would be back to the draft board for him and back on the road for her.

Not unexpectedly, Mary soon discovered that one army camp tended to look much like the rest: an elderly brick building or two, a too-small parade ground, new wooden barracks that had been flimsily thrown up, often without adequate ventilation, some of them dangerous firetraps. At one camp she visited, she saw the sentries making their nightly rounds with fire extinguishers at the ready. Some camps were scrupulously maintained, others ranged from untidy to chaotic; Mary couldn't see that the housekeeping had any discernible effect on the quality of training or the morale of the recruits. She found the floor in one camp kitchen greased like a skating rink with scraps of raw meat and the sinks too revolting to describe, but she did say the food that came out of that hovel was first-rate and morale was correspondingly high.

As Secretary Baker had anticipated, camp commanders were of two distinct breeds. There were those who understood that the widely assorted recruits they were getting now must be handled differently from the submissive rookies they'd dealt with before the war. Then there were the diehards, who thought they could go along in the old autocratic way where the officer's word was law and the lower ranks had no choice but to obey without question. Mary was surprised to note that the older officers, particularly the generals, understood the need for flexibility better than the young ones did.

Mary herself felt the need of some basic training, and took to carrying around a manual called *Studies in Minor Tactics*. After some hard plugging, she felt reasonably confident that she could, in a pinch, order out a batallion and destroy an army hiding behind a barn. Perhaps batallions were smaller then, or barns were larger. Or possibly, like so many new recruits, Mary hadn't quite grasped the logistics. In *My Story*, she told how, during a sham battle, one rookie threw a sham grenade (i.e. a rock) into a clump of real bushes. A second rookie rolled out of the clump yowling a most unmilitary "What the h——?" (Well, that's how Mary wrote it down.)

"Your machine gun's jammed and you're out of commission," yelled rookie number one. "Roll back in there and die."

Mary saw a good many things that she didn't dare publish. Some of these neophytes were finding the heat, the bodily discomfort, the unrelenting hard work, the strangeness, the loneliness just too much to handle; there were more suicides than ever got reported. It was a terrible time for Mary, hard for all those mothers who kept writing her letters, perhaps hardest of all for President Wilson, who had to contend not only with the horrendous burden of the war but also with the profiteering and one-upmanship in his own administration.

Now that mobilization had begun, America's earlier foot-dragging about preparing for war was showing its bad effects: too much friction, too much waste, too much delay, and far too few soldiers ready to fight. In May 1917, Gen. John J. Pershing had gone to France with just 2,000 fighting men at his command. At the end of that year, he would still have fewer than 200,000, of whom 7,000 were marines. It would take a full year, until May 1918, for the American army to come up to full strength.

And still the war went on, and so did Mary Roberts Rinehart. By now she'd earned a reputation in government circles as some kind of wonder woman. Herbert Hoover asked her to join the Food Administration. She had to turn him down. She was still visiting army camps, still writing her articles, still hoping to be accepted as an overseas nurse, the one job she really wanted and never got.

In August, Dr. Rinehart became Major Rinehart. Mary saw him off in his new uniform with his officer's trunk strapped in the back of his car; she was somewhat comforted that Stanley Senior was on his way to the same camp where Stanley Junior was already getting his basic training. The major, on the other hand, was worrying about Mary. Her downtown office had been broken into and searched, not just once but several times. Nothing had been taken except a photograph of her, but her files had been rummaged through again and again. The reason was obvious enough. Because of her involvement with the military, somebody thought the inquisitive Mrs. Rinehart must have got hold of secret information, which she hadn't and wouldn't have been fool enough to leave kicking around her office if she had.

This was by no means Mary's only brush with espionage. The War Department had been getting reports that morale in one of the officers' training camps was showing a sudden inexplicable decline, and Mary was sent there as a troubleshooter. For the first few days, she did nothing but look and listen; those reports of lowered morale had not been exaggerated. She began to suspect the cause when she kept hearing the name of a certain officer. One night at a dinner dance, when he'd had a little too much to drink, he sat down at her table and started right in asking improper questions, mostly about troop sailings. Mary tried to shut him off, but the officer was drunk enough to persist. He began extolling the

Germans, decrying the War Department, insisting that the army he was allegedly helping train was already beaten; they might as well quit before they got killed. Mary's patriotism got the better of her discretion. She told him flat out that he was talking sedition and heading for serious trouble.

That sobered him up. He disappeared from the party and Mary left the next day for Washington, with a full written report of the encounter in her dressing case. On the train, a middle-aged man persisted in trying to make conversation with her. She assumed it was for the usual reason, so she snubbed the old goat pretty thoroughly and thought no more about him. However, she did take the precaution of taking her dressing case into her berth before she went to sleep. Waking early in the morning, she found her case out in the aisle and the report missing.

That settled the matter. The inquisitive officer was thenceforth under surveillance. He kept his nose clean after his big gaffe, but never got to France. Military intelligence had checked him out and discovered that he'd been one of a dozen or so young German officers planted in the U.S. Army as subversives some years back. Undoubtedly, the Germans were thorough. But not quite thorough enough. They ought to have taken into account the fact that a woman who'd written mystery stories for a living must be a hard person to fool.

CHAPTER 25

Far Too Many Cactus Plants

Early fall of 1917 found Mary's finances once more in a state of crisis. There was no way she could carry on at the Bluff without her husband's help. On the same night that she'd seen Alan off to Harvard and Ted to prep school, she went back and told her mother that she was closing the house. Cornelia could accompany Mary to a New York hotel or go to Olive's with her maid. She chose Olive's. Mary, her war work seemingly over, booked a small suite at the Hotel Langdon and filled her fountain pen.

She meant to write a book, in fact she had to write a book. But what could she write? Nothing was in her mind except her family and the war; she decided to write a romance about the war, based on her overseas experiences. Its heroine would be an idealistic young American girl who would wangle her way to Belgium and set up a soup kitchen in a bombed-out house while her worthy but bullheaded fiancé back in the States nursed his grudge and envisioned her being mauled by dirty foreigners. The hero would be a sort of Scarlet Pimpernel who ran dangerous missions on behalf of his beleaguered homeland when not scrounging whatever meats and vegetables he could find to keep his fair lady's soup kettle at the boil.

The Amazing Interlude starts off a bit lamely but soon the reader is struck full force by the starkness, the misery behind the battle lines, the small acts of heroism that made up everyday life in a country where little else than courage and fortitude still existed. For Mary, the book must have been a catharsis. She said herself that it became an obsession. She worked as much as fourteen hours a day, going out only to get a breath of air or to spend a quiet time at a little Episcopal church nearby. She realized that, when she prayed, she was too often performing an empty ritual, going through the motions because she harbored a vestigial fear lest that wrathful God of her grandmother's might yet exist and require placating. But she didn't dare stop. Her menfolk were too precious to her, she had to do what she could for them.

Ted's school was outside New York. With her book well underway, Mary sneaked time off to visit her youngest son. She found him in bad shape, jerking with nerves, looking like death warmed over. Examination revealed a dilated heart and incipient chorea. Mary admitted Ted to Roosevelt Hospital and divided her time between her book and his bedside. It occurred to her that Ted's illness might have been brought on at least partly by nervous strain. Boys his age, almost but not quite old enough to enter the service, must have suffered a greater sense of frustration in this time of crisis than their parents realized.

By Christmas, however, Ted was back on his feet. Alan came on the train from Boston and they all three went to spend the holidays with the two Stanleys at Camp Sherman. Being together was the best Christmas present of all, and one of the family's treats was their being allowed to sit in while Major Rinehart delivered a scientific paper to a large medical group. His subject was capillectomy. As he rolled off his learned discourse, Mary and the boys heard murmurs from the physicians around them. God, how rusty one got in a speciality! What was a capillectomy? None of the doctors could remember. It was not until the major wound up in high glee presenting two cases, one man with long hair and a virgin beard, the other freshly shaven and barbered, that his colleagues caught on. A capillectomy was a haircut.

Sergeant Stanley Junior, by now six foot two and a bit, presented his own form of entertainment, which was to stand at attention in his father's office doorway and make Major Rinehart return his salute in accordance with military protocol. He'd then march off, returning five minutes later to salute again, and again to an increasing volume of army-style expletives, until the major lost it completely and threw him out of the building. Even Jock the Airedale contributed his bit to the hilarity, chasing off with a machine-gun company, getting himself lost, being brought back under military arrest and officially ordered by General Glenn henceforth to wear a dog tag.

Partly through a serendipitous ignorance of certain army rules, Major Rinehart got hold of two riding horses for himself and Mary. Great was the joy of some privates on the bank when the major's horse tried to lie down in the middle of a stream. Another night, husband and wife rode out on maneuvers with an artillery squad. Mary listened to the familiar noises of pounding hooves and creaking gun caissons and felt herself hauntingly back in France.

The holidays over, alone in New York, Mary gave way to exhaustion and came down with bronchitis. Howard Eaton must have had his sensors out; he dropped by in his casual way and proposed a trip to the Southwest. She began to feel the call of the wild, and why not? Ted was back at school and doing fine. Mary had collected a healthy advance on The *Amazing Interlude*. She'd also sold a story to the movies and been paid in cash with three one-thousand-dollar bills, the first she'd ever seen. Her living expenses were down to a relative pittance, her bronchial tubes deserved a quiet vacation in the sunny Southwest. Clearly, this trip was meant to be.

But what was meant was not what happened. Mary had a part-time neighbor at the Langdon, none other than her erstwhile political acquaintance, Col. Theodore Roosevelt. Former President Teddy had resumed his old military title in the hope of taking a division to the front, but there would be no place in this new army for the old Rough Rider. Roosevelt and Mary, both of them rather at loose ends, became fairly well acquainted. When Howard Eaton came to see Mary, she sent word down the hall to the colonel that a mutual friend of theirs had arrived; in no time, the two men and the lonely woman were knee-deep in plans. They'd get up a riding party and a pack outfit, forget the war, and go looking for bighorns south of the border.

When the time came, however, Roosevelt was not free to go. Somehow or other, this had turned from an innocent hunting trip into a government project. Mrs. Rinehart's quasi-military connection made her eligible to participate. Her traveling companion would be a Miss Mary Elizabeth Evans, rank and serial number unknown. An army intelligence man had signed on as interpreter, a border officer was going to hunt for smugglers. While the War and Treasury departments were messing around with the itinerary, the State Department was having fits about the expedition's going at all, not so much because of the participants' very good chance of being killed by bandits as that any such untoward incident could hypothetically affect international relations in a decidedly negative way. Eventually, even the navy got involved. Mary wondered why Agriculture and the post office failed to horn in, but that gap was filled at the last minute by the none-too-trusting Mexican government with two of their own army officers, three sergeants, and two privates, all in uniform and on horseback, all of them armed to the teeth.

The Mexican soldiers had nothing on Mary. A rash of alarming headlines had recently erupted, each new scarehead had inspired another addition to her personal armory. She carried a Winchester .30-30 rifle in a scabbard under her right stirrup, a small combination rifle-shotgun hung on her saddle horn, and a .38 Smith & Wesson revolver stuck in her belt, plus ammunition enough to start her own war.

Any notion that this would be a pleasure trip was long gone. They were after spies, saboteurs, and assorted bad hats; all they would find were a few American draft dodgers and far too many cactus plants. The route laid out for them was arduous in the extreme. They were not equipped for the weather, they had no tents nor even umbrellas. They'd pictured the desert as hot and dry, they had not reckoned on freezing cold nights and an occasional cloudburst. They'd thought they were hiring a cook, he turned out to be a barber.

It was marvelous what bureaucracy could achieve, but Mary's previous camping experiences had prepared her for anything. She was jogging peacefully along one day, wearing dark glasses and a green mesh veil to protect her face and eyes, when the intelligence officer pulled his horse up beside hers. He wondered, he said, whether Mrs. Rinehart had ever read any stories about a woman named Tish. Somehow or other, he'd noticed a resemblance between the two.

There were some good times. One day they discovered a small hot spring, the two women hung a blanket around it and took turns. It felt like bathing in a midget volcano crater, Mary said, but it did help to get the kinks out. Then there were the bad times. Miss Evans's horse fell with her on a precipitous mountain trail, and she narrowly missed being killed. Mary caught sight of a mountain lion, or thought she did, and picked up her rifle. As she was drawing a bead, somebody yelled, "Don't shoot! That's the cook."

On their last day out, both humans and animals were worn out and suffering badly from thirst, until they topped a rise and saw below them the Pacific Ocean and the hospitable town of Ensenada. The American consul was the only person who wasn't glad to see them: he went away for the weekend while the townsfolk threw a dance for the visitors and the town band serenaded them in the wee hours while they were trying to get some sleep.

Monday morning it was *adiós, muchachos*! Members of the pack train who had been checked into the town lockup in the interests of sobriety were liberated. As they lined up to start home, every single member of the expedition, including Mary and Miss Evans, was presented with a quart bottle of mescal. An hour or two later, the pack train was in total disarray. Even the mules were drunk. Mary and her sober companions urged their horses into a canter and left the revelers far behind.

Late that night the laggards caught up with the leaders. Crossing the border was no problem. It was not until they got to San Diego that Mary learned the consul at Ensenada had come back from his weekend and sent a panicky wire about a woman with a German-sounding name who'd led a horde of desperados into his town. At that very moment, a U.S. Navy gunboat was steaming southward to arrest the dangerous Mrs. Rinehart and her sinister cohorts.

Back in New York, Mary had a surprise waiting for her, but not the one she'd wanted. She'd finally been accepted as a Red Cross nurse, though not for overseas duty. This was a blow, as her whole intention in volunteering had been to get sent to France in case any of her menfolk needed her at the battle front. Now young Stanley was about to go over with his division and his mother wouldn't be with him. Nor would his father. Major Rinehart had made the mistake of being too good at his job. He was stuck in Washington with the surgeon general, discussing some innovations with which he had experimented at Camp Sherman and which would soon have an effect on the entire Army Medical Corps.

Feeling bereft and thwarted, Mary went back to *The Bat*. Committing imaginary murders got rid of some of her frustration; she'd managed to finish two acts and rough out a third before depression overtook her and she simply could not go on. So she wrote a funny story. Laughter is, after all, the best medicine; some of the most hilarious fiction comes out of a writer's deepest grief.

Mary let the seesaw swing pretty high with *Twenty-Three and a Half Hours' Leave*. A year or so later, she slipped into a movie theater and listened to a packed audience roar its collective head off at the antics of a young soldier who'd bet he could eat breakfast with his commanding general on his final leave. The story of how he won his bet but lost both his heart and his uniform and had to make his farewell appearance in nothing but a slicker gave even the author a few chuckles.

Summer was coming. Alan and Ted would be out of school, it was high time to give Olive a break from mother-sitting. Mary decided to rent a house on Long Island where the family could enjoy the ocean breezes and she could work on another wartime novel. This one featured a munitions manufacturer with a conscience; she called it *Dangerous Days*. The War Department didn't want her this summer of 1918, but she did go to Washington as often as she could, to boost her husband's morale. Major Rinehart was still hoping to get overseas, but still not succeeding.

In June, Mary moved the boys, her mother, her secretary, two maids, and a cook into the rented house. The house was big, sunny, and comfortable but isolated from the highway by a long road; the cook didn't like it. It wasn't that she minded them walking around all night in the empty room overhead, she explained, but she did feel uncomfortable when they came and sat in the rocking chair beside her bed. Mary asked who "they" were, the cook replied, "I'm not saying."

Mary begged the woman to keep right on not saying, particularly to the other servants, but that didn't solve the problem. One night at bedtime the laundress raised a ruckus, claiming that she'd seen a man going upstairs in front of her. Alan grabbed his shotgun and they searched the house but found nobody. Then the actress Marie Doro came to spend a weekend discussing the role she was to play in a drama based on *The Amazing Interlude*. The morning after her arrival, Miss Doro brought her breakfast tray into Mary's room, complaining that she hadn't slept a wink because somebody kept walking up and down outside her door all night long. Mary said it must be rats. They set traps and caught nothing.

The truth was, Mary hadn't expected to catch anything. She'd been having some odd experiences of her own. The room where she slept was joined to a small boudoir that she used for a study. Accessible only from the bedroom, its only furnishings were a wooden chair and a kitchen table with a brass lamp and Mary's writing materials on it. At night, Mary left the connecting door open. She often thought she heard sounds of the lamp being moved around. When she got up and turned on the overhead light, however, the lamp was always just where she'd left it.

Alan was wakened one night by heavy footsteps slowly thumping up the stairs and stopping at his door. He jumped out of bed, grabbed his gun, and switched on the light practically in one lightning-fast movement, but found nothing to shoot at. It was spooky but also, at times, ludicrous. One night Mary's secretary, a no-nonsense young woman with long red hair who scorned all this supernatural nonsense and didn't even balk at going downstairs in the dark for a glass of iced water, burst into Mary's room with her hair flying and blurted that somebody was hiding in the laundry hamper outside her door. While brushing her hair, she'd heard the squeaky lid being raised and lowered twice.

Mary snatched her revolver and ran to confront the hamper. "Come out or I'll shoot," she ordered. The hamper didn't even squeak. Very carefully, gun at the ready, Mary raised the lid. She found nothing more eerie than the family wash.

Mary sometimes wondered why, during that oddly disturbing summer, none of them accidentally killed somebody else. They all tried to laugh off the noises, even when something or other beat a monotonous tattoo on the antique warming pan that hung beside Mary's bedroom fireplace. One day she put a tentative question or two to the gardener who lived in the small house down near the road. He wasn't a bit surprised. His wife had tried to sleep there overnight once, he said. After something had come along and dragged the covers off her bed, she'd rushed downstairs and rung the big bell outside the back door for him to come and get her. She wouldn't stay in that house again for a million dollars, cash on the barrelhead.

The gardener suggested that Mrs. Rinehart try moving one of the pictures from the living room wall. Sure as shooting, he promised, she'd find it back in place the next morning. Mary preferred not to make the experiment, especially after she'd been wakened by a cold air blowing over her, a tremendous thud that rocked the bed she was lying in, and the sound of her dressing table rising up and crashing back to the floor. When she'd got up courage enough to turn on the light, she found the table where it belonged, with not so much as a tipped-over cologne bottle to prove she hadn't been dreaming.

Their scariest time came after a dog belonging to the estate was shot. Since ghosts do not usually carry revolvers, Mary wondered whether, after all, some human agent was behind these allegedly supernatural happenings. She arranged an ambush, stationing the boys in the living room with the shotgun, the gardener in the gunroom in the opposite wing of the house, and Mary and her secretary in the dining room with a window open. Here they had a clear view of the stairs and the hallway where a single candle burned. At one o'clock, with everyone keyed up to the shrieking point, a weird and shapeless figure crawled through the living room doorway.

"Stop or I'll shoot," Mary quavered. The weird and shapeless figure leaped to his feet. It was Ted in his bathrobe, lamenting that his mother had scared off whoever was in the garden.

No, she hadn't. A round, white light was bobbing away from them across the lawn, as if somebody was walking backwards holding a flashlight. But why? They watched the light until it disappeared into the marshes about 200 feet away.

Since the eldritch disturbances kept her from getting much sleep, Mary put in a good deal of time on her new novel. By late August, *Dangerous Days* was finished and she felt entitled to accept a few dinner engagements. One night at a neighbor's, Mary entertained her fellow guests with a partial account of what had been happening in her rented house. The following day, she had a surprise visit from her hostess of the night before. Now that the Rinehart ménage would be moving out, the lady felt free to let Mary know that the house had been reputed for years to be haunted. There had even been a piece about it some years back in a New York paper.

Perhaps this was cold comfort, but even things that go bump in the night have their uses. Six years later, Mary would make $40,000 out of a mystery novel laid in that house. Remembering those odd noises in her improvised office, she named her book *The Red Lamp*.

CHAPTER 26

An End to the War to End All Wars

During that summer, Mary had kept in touch with the Theodore Roosevelts. On September 12 she was invited to lunch at Sagamore Hill. She was reluctant to go, she was too well aware that their youngest son, Quentin, had been killed in France less than two months before.

But she went, of course, riding out from New York with the colonel and his wife in their car, trying to make light conversation while the former president sat up front with the chauffeur and didn't say a word. Mrs. Roosevelt knitted. When at last she spoke of her dead son with loving resignation, it was Mary who cried. In her memoirs Mary paid due credit to the "shadowy partner" to whom much of the credit for the spotlighted half's fame is so often owed. She saw this quiet strength in Mrs. Roosevelt, and she was everlastingly grateful for it in Stanley Marshall Rinehart.

Back in New York and alone again, Mary took another poke at *The Bat*, but the perverse little creature refused to fly. Alan had found out at Harvard that he was now eligible to join the marines, and he informed his mother by phone that he'd already enlisted and was heading for boot camp. Ted, still too young for active service, signed up with the National Guard to protect bridges and railroad tracks from possible sabotage. Mary felt rather desperate about having all four of her men on active duty and herself fiddling around in a hotel suite.

Then she got a long-distance telephone call. The secretary of war was on the line. Could Mrs. Rinehart sail for France in three days' time? That same night, Mary was on the train to Washington to kiss her increasingly frustrated husband good-bye and get her passports in order. Again in New York to pack her bags, she squeezed in a luncheon with Avery Hopwood and asked him to finish *The Bat* for her. A special airplane flew up from Washington with her letters and credentials, she boarded a French ocean liner.

This trip was a far cry from her maiden voyage on the *Franconia*. They had no convoy, but airplanes saw them safely down the bay. Boat drill was rigidly carried out; scads of women showed up for it along with the men, all in the uniforms of various welfare organizations, all claiming the war would soon be over. Mary didn't believe them but didn't argue the matter, she was too taken up with wondering how to locate Stanley Junior. She knew that her son had finished training school and been commissioned as a second lieutenant, but nothing more.

At Bordeaux, she was heartened by meeting two French officers sent by André Tardieu, the new premier. They gave her to understand that the arms of France were flung wide to embrace Madame Rinehart, her slightest wish was their command. Having heard that Paris was mobbed, Mary asked the officers to phone ahead to the Ritz and reserve her a room. Alas for chivalry! When she got there late the following evening the Ritz had never heard of her, they couldn't offer so much as a bathtub or a billiard table to sleep on. Furthermore, they didn't even care. *Tant pis, Madame. Allez-vous en, Madame.*

Two men whom Mary had met on the ship, a clergyman and a polo player, got the same cold shoulder as she had. The man of the cloth remembered a small but good hotel nearby at which he and his wife had spent their honeymoon. There the manager gave Mary an extremely fishy stare and wouldn't let the three in until he had rooted through an old register and verified the minister's honeymoon visit. At last he confessed that he did have a suite with two bedrooms and bath on the top floor. He failed to add that the bath could only be reached through the bedrooms.

Here was a contretemps most serious. Should Mrs. Rinehart have the outer room and be required to pass through the men's sleeping quarters, or should the one next to the bathroom be hers? They settled on the latter. Mary sustained the proprieties by ducking under the covers and pretending she wasn't there. The following morning, to the relief of the manager, she set out to find less iffy quarters.

At eleven o'clock on the morning of November 11, 1918, Mary happened to be standing on a curbstone on the Rue de la Paix when she looked up and saw a German airplane doing loops and barrel rolls in the sky. Then she heard the booming of the signal guns, and knew. This was the Armistice. The war to end all wars was itself ended.

All traffic stopped. All Paris grew silent. Then a young poilu in uniform rushed into the center of the avenue, shouting out the news of victory. A man in civvies joined him, then a girl, then a whole procession, all smiling, all quiet.

But then the excitement began to build. Having no bands left to play for them, the Parisians brought out toy drums, cooking pots, spoons to beat them with, anything and everything that could make a joyful noise. A file of American doughboys goose-stepped down the Avenue de l'Opéra, led by a corporal with a tin trumpet and a sergeant with a big cigar. They broke ranks and snake-danced through the crowd chanting, "Hail, hail, the gang's all here! What the hell do we care now?"

An Algerian soldier straight from the battlefield, ragged and filthy, kissed a British admiral. A French soldier reeking with *vin ordinaire* kissed Mary. Then, along toward twilight, came the parade of the *mutilés*, the halt leading the blind, Red Cross nurses pushing the wheelchairs of the legless. Mary cried.

She still hadn't found her son, and she was hearing tales of certain officers who'd kept up the fight to the very end, of soldiers killed within moments of the armistice. How could she celebrate until she knew? Fortunately she was soon able to locate Stanley through the American service paper, the *Stars and Stripes*. They sat down together to the biggest, most expensive meal they could find in Paris; that was when Mary Roberts Rinehart signed her own armistice.

But the wounds were yet to be healed. November 14 found Mary off to Chaumont on a jam-packed train that poked along at the speed of a tortoise. At last they arrived; Mary's escort, a young officer who'd lost an eye to an exploding hand grenade, took her straight to General Pershing. Black Jack looked thin and tired but greeted Mrs. Rinehart warmly and described the strategy of the Allies' final all-out attack. On the fifteenth, she began a tour of battlefields still littered with the debris of that last grand assault: broken-down tanks and transport, dud shells, barbed wire, discarded equipment, even personal letters. In an abandoned observation post Mary found a notebook with meticulous records of that last, fateful morning: German reconnaissance flights, an observation balloon, and finally, on the stroke of 11 A.M., guns ceased firing. Mary took the book and kept it.

This was a sad journey and far from a comfortable one. Things were much the same everywhere Mary went. The weather was cold and gloomy, shelter hard to find, food neither good nor plentiful. A meal might be no more than a piece of dry bread and a cup of water. Sometimes Mary spied a column of marching men, more often she saw nothing worth recording. The German line of retreat was total desolation, the vanquished *Wehrmacht* had cut down telephone poles, lifted railroad tracks, set fire to ammunition dumps, wrecked guns, tanks, vehicles, destroyed absolutely everything, except the former headquarters of the German crown prince in the Argonne. This was an amazing mix of concrete dugouts with stairways that led down to heavily protected subterranean chambers and, above ground, a cozy beer garden set out with tables, chairs, and rustic arbors. But the plants were all dead.

Back in Paris after a harrowing visit to Verdun, with its thousands of graveyard crosses set out in tidy rows, Mary found a mood of gaiety that verged on abandon. Drunkenness was rife, prostitutes lined the sidewalks. Montmartre was thronged with rowdy celebrants. One night at the Folies Bergère, Mary watched a gang of soldiers form a flying wedge and surge through the audience, knocking down chairs and patrons like candlepins. When they began throwing things, she wisely decided it was time to leave. There were taxis, but hailing one was impossible unless the would-be passenger knew the magic signal. Mary was well schooled; she simply stood at the curb and held up a pack of American cigarettes.

The big news now was President Wilson. For the first time in America's history, an incumbent president was going out of the country. But not out of touch with his office. Here was another historic first, a transatlantic hotline made up of telegraphic relays stretching all the way from Washington, D.C., to Sydney, Nova Scotia, the North American terminus of the Atlantic Cable, and thence to Europe. One day in early December, Mary stood behind an honor guard of soldiers and watched Mr. and Mrs. Wilson drive by in an open car. Whatever might later befall his hopes for a just and lasting peace, on this day Woodrow Wilson was the hope of the world.

Mary would not be covering the treaty negotiations at Versailles. She went back into Germany, was ignored by stolid peasants trying to pick up the pieces of their shattered lives, had her car stoned by yelling boys, visited hospitals both good and bad. She spent a tragic night helping to make cocoa for a crowd of ragged, skeletal former prisoners of war who'd been let out from German prisons with nothing to eat, no money to buy anything, hardly boots to their feet. They were a polyglot crew, some Russians among them. Would they ever get back to their homeland? Did they still have a homeland? Did they know about the Bolshevik Revolution, the assassination of the czar and his family? Mary never found out what happened to the ex-prisoners; perhaps it was just as well.

Mary had authorization to stay longer, but her son was being demobbed and home ties were tugging. She had already wheedled a berth on Stanley's troop transport when she got a cablegram asking her to succeed Edward Bok as editor of the *Ladies' Home Journal*. The offer was tempting. For a freelance writer, nothing comes in unless the work goes out; a steady job with a regular salary and paid vacation was a temptation.

However, the money wouldn't be so good. Lord Northcliffe had told Mary Roberts Rinehart that she was now earning more than any other living writer except possibly J. M. Barrie. Mary did want a big lump of cash in a hurry, because George Doran had offered her eldest son a junior partnership and she wanted to buy Stanley Junior a percentage of the publishing company's stock. She was still weighing the pros and cons when the troopship put out from Brest.

It was a ghastly voyage. The seas were enormous, the weather was terrible, so was the food served to the passengers. Anticipating this, Mary had brought aboard a big hamper crammed with edibles: bread, butter, fruit, baked ham, cooked chicken, lots of tinned goodies. Her cabin, obtained by evacuating the assistant engineer, poor man, became the most popular spot on the ship. It was also Stanley's sleeping quarters. He hadn't fancied his berth in the hold next to the engine room, but the pitching and rolling in a sleeping bag on his mother's cabin floor presented its own problems. Mary offered to nail her son to the floor, but he demurred and kept on rolling.

Once in the States, the two made a beeline for Washington. Dr. Rinehart was still with the surgeon general's office, still a major. He had been up for a colonelcy, which he'd wanted very much, but an across-the-board cancellation of promotions after the Armistice had dashed his hopes. Mary was somewhat dazed to see her husband living frugally on his army pay in a small bachelor apartment, making his own coffee in an electric percolator. Ted and Alan had spent Christmas with their father, bought presents, decorated his two rooms. This was all they'd had by way of a home; it was clearly time for their mother to turn down the *Journal*'s offer and go home and air the mattresses.

The Bluff had not taken kindly to neglect. It took Mary and the servants three months to get rid of the accumulated grime. Cornelia was with her now, Major Stanley and the boys would be coming home. Mary knew she ought to begin another book but all she could think of was the war, and readers were sick of the war. To deepen the gloom, Congress had passed a new Eighteenth Amendment to the Constitution. America had gone dry.

The timing was stupid, and a total ban on the sale of liquor was far too stringent. People were still burdened with wartime taxes, they'd had enough of privation and sacrifice. Young men and women who had served in the military or as civilians had learned all too well how brief and tragic a life could be. They wanted to snatch at any pleasure, however evanescent. So the less well heeled made home brew or distilled something horrible that they called bathtub gin. As for the rich . . . well, even Bab would soon be prattling quite matter-of-factly about Daddy's bootlegger.

Running battles between T-men and rumrunners were not in Mary Roberts Rinehart's line, but these were not the only villainies afoot. She recalled a furtive conversation she'd had with a very frightened man in Los Angeles at the end of her Mexican trip. During her own service with the War Department, Mary had learned plenty about agents provocateurs, incendiary propaganda, and sabotage. Like a great many other Americans, she blamed it all on Bolshevik Communist infiltrators. She cited one pamphlet she'd seen that suggested arson, pillage, and rape as acceptable working tools for establishing a true government by the people, which is to say by those who were gullible enough to adopt the Party line and thenceforth pay mindless allegiance to their self-appointed leaders. The phenomenon is not unfamiliar.

The Seattle shipyard had been targeted as a logical starting point for the Revolution. Mary's confidant had been a shipyard worker there, and he'd walked out with the rest when the strike was called. Organizers had taken it for granted that the police and militia would at once join out of sympathy for their oppressed brothers, take over city hall, shut down power plants to halt the streetcars, and cut off the water supply until everybody capitulated; as of course they would, it being axiomatic that a few armed men could easily bring an unarmed populace to its knees. From then on it would be a piece of cake to spread the Revolution across the entire country to the glory of the Communist party and its dauntless leaders.

This man had been given the impression that the Revolution would be bloodless. He had willingly joined the striking union, the IWW (Industrial Workers of the World, also known as the "I Won't Work" party. Its members were contemptuously called Wobblies). Now he was in a state of extreme agitation. He kept insisting to Mary that he was no traitor, but . . .

His wife and children were safe in Tacoma. But what if, like so many other shipworkers' families, they'd been in Seattle when the takeover occurred? He'd got the message that tonight was the night. The power plant would be cut off, the city would go dark, then the looting and burning and—he couldn't say what—would begin. He could not bear to let this happen. He hadn't dared alert the police, at last he'd gotten up nerve enough to telephone city hall. When the Wobblies marched that night, they were accosted by ex–Texas Ranger and present mayor Ole Hanson with a posse of armed civilians. A few shots were fired, then they all went home. *Sic transit* the Revolution.

Just why this disaffected ex-IWW member had chosen to trust his story to Mrs. Rinehart can only be conjectured. The man might have hoped that she'd spread the alarm about would-be insurrectionists who might threaten other cities. Perhaps he'd felt a need to confess and she'd seemed like the sort of woman who would understand. Maybe he'd just wanted to meet a celebrity.

Mary had said the right things, no doubt, and shoved the incident to the back of her mind. Now that strange conversation came back to her and the creative juices began to flow. *A Poor Wise Man* is rather a prissy title for a book about sabotage but the convoluted story of how a young drugstore clerk mobilized a town is grim enough, except when the bluebird of happiness makes a cameo appearance at the end of the story.

In April, Mary had a happy ending of her own. Dr. Rinehart was at last discharged from the surgeon general's office and free to come home. She went to meet him in Washington; on their twenty-third anniversary they drove home together in the major's car to pick up the pieces of their life together.

But, they had to face it, life would not be the same. Their eldest son was, of all incredible things, getting married! They could hardly fault Stanley Junior's choice of a bride; she was the daughter of publisher George H. Doran. Stanley was only twenty-one, but Mary had to concede that young men matured fast in wartime. Alan, now eighteen, was to be best man. Even Ted at fourteen could hardly be called the family baby anymore. He was shooting up like his brothers, his voice was as deep as a man's.

Reconciled to being a father-in-law, Dr. Rinehart went back to work at the dispensary and began rebuilding his private practice. Mary's thoughts turned once more to *The Bat*. She was understandably chagrined that Avery Hopwood had not lived up to his promise to work on the last act while she was in France. He was ready now to make amends, though; she laid aside her novel and the two of them went to work in her downtown office. Nothing much happened. In June they were still not happy with what they'd done. Hopwood was willing to keep on trying but Mary said sorry, she had a train to catch.

Out in Hollywood, Mr. Samuel Goldwyn had had an inspiration. He was starting a collection of Eminent Authors in order to show the world what an erudite lot moving-picture producers really were. There were even rumors that the Eminent Authors would be permitted to adapt their own books for the silver screen. Furthermore, Goldwyn was offering his Eminences each a guaranteed three-year contract at $15,000 a year plus royalties, if there were any. Captivated by the glamour of filmland and the chance of some steady money, Mary signed. In July she set out by train for Los Angeles. Nearing her destination, she got a telegram. Would she mind being met at the station by a baby blimp instead of a taxi? Yes, she would indeed mind, she replied, so her promoters settled for an open car and armloads of flowers. Even this much ostentation seemed bizarre to the Eminent Author from Pittsburgh, but the locals took it calmly enough.

Perhaps Mr. Goldwyn honestly believed that a successful

author could be trusted to develop her own work into an acceptable scenario, but the professional screenwriters chose not to. The man assigned to her did not want her ideas, or her story, either. What the studio did in fact want was for Mrs. Rinehart to pose for a great many publicity shots and then go home until it was time to take some more pictures. They did lavish a good deal of time and attention on her appearance; she found it interesting to have her whole face redesigned by a makeup artist, although she did complain that the heavy beads of mascara on the ends of her eyelashes kept getting caught in the veil of her hat.

And she got to socialize with the movie stars. Douglas Fairbanks was already on the Rineharts' Christmas-card list. He offered to give her and Stanley a plot of land next to his so that they could build their own house and be neighbors. One day in Cecil B. DeMille's office, Mary shook hands with a sweet young thing named Mary Pickford, who would become not only Mrs. Douglas Fairbanks but also for many years America's sweetheart, notwithstanding the fact that Miss Pickford was born in Toronto, Ontario. In Hollywood, Mary Roberts Rinehart learned, things were seldom what they seemed.

CHAPTER 27

Playtime

Certainly Eminent Authors didn't get to write. Fed up with trying to buck the system, Mary wiped the mascara off her eyelashes and went home to round up the family for another holiday at Eaton's ranch. Stanley Junior and his bride had other things to do, but Cornelia Roberts and her maid came along for a change. These two occupied the only bedroom of a cabin built over a rushing stream; this cabin would become the Rineharts' regular summertime retreat for some years to come. Stanley Senior, Mary, and the boys bedded down in a row on the back porch. Mary got around the proprieties by staying asleep until her menfolk were up, dressed, and ready to ride.

She was relieved to note that even the cowboys had moved with the times. It was now acceptable for female dudes to wear riding breeches instead of those cumbrous divided skirts. Mary bought herself a pair of gray leather chaps, a pair of high-heeled cowboy boots, and a Stetson hat to replace the tired old brown velour hat into which so many fishing flies had been stuck, and which had so often served her for everything from a potholder to a drinking cup.

Perhaps because Cornelia was along, perhaps because parents and offspring alike were wrung out from their taxing wartime experiences, none of the Rineharts seems to have been up for anything more hair-raising than a short gallop or a day's fishing. Then it would be back to the ranch for another good meal, a quiet night's sleep, and the happiness of being together in a place they had all grown to love.

Too soon it was fall, back to school for Alan and Ted, back to work for their father and mother. This was when Mary took time out to fight that previously mentioned battle of words with Irvin S. Cobb, thinking as she wrote how very much she knew about men, what fun she was having putting some of her knowledge down on paper, and how prudent she was being not to mention the rest. She finished *A Poor Wise Man*, didn't like what she'd done, wrote the whole book over from start to finish, and packed it off before she could change her mind again.

She also produced a sort of novella that she called *The Confession*. This is not the best piece she ever wrote, but it does have an interesting history. Pittsburgh's district attorney, a relative of Cornelia Roberts, wanted Mary's opinion on the authenticity of a note that some workman had turned up during the renovation of a building that had once been a house of prostitution. Folded into a tiny square, hidden in a dark rear hallway underneath the battery box of a telephone, the note purported to be a confession by the one-time madam. She had, she said, killed a woman in that house. She'd given the date and the year, ended with the words *If this is found, may God have mercy on my soul*, and signed her name in full.

Mary took the note seriously. If this was supposed to be a hoax, or had been written by someone else out of malice, what would have been the point of hiding the scrap of paper so well that it might never have been found?

The district attorney had verified the fact that the woman named had indeed kept a bawdy house in that building at that time. Mary had nursed enough girls from the red-light district during her student days to know all about their jealousies, their sudden rages, their hair-pullings, fistfights, and worse. She'd seen two of them brought in together, each bleeding from razor slashes inflicted by the other, both of them sorry for what they'd done, both ready to forgive and forget. She noted the date of the letter—Decoration Day—and remembered how drunkenness and license had run rife on holidays in Pittsburgh's Tenderloin, how frantically overworked the ambulances and the police had been. So had the girls, no doubt; it would have been an ideal time for a murder in a whorehouse to go undetected.

Having met that terrified shipyard worker in Los Angeles, having just finished the book that his confession had inspired, Mary could understand readily enough why an uncaught murderess might have felt the need to shrive herself by writing out a confession and squirreling it away, leaving the outcome to the God of Justice of whom, Mary remembered too well, plenty of girls from the houses had poured out their terror during those long nights on the wards.

The ex-madam was still alive. She had gone straight and adopted a little girl. A signature of hers found on the lease of a place she had later rented matched the writing on the note. The cellar of the former brothel was dug up, but no body was found. With no case to pursue, the matter was dropped, to Mary's secret relief. She suspected that the murder had really happened and that the body had been dumped in the river. She was sure that by now the perpetrator had been punished enough by her own tormenting conscience.

Speaking of punishment, Mary was called back to Hollywood, actually to do some writing. Her picture was all filmed. This being still in the days of the "silents," however, captions were needed, and she, who hadn't been allowed to write her own scenario, was somehow now obligated to write them. The book that the screenwriters had allegedly adapted was *Dangerous Days*. What Mary saw in the final version bore no resemblance to her original work and made, she thought, very little sense. She did what she could, then packed to go home.

Dr. Rinehart had come with her this time, which was a good thing. Less than a day before they were to catch their train, some bright soul realized that the sabotage theme, almost the only part of Mary's book that the scriptwriters had retained, might be offensive to labor. Mrs. Rinehart needn't get any silly ideas about their shooting the film over, her job was to rewrite all the captions, getting rid of the hypothetically inflammatory material while making the words appropriate to the existing photography.

At that, Mary did the only sensible thing. She went back to bed. Dr. Rinehart pulled up a table beside her and took up his pen. Together they proceeded, as she bitterly recorded in *My Story*, to enfeeble the already moribund, and to suffer the indignity of having the result shown to the world as Mary Roberts Rinehart's own work.

This was the last time Mary would get herself into such a position. For the next Rinehart film, she asked the studio to find a scenario writer who was willing to come and work with her in Pittsburgh. That was fine with Mr. Goldwyn. He sent a nice young married couple with a proven record of successes. They and Mary developed a pattern of talking over the day's work in the morning. After their chat, Mary would go to her own work and the scriptwriters to theirs. When they'd finished, the couple headed west with a well-plotted, technically correct scenario ready to roll.

The scenario department paid them off, threw out the whole business, and wired Mary that they would have a complete rewrite ready in a week. Mary wrote back telling them to tear up her contract. They wouldn't do it. Mr. Goldwyn still believed in his great experiment and just couldn't understand why his Eminent Authors kept turning out such disappointing scripts.

Meanwhile, *The Bat* was still hanging by its toes. Avery Hopwood came back to Pittsburgh. He and Mary finally conquered that recalcitrant last act, only to realize that their success with Act 3 meant having to make changes in Acts 1 and 2. And the timing was critical; they must check it to the second. And Alan had flunked out of Harvard and gone out West to be a cowboy. And other family matters were, as Mary put it, at a critical point, which may have meant that Dr Rinehart's well-known temper was coming to the boil again, as well it might. Mary checked in at a New York hotel.

At five o'clock one April afternoon, the curtain fell on the absolutely last, final, and totally satisfactory draft of *The Bat*. As the two playwrights reached to shake hands on a job well done, the telephone rang. Stanley Junior was on the phone—Mary's grandchild was on the way. She rushed to the hospital and sat for eight hours at her daughter-in-law's side, observing at firsthand the benefits of twilight sleep. At three in the morning she saw her granddaughter into the world, then took her son back to her hotel, made him eat a sandwich and drink a glass of milk, and tucked him up on her sofa. What, after all, was a grandmother for?

The next day, the New York papers announced that publisher George Doran and his best-known author were cograndparents. One of them published a photo with the caption *Who would believe from this picture that Mary Roberts Rinehart is a grandmother?* Not many, probably; the unknown person in the picture was wearing a totally masculine full beard.

Becoming a grandmother was a solemn business. Mary had to face the fact that she and her husband, whom she'd always thought of as one of her boys, were over the hill, not precisely heading for the last roundup but definitely going hand-in-hand into the sunset. Well, it happened to everybody sooner or later. In the meantime, she had plenty to do.

Fully convinced at last that they had a hit, she and Avery Hopwood each retained a quarter interest in *The Bat*. The team of Wagenhals and Kemper would be the producers, and they would do an outstanding job. The only problem was the title. The management didn't like it and opened the play in Washington as *A Thief in the Night*. Mary wasn't standing for that. When they opened in New York, *The Bat* was back.

She hadn't bothered to stick around for the opening. Along with her husband, Ted, her mother, and the maid without whom Cornelia could not have managed, she went west to their cabin. At the train they were met by a burly young puncher wearing plaid pants tucked into reprehensible boots, a well-aged Stetson, and an old blue shirt that belonged to the camp cook, with whom he was bunking. Alan greeted his loved ones with the mild condescension of the dude rancher to the dude, then started hefting their luggage while the rest of the family lined up and cheered. His brother Ted magnanimously tipped him a quarter.

For the first month or so, the Rineharts took things relatively easy. In August, Howard Eaton organized another of his jolly little camping trips, this time into Arizona and New Mexico. Because of the long distances involved, they would go by car instead of on horseback, some twenty of them, including a full complement of Rineharts; Ted had elected to join the party. Their motorcade of eight cars and three trucks full of camping gear left Flagstaff heading for the Grand Canyon. By the time they'd made their way through 700 miles of sand and mud, they'd got lost, run perilously short of gas, gone tentless one night when a truck broke down, experienced the unique discomforts of a sandstorm, had to be dug out of a hundred or so dry creek beds, got stuck fording the Little Colorado River, and been roped out by a team from an Indian school directed by a policeman wearing a big revolver and a magnificent parure of turquoise and silver earrings, necklace, and bracelets. They'd run out of water, got sick from bad wells, and watched an Indian kill and dress a prairie dog for his supper.

In New Mexico, Mary got her first news of *The Bat*. Audiences loved it, critics on the opening night had not. Mary took the news calmly, for she was preoccupied with more immediate problems such as how to take a bath in an irrigation ditch and get into one's nightgown with suitable decorum before an admiring audience of Native Americans. Stanley Senior and the boys also had their troubles, trying to change from pajamas to day clothes without revealing anything not meant to be seen. Since they themselves were tourists who'd come to gawk, they could hardly fault the natives for gawking back. One of Mary's fondest memories on that trip was the story she told of her husband sitting inside an open tepee in his BVDs, mending the seat of his pants with adhesive tape, quite unabashed by an audience of six curiously watching Indian women and two babies.

As the autocade went on, Mary kept getting more telegrams, brought by horseback riders, truck drivers, or swift-running Zuni messengers. *The Bat* was flying high; by the weekend, those critics who'd panned the show on Monday were lauding it to the skies. The producers were already starting to audition road companies. Audience members who couldn't handle the suspense were ripping the arms off their own seats and shoving the debris under somebody else's. Everybody was too caught up in the plot to be aware of anything but what was happening onstage. After the bemused playgoers had staggered from the theater, ushers would discover that they'd left behind them everything but their false teeth.

One telegram told how a group of gamblers had each put a hundred-dollar bill in somebody's hat at the end of the first act and added their guesses as to who the criminal was after the second. At the end of Act 3, each man had had to take his money back because not one of them had got it right. Mary tossed the telegram into the campfire and took another admiring look at the Grand Canyon.

By the middle of September, though, back in Sewickley, Mary was hard at work on another play. Wagenhals and Kemper had acquired the rights to an old Spanish play called *Maria del Carmen*. The script was dreadfully outmoded for American audiences. Avery Hopwood had taken a stab at updating it, but work was still needed. Mary, the veteran play doctor, had risen to the bait once more.

And a good thing, too. While Mary was out West, the two producers had been traveling in Spain. They'd brought back some wonderful Spanish costumes and a troupe of genuine Spanish dancers. Wagenhals and Kemper were making innovations at the theater as well, turning the orchestra pit into a forestage, which would be the first of its kind in America. Even more daringly, they'd have some of the characters entering not from the wings but down the aisles from the rear of the theater, speaking lines as they came. This would cause no end of a stir until audiences caught on that the chattering intruders were part of the show.

Thanks to a vastly improved script, inspired production, and some superb acting, they had another hit. Particularly outstanding in the cast was a budding actor named William Powell, who played his role of a tubercular young man so convincingly that

Mary feared he might not survive the run of the show. But *Spanish Love* stayed on the boards for a solid year and, and after it closed, Powell went on to become one of the shining lights of Hollywood.

Mary remarked in her autobiography that, while good playwrights and producers could turn actors into stars, it was only fair to add that good actors could also enhance the reputations of the playwrights and producers. She felt it was time to give credit where credit was surely due.

That winter of 1920–21, Mary Roberts Rinehart would be on more playbills than she'd bargained for. While *The Bat* and *Spanish Love* were drawing full houses, Helen Hayes was playing in a dramatization of *Babs* by Edward Carpenter, while May Robson, Mary's erstwhile sparring partner, starred in Edward Rose's farce, *Tish*.

For years, Mary had neglected her bookkeeping; her business affairs were in an almost impossible welter. At last, to her ineffable relief, Dr Rinehart took over as her business manager. The volume of mail that Mary received each day had become overwhelming; even with a secretary she couldn't begin to handle it all. Still less could she handle her money, and she'd made some terrible mistakes in her income-tax returns.

Besides maintaining an extravagant lifestyle, she'd literally thrown away thousands and thousands of dollars on bad investments and smooth-talking con artists. Her husband set to work to curb Mary's enthusiasm for thrusting money at anybody who held out a hand. Stanley's endeavor was to build her an estate to fall back on when she grew older and couldn't keep up her heavy workload. Ten years the elder of the two, himself not in the best of health, he was determined to leave his wife properly provided for. Though it was some time since he'd been the family's chief breadwinner, Stanley Marshall Rinehart was still, when it counted, the Head.

CHAPTER 28

A New President,
A Changing World

Now that her husband was getting her finances under control, Mary decided, as she tended to do every so often, to reorganize the household and simplify her life. Her first move was to hire a personal maid for herself and her mother, to make sure that their clothes were always pressed, Mary's fabulous hats neatly set on hat stands, her shoes properly treed. She set a regular weekly schedule for her manicure, shampoo, and wave. She resumed her demon housewife role, inspecting her pantries, running an exploratory finger over furniture and woodwork to make sure that no housemaid was lagging on the job. She'd just got everything nicely regimented when fate hurled another bombshell, this one via the Republican National Committee.

Nineteen twenty was again a presidential election year. Woodrow Wilson was in no shape to run again, the Republicans were determined to win this time. In June, two equally worthy candidates were deadlocked. Frank O. Lowden was the brilliant young governor of Illinois, a reformer with an independent mind. Gen. Leonard Wood was a Congressional Medal of Honor winner with no political experience but plenty of popular appeal; Theodore Roosevelt and Colonel Procter, the Ivory soap king, were both backing him.

The Old Guard, headed by Sen. Boies Penrose of Pennsylvania, the single most powerful and most corrupt Republican party boss in the country, wanted neither Lowden nor Wood. What the Republicans wanted, and were determined to get, was an obedient party hack who could present a plausibly statesmanlike appearance, reel off a stirring oration without saying anything of substance, and do as he was told. After due consideration and a keen scrutiny of the field, Penrose selected handsome, genial Warren G. Harding, then senator from Ohio, as his man.

Harding himself was reasonably honest, and able enough to have worked his way up from the proverbial humble beginning through state government to the U.S. Senate. This was where he wanted to be. He had no further ambition but to improve his golf game, to play poker with his cronies as often as possible, and to play other games with certain obliging ladies about whom his wife was not supposed to know. The senator wasn't much for work; he liked to "bloviate," sitting on his front porch back in Marion, spitting tobacco juice over the railing, chatting about nothing in particular with any neighbor who happened along. Harding was afraid of responsibility, he didn't think he was fit to be president, and wasn't. In short, he was all that Boies Penrose could have wished for.

Anybody interested in the wheeling and dealing by which Warren Gamaliel Harding, after an abysmal start, won the nomination and the office should read Francis Russell's remarkable biography, *The Shadow of Blooming Grove*, published by McGraw-Hill in 1968. Suffice it to say that, despite his protests and even his confession to Penrose's sidekick, Sen. Jim Watson of Indiana, that his blood pressure was 185 and he had sugar in his urine, Harding was doomed to be president. His mentors planned his campaign. They knew better than to let him run loose—too many genuinely qualified candidates were already barnstorming the country. Harding must stick to his own front porch and let the country come to him.

This was showmanship of the highest order, or the lowest,

depending on one's political point of view. Anyway, it worked. There were glitches to be ironed out, of course. In September, Mary Roberts Rinehart, a Republican like her husband, got a telegram from the National Committee. The party had suddenly remembered that women were now enfranchised, it might not be a bad idea to put a female-oriented plank in their platform. Would Mrs. Rinehart come to Marion as one of a party of big, broad, forward-thinking women and help to introduce plans for a department of public welfare?

How could she refuse? Mary traveled with Mary Flinn Lawrence, who was already making her mark in Pennsylvania politics. They planned to spend the night in Columbus. Little did they know how many other forward-thinking women had the same idea. They wound up sleeping on cots in a hotel's sample room. In the morning it was on to Marion, where they met up with Colonel Roosevelt's daughter Alice Longworth, Mrs. Gifford Pinchot, wife of a former chief forester in the Department of Agriculture, Ruth McCormick, daughter of Senator Hanna and married into a rich and influential family; along with some others whose names Mary didn't mention in her memoirs.

When the delegation arrived, they were startled to find the street and the Harding lawn, which had been covered with limestone chips to keep it from turning into a morass, packed with women from every state in the Union. The Hardings were informal and folksy. They offered Mary's group the hospitality of the house, a plain but solidly built two-story dwelling. After Harding became state senator, its once-simple porch had been replaced by a far more impressive one that ran the length of the house, was supported by Ionic columns in pairs, had an ornate railing, and ended in what Francis Russell described as a "rounded protuberance" that suggested a bandstand.

Mary washed her face and powdered her nose in a small upstairs bathroom, then joined her party on the porch. The rounded protuberance made an effective podium for the big, handsome man with the silvered hair and the golden voice. Regrettably, the bright sunlight didn't do much for his wife. Florence Kling DeWolfe Harding had never been much to look at; her most attractive attributes had been a strong mind and a rich father. The Duchess, as her husband called her, was older than he and showed it. The broad ribbon choker she wore did little to hide the crepiness of her neck. According to Mary, though, on this day the pride and hope that shone from behind the wrinkles in Mrs. Harding's face made up for her lack of feminine charm.

Senator Harding made the expected speech. All the women applauded, even though some of them might not have understood everything he said. Few listeners ever did. He had a tendency to let rhetoric overcome coherence, and to garble his words. It was through one of Harding's linguistic gaffes that the bastard word *normalcy* has by this time managed almost to oust the legitimate *normality*.

Mary also spoke. Being no orator, she thought she must have made little if any impression. She had her picture taken standing between the two Hardings, she said she looked rather frivolous. She dined that night with a Marion neighbor of the candidate's and was taken to the train by a Colonel Forbes, who was slated to take charge of the new Veterans' Bureau if Harding won the election. Had Mary but known, this brief encounter was soon to bring about a startling change in the Rinehart family's life.

Perhaps it was time for a change. Alan had got over his cowboy phase and gone back to his studies at Harvard; Ted was with him as a freshman. Mary was not feeling well. She was worn out from the hectic life she'd been leading for far too long, but she couldn't make herself slow down. Every so often she would suddenly be wracked by a ferocious burst of pain and have to be given a shot of morphia, which sent her mind spinning off into grandiose daydreams.

Then she made the terrible mistake of going with Samuel Goldwyn to a sneak preview of the movie that had been made from the scenario hurriedly scrabbled together after the excellent one written in Pittsburgh had been so cavalierly rejected. The film was every bit as awful as Mary had anticipated. As she left the theater, her ailing gall bladder, the source of the pain, put on its own smashing grand finale.

She didn't remember much after that except something about

an ambulance and being rushed into an operating room. Stanley Junior was holding her hand, Dr. Rinehart was rushing in from Pittsburgh. Mary knew she was going to die and didn't much care. She felt like an old crone, she was too tired to fight any longer, but she did hate to worry her husband and sons. She tried to send them some kind of last message via the hospital staff but somebody clapped an ether cone over her face. She knew the routine; she breathed deeply, felt herself rushing into the light at the end of the tunnel. This, then, was death.

No, actually it wasn't. By July, Mary was convalescent enough to be taken to the ranch in a Pullman berth. For days and days, she was content to sit on the cabin porch gazing idly at the mountains in the distance and the chipmunks playing around the cabin, soaking up the peace. Mary had all the time in the world now, time enough to think about the things that counted, to realize how sorely out of balance her life had become. She resolved to forget about that offer from the *Ladies' Home Journal*, to write less, to keep out of the moving-picture studios, to quit rushing madly around on so-called important assignments and then, stricken by guilt and homesickness, rushing madly back to her family.

Turning down the *Journal* did bother her a little. The magazine would have provided an ideal forum from which to air her opinions on alien registration, on adequate child labor laws, on family planning, on the jazzed-up, profligate, pleasure-chasing lifestyle that some Americans mistook for modernity. She could have talked about how active participation in wartime pursuits had changed women's attitudes about themselves and the lives they wanted to lead, had disproven the outdated thesis that marriage was women's only meaningful goal, homemaking and motherhood their only occupations worthy of respect. But other writers were saying these things too. Why not just let them?

Now that she'd got her priorities straightened out, Mary began to perk up. Ted left a fishing rod lying on the porch one day; his mother eyed the tempting wand for a while, then inched her way over to it. She was still not able to walk much, so she crawled down to the stream in her nightgown and negligee, dragging the rod after her. When her menfolk came home, they found Mary back in her chair, bedraggled but cocky, with one small fish laid out at her feet.

One triumph led to another. Mary wasn't supposed to ride but surely a little amble along a familiar trail on a thoroughly reliable horse couldn't really count as riding. So one of the boys brought her a chair to mount from, another held the horse, and she was back in the saddle again.

The Eaton ranch worked its wonders, as always. Mary returned to Sewickley fully cured and eager to get on with her priorities. She finished up a novel called *The Breaking Point* based on Dr. Rinehart's long-ago tale of an amnesiac. The case history that had inspired her first successful short story and launched her as a professional writer was still worth retelling, and she told it well. That done, she settled quietly to polishing up some of her travel articles; these would be published in 1922 as a collection called *The Out Trail.*

Now came a chance to test her new resolve to slow down. Actually it wasn't much of a test; she was asked to report on the International Disarmament Conference in Washington for national syndication. After so many trips back and forth from Pittsburgh to the capital during recent years, this must hardly have counted as going away. Mary drove down in the car with her secretary and a full cargo of maps and reference books. They arrived in time to witness the burial of the Unknown Soldier. Mary saw the elaborate ceremony as a bitter farce, she could think only of the countless tragedies it represented. As the drumbeats rolled and the flags went by, she gave way to angry tears.

The conference opened the next day. Mary had no great expectations that a miracle would occur, but there was always a small hope that some good would come of all the talk. What came was about what she'd expected; after listening to three weeks of diplomatic bickering she gave up and went home. Not quite empty-handed, however. Colonel Forbes, the man who'd given her a lift to the station that night in Ohio, was now, as Harding had wanted him to be, head of the Veterans' Bureau. He was eager for

Dr. Rinehart to come to Washington and become his consultant on tuberculosis.

This would mean leaving the Bluff and changing the Rineharts' whole way of life. Stanley Junior, now permanently settled in New York, liked the idea. Their transferring to Washington would bring his family nearer to him. Alan, always the adventurer, was all for the move. Ted was not—he didn't uproot easily. Mary herself found the prospect rather exciting but Dr. Rinehart, the one who must cast the deciding vote, was none too keen. He'd long ago got over his resentment at what the Bluff had cost Mary in money and slaving to meet endless expenses. Now the big estate was home, and always would be, even when they came to speak of it in the past tense.

However, Dr. Rinehart knew that his career in Pittsburgh had peaked. There was no higher state position for him to attain. To employ his abilities on a national scale, to contribute his knowledge and skills to making life a little easier for those returning veterans who still needed and perhaps would always need medical care, would be a service worth some personal sacrifice. The doctor went down to Washington, had a long interview with Colonel Forbes, and accepted the offered position.

On Christmas morning of 1921, William the old retainer wore his red velvet Santa Claus suit for the last time. That afternoon the Rineharts held open house for their Sewickley friends and neighbors. They would come back, they kept telling their guests. But they never did. Ted and Alan eventually joined their elder brother in New York, and Mary found plenty to intrigue her in the intricate convolutions of capital society. Cornelia, poor woman, missed the Bluff terribly. Dr. Rinehart was unhappiest of all, and had better reason to be than he would be aware of for another year or so.

Warren G. Harding, when still a newly elected senator, had met Charles R. Forbes while he and the Duchess were on a fact-finding mission to Hawaii at the government's expense. At that time, Forbes had been appointed by Woodrow Wilson to direct construction of a new naval base at Pearl Harbor. The reason why

Wilson picked him seems never to have been explained. Forbes's army record was a strange one. He had enlisted as a private in 1900, gone over the hill two months later, and vanished from sight for four years. In 1904 Forbes was restored to duty, apparently without so much as a tongue-lashing. In 1907 he was honorably discharged with the rank of sergeant. When the United States entered the war he went back in as an officer with the American Expeditionary Force and emerged as a colonel.

Forbes's exploits seem to have been legendary, some of them possibly more exploitation than exploit. He was a master at self-promotion. He must have spotted the Hardings as likely prospects, and he'd lost not a moment in attaching himself as tour guide and boon companion during their stay in Hawaii. Captivated by his personality and his skill at poker, Harding had never bothered to check out Forbes's stories or examine his past record before making him head of the Veterans' Bureau. Dr. Rinehart, never dreaming that his country's new president could have been so careless or so gullible, naturally assumed that Colonel Forbes was as dedicated as himself to improving the lot of sick and disabled veterans.

Forbes was dedicated, all right, but the only veteran he intended to serve was himself. Frederick Lewis Allen's book *Only Yesterday*, first published in 1931 by Harper & Brothers, gives a hair-raising account of how the charismatic colonel managed to squander more than $200 million of government money during the two years he was head of the Veterans' Bureau, junketing around the country, supposedly to find suitable sites for veterans' hospitals, tossing out wads of money to any smooth operator willing to cut him in on a third of the take.

In 1926, Colonel Forbes would be tried for fraud and sentenced to Leavenworth Prison. At this early stage, it was still possible to mistake arrant piracy for bureaucratic bumbling. Even after Forbes resigned in disgrace, the pork-barreling would go on in the Veterans' Bureau, as in most other departments of an administration that had turned into a vast, bottomless grab bag. Harding himself was not a crook, but he did have a magnetic attraction to good old boys who knew all the bad old ways of getting their hands in the till.

Some of the veterans themselves learned how to cheat. Mary served for a while on a committee investigating a rehabilitation program that had been formed to teach returned servicemen skills that would equip them for civilian jobs. They were given free instruction, free books, and a stipend of $100 a month until they had completed the chosen course. By failing to complete one course before signing up for another, they could keep the gravy train running overtime. Mary's committee turned up veterans who had thus wangled themselves into twenty or more different courses. She cited one diligent student who had acquired a smattering of subjects that ranged from dentistry to playing the pipe organ.

Like the other consultants in the Veterans' Bureau, Dr. Rinehart found himself being given plenty of responsibility but no real authority. He was determined to staff his tuberculosis hospitals with fully competent personnel; he worked out a comprehensive training program but it got lost in the shuffle, perhaps because there was nothing in it for anybody except the veterans. He doggedly put his plan back together and drove it through. Not long after the doctor had lined up a team of the best men in the country to lecture and instruct for nominal fees, he was informed that his project was too expensive and would have to be killed.

Eventually, Dr. Rinehart would be driven by exasperation to send in his resignation and open a private practice in Washington. In those early days, however, he was still determined to honor his commitment. Tuberculosis hospitals required a particular kind of environment, therefore he often had to go out prospecting for appropriate sites, continually dealing with politicians who pressured him to opt for locales that would gain them favor among their constituents but would not be desirable for the patients. These hunting trips took him away from home for as much as ten days at a time and happened far too often for Mary's liking. Apparently she felt that one gadabout in the family was enough.

The Rineharts' first Washington address was a service apartment at the Wardman Park Hotel on Wyoming Avenue. The floor above them was occupied by the old Pennsylvania party boss, Sen. Boies Penrose. No longer was Penrose the 350-pound hulk who'd bragged that his photograph had graced every brothel in Harrisburg and Pittsburgh, who'd been known to eat seven pounds of steak at a sitting and wash it down with a full quart of bourbon. His dissolute life had caught up with him. The Rineharts had not been in Washington very long when there was an obituary in the papers and a vacancy on the next floor, far better suited to their needs than the too-small apartment they were in. As soon as the necessary changes were made, they moved upstairs.

It started the very first night. Mary and Stanley had just turned off their reading lamps when something like a black curtain blowing in the wind swept across their bedroom. But the air was still and the curtains were only narrow hangings held tight to the wall by heavy bands. This was a puzzler. So was the maid's appearance at seven o'clock the next morning with her mistress's coffee.

Mary, wakened from the exhausted sleep of the newly moved, was not happy. Marie, who was Cornelia's maid and at this time the only live-in servant, insisted she'd heard the two short rings that were Mrs. Rinehart's signal. This was odd. Either Marie had been dreaming or Mary had rung in her sleep, or else there was a short circuit in the wiring. After a few more such incidents they called in an electrician. He found nothing wrong with the bell, which had been installed after Senator Penrose had become bedridden. The ringing kept on.

CHAPTER 29

The Unexpected

Mary had always tried to keep to her original vow of not writing while her husband was at home. Now that he was gone so much, she either wrote in the study during the evenings or went to bed with a book. Alone and quiet, she began hearing odd noises. Sometimes they sounded as if furniture was being moved, which it wasn't. Once she heard the apparent crash of a heavy fern basket falling on the porch, when no fern had fallen.

A friend interested in spiritualism told Mary that the proper drill on such occasions was to go and ask the noise what its problem was and whether she could be of help. Mary didn't think much of that notion, but one night when she'd seemed to hear a living room window close without human aid she forced herself to enter the room. Pressed back against the wall, she addressed the intrusive spirit in a weak and trembling tone. At once the bell pealed out, and kept on ringing until Mary at last caught on. She was leaning against the bell-push.

This farcical episode did not clear up the problem. One day when Mary had a visitor, Keno, the resident bull terrier, climbed up on her lap and cowered there, growling, trembling, staring fixedly into one corner of the room for no apparent reason. Another time, when Alan, alone in the apartment, dressing for a party and in need of a buttonhook to cope with a heavily starched shirt collar, started into his parents' bedroom, Keno bounced in front of him, then wheeled and crawled back out on his stomach, whining in abject terror. Alan decided he could manage without the buttonhook.

The phenomena went on. Two of Mary's visiting aunts were startled by raps on the headboards of their beds and by a phantom typist tapping late at night in the dark, empty study. When Stanley Junior came to attend a ball with Alan, the hall floor had recently been painted and the furniture set back only that day. Stanley returned in the early hours, went straight to sleep, and was wakened by hearing a heavy leather armchair outside his door creak and scrape nonstop for about an hour. Mary found him in the morning trying to figure out how that chair could have scored the pristine floor so heavily in a circle about six inches wider than the chair.

One night when the Rineharts gave a dinner party, Mary made the mistake of chatting about their resident poltergeist. Thanks, very likely, to one of the hired waiters, the next day the Washington papers carried a story about the ghost of Senator Penrose, still ringing his bell. Somebody from the Senate Office Building corroborated the story. That bell in his private office had continued to send out its two short peals for some days after the senator's death. Senate pages wouldn't enter the office because they were afraid of ghosts.

These were Halloween yarns, a little bit scary, a little bit laughable. Now would come the genuine nightmare, bizarre, incredible, unutterably tragic.

Ever since her stroke fourteen years before, Cornelia Roberts had not only been mute but had dragged one foot and been totally without the use of her right arm. Never once had she tried to get into a bathtub by herself, and nobody had dreamed she ever could. But there it was.

Mary had left Washington earlier that day, on her way to spend a few days by herself at Eaton's ranch before the family arrived. Marie, as always, was taking care of Mrs. Roberts, and they had spent a happy day checking over Cornelia's clothes in preparation for her vacation at the ranch. At bathtime, Marie turned on the hot water and let it run while she was called away on a brief errand. Somehow, during those few minutes, Cornelia contrived to get into the tub. Unable to scream or to help herself, she suffered such terrible burns from the scalding hot water that she died in the hospital a mercifully short time later.

Mary had rushed back as soon as the telegram reached her, and was at the bedside when her mother died. They took the body back to Pittsburgh. Cornelia Gilleland Roberts would lie in familiar soil along with her husband, her mother-in-law, the little granddaughter who had drunk poison, the little niece who'd been hit by a train, with Sade and John. So many dead, so many violent deaths. Mary thought of Stanley's half-brother Ed, dying of burns like Cornelia, saying, "I think I'd like to smoke."

She felt again her old uncertainties. She still did not quite trust life, she prayed always for the ones she loved, asking only that they might be safe. She never quite shook her superstitious feeling that, should she fail to offer up her nightly petition, something awful might happen to them.

As a footnote, Mary found it worth mentioning that, after her mother's death, those uncanny disturbances ceased.

The Rineharts went into mourning. Mary was feeling her mother's death grievously; blaming herself, as people do, for all the little attentions she hadn't given. She was missing the Bluff, her friends and relatives back in Pennsylvania, her sons now away from the nest. She was experiencing, like countless others, the bleak letdown of the postwar period. She found it next to impossible to get any work done, but she did begin to learn things about life in Washington, including the fact that, should she and Stanley decide to make the District their permanent home, they would lose their right to vote. Gradually the Rineharts began to mingle in society and to do a little entertaining themselves, always having to be mindful of the eternal Washingtonian protocol.

Before Stanley had got thoroughly fed up with the Veterans' Bureau and begun to make his feelings known in his own uninhibited fashion, the Rineharts had developed an acquaintance with a neighbor who was also a colleague of Stanley's. Charles F. Cramer was a lawyer whom Forbes had brought with him from California to be the attorney for the Veterans' Bureau. Francis Russell described him as a tight-lipped little fox with a pompadour brushed up to mask his receding hairline and a pince-nez that gave him almost a womanly air. Cramer and his wife had bought the Hardings' former dwelling on Wyoming Avenue for $60,000. Living so nearby and being so closely connected through the bureau, the Cramers often joined the Rineharts for a quiet dinner or a game of bridge.

By the end of his second year as head of the Veterans' Bureau, Charlie Forbes's grand-scale looting had become too flagrant to go unnoticed. Rumors were going around, and they were all true. Eventually Harding's attorney general and close friend Harry Daugherty had to let the president know what was going on. Harding took it badly; he flatly refused to believe that his great pal and poker buddy would knife him in the back. Daugherty told Harding to check Forbes out for himself; the evidence was too clear for even the Great Bloviator to overlook.

The following afternoon, as Russell tells it, a visitor with an appointment to see the president had been misdirected to the Red Room. As he entered, the visitor was appalled to see the president throttling a man he had pinned against the wall, yelling "You yellow rat! You double-crossing bastard!"

The yellow rat was Charlie Forbes, and the unnamed visitor may have saved Forbes's life. When Harding realized someone else was in the room, he let go, pulled himself together, and took his visitor into the next room. Forbes staggered away, his face blotched, his breath coming in gasps.

In the hope of averting an open scandal, Forbes was allowed to leave for Europe, ostensibly on business connected with veterans still in overseas hospitals. On January 31, 1923, a reorganization of the Veterans' Bureau was instituted. On February 1, Attorney Cramer tendered his resignation. On February 12, the Senate passed a resolution for an examination of the allegations that were being made. On the fifteenth, Forbes cabled his resignation from Paris, and Harding accepted it.

Early in March, Charles Cramer drove his attractive young wife to Union Station to catch a train for New York. He then went home, asked the maid to get him some stamps, and sat down to write letters. Cramer seems to have spent most of the night writing letters, then early in the morning he went into the bathroom and shot himself.

Russell says that Mrs. Rinehart heard the shot, ran over, saw the pile of letters on the desk, and found Cramer dead on the bathroom floor. Mary's version in *My Story* was that Stanley answered an early morning phone call from the Cramer house, turned to Mary, and said, "Charlie Cramer has killed himself."

Whoever phoned had asked both the Rineharts to go over. The doctor was there before them, and they discovered that the butler, for some reason, had carried Cramer's body from the bathroom to an upper back porch. Mary mentioned how bizarre it seemed to see their dead neighbor lying there in the bright sunlight; she and Stanley had him moved back into the house and laid out decently on a bed.

Sometime in the general confusion, the letters that Cramer had written disappeared. Perhaps they were abstracted for political reasons. The simplest explanation is that the maid who'd fetched the stamps simply mailed them as a final service to her late employer. Gaston B. Means, a Washington character known for his uninhibited narrative style, was later to allege in a book called *The Strange Death of President Harding* that Cramer had been murdered. Means also averred that, later on in San Francisco, Flossie Harding had poisoned her husband to spare him from going back to Washington and being impeached. Means's effrontery was boundless; his amanuensis was a lady whom he'd met while he was serving a term in an Atlanta jail. This woman also wrote for a confession magazine, and it need hardly be said that their collaborative effort made the best-seller list.

Cramer's death couldn't have done much to lift Mary's depression, but she did go back to work on a play based on her novel *The Breaking Point*. It finally opened in Washington on a sweltering summer evening, to standing room only and roses all the way for the playwright. At last Mary Roberts Rinehart, who had been dodging her own first nights for the past fifteen years, stood on a stage and received an ovation, knowing as she bowed and smiled that the play was not going to make the grade.

While the critics were still lauding *The Breaking Point*, the playgoers themselves had already begun to slip quietly away in search of livelier entertainment. This was not the time for a searching drama of human emotions; what they'd hoped for was another *Bat*.

Rewriting didn't help much. The play went to New York, ran for a month, and walked for a month. By the end of the third month it had crawled to a faltering finish. Mary would know better next time, if there was ever to be a next time.

What with the upheaval in the Veterans' Bureau and the sad demise of Mr. Cramer, the Rineharts now accepted the fact that, much as they loved the Bluff, they were never going back there. They were succumbing to the charm of the capital city, and they liked being closer to their sons.

Alan was still living with them. He had been working for one of the Washington papers, chasing down stories in his disgraceful old jalopy except on those occasions when he enhanced the paper's reputation while saving it money by borrowing his parents' impressive car to ferry visiting VIPs to their interviews.

Now Alan was making noises about sailing alone around the world in an eighteen-foot boat. Mary knew better than to voice her motherly alarms; she talked her son out of it by giving him a graphic word picture of how unutterably boring such a voyage would be. So he decided instead to go and write up the Haitians. This didn't sit well with Mary either. She didn't want any of her boys to be a writer; she knew too well what the penalties were. But when Alan came back from the Caribbean with a sheaf of pieces that were eagerly grabbed up by *Cosmopolitan* magazine, Mary had to face the awful truth.

Ted was less of a shock to his mother. He was nearly through at Harvard, it was time for him to get serious about a vocation.

He seems always to have felt that he ought to become a doctor, not so much from personal inclination as out of respect for his father. One day he asked his mother if she would like him to study medicine. Her answer was no, not unless he himself wanted that more than anything else. In that case, he decided with great relief, he'd prefer to go into publishing with his elder brother.

So Ted would also be settling in New York. His mother and father might as well put the Bluff up for sale and begin house hunting in Washington. They were in no special rush, however. The apartment was peaceful with just the two of them, perhaps a bit lonely at times, but they had each other. Their marriage had been in the truest sense of the word, a labor of love; a determined effort by two strong individuals to keep their relationship in good repair. Being sensible parents, they were not trying to keep their sons tied to them, but the ties that held Mary and the doctor together were far too strong ever to be broken, however great the strain.

They went back to Sewickley for the last and final time, making decisions about what to keep and what to get rid of, tying tags to some shrubs that they wanted transplanted to their new house on Massachusetts Avenue. The white lilac tree that Stanley had given his wife once at Eastertime when they were still, as Mary said, young marrieds just scraping along would have to go with them. The lilac had got used to being moved; it would survive another uprooting and so would they.

There were at that time plenty of places to ride horseback around Washington. At Christmastime, Stanley had given Mary a saddle horse and she had reciprocated in kind. Mary's was a reliable mare. The horse she'd bought for Stanley had come with all sorts of guarantees, but somehow she'd always been a trifle wary of the creature. One day when they were out together, Stanley happened to slip one foot out of his stirrup. Not noticing what he'd done, Mary began to canter. Seeing the mare speed up, Stanley's mount followed suit. The empty stirrup began to swing, hitting the horse in the side and hurrying it on as the rider groped in vain with his foot to solve the predicament.

Then Mary saw her husband flash past and realized he was

on a runaway. She chased after him but couldn't keep up. Horse
and rider were soon out of sight. There was nothing she could do
but keep on; coming to a paved road she was horrified to see her
husband lying there unconscious, bleeding from a head wound.
She sat down in the road and cradled his head in her lap, loosened
his collar, took off his tie, sure all the time that it was no use. Her
best-beloved was dead! She'd murdered him by giving him the
wrong horse.

About the time people began to gather, the corpse sat up and
demanded indignantly, "What happened?" From the evidence,
the bolting horse had tried to swerve from the bridle path to the
pavement, throwing his rider headfirst onto the concrete, then
falling on top of him. Somebody called an ambulance, and Stanley
was carted off to the hospital with a bad concussion and a broken
leg. The leg mended, Stanley insisted on being active as usual, but
for the next six months or so he was, as Mary put it, distinctly
queer. Once back to normal, he remembered next to nothing
about his half-year in a fugue state; Mary thought it was just as
well he didn't.

Ted was being graduated from Harvard that year, class of
1924. There would be no visit to the ranch. Dr. Rinehart was still
having occasional dizzy spells and, all things considered, neither
he nor Mary could have been hankering much for long days in
the saddle. Instead, they decided to rent a house for the summer
on one of the many islands off the coast of Maine. As soon as Ted
had secured his diploma and shed his robe and mortarboard, they
all set off for the island.

They found island life much to their liking. Among this one's
various amenities was a separate studio, sitting among the scrub
pines and facing out toward the ocean. Mary appropriated this
convenient aerie for her office and, knowing that the boys always
enjoyed having their father to themselves and would keep him
well occupied, went off every morning to work on a new mystery
novel. Maine mornings, even in high summer and particularly on
the ocean, can be cold and foggy. Mary provided herself with heat
of a sort by lighting a big oil lamp and setting it on the floor near
her feet.

Rinehart fans may have thought—may still think, since the book is yet again in print—that *The Red Lamp* was an odd sort of book for their idol to have written. It may have been inspired to some degree by the late Boies Penrose's strange legacy. However, the venue of the quick and the possibly undead at a big old house on the water is reminiscent of that other haunted house she'd rented six summers before and the red lamp a small tribute to the one that had given her some uneasy nights there.

Mary was not one to waste a picturesque setting. She had a suitably eerie plot, an ingenious solution, some excellent characters—all the necessary ingredients for a highly readable novel, which *The Red Lamp* still is, but somehow it comes off just a bit logy, like the old rowboat that had its own small part in the narrative.

This is not strange. Mary was going through another bad patch. She was tired all the time, her handwriting was deteriorating, she worried too much over things that might never happen, she had shaking spells. Mary was forty-eight years old that year. Surely she, a nurse, and Stanley, a doctor, must have recognized the symptoms; but in 1936, when *My Story* was first published, the word *menopause* would not have been the sort of thing a gracious lady with an international reputation could comfortably put into her memoirs.

All symptoms to the contrary notwithstanding, Mary finished the book and got it off. *Cosmopolitan* magazine bought the serial rights for $40,000 and George Doran published the hardcover book. This first Christmas in the new house on Massachusetts Avenue began to look brighter. Cornelia would not be there, but all the boys would be at home, as well as young Stanley's wife and the little daughter whom her parents had nicknamed, for the most reasonable of reasons, Bab. Mary went out and bought Bab a toy drum, not that the child needed one but just because there'd always been a drum under the tree when the boys were small. Locales might shift with the changing times, but family traditions could still remain.

CHAPTER 30

Shipped to the Desert
and "Strong as a Lions"

One day shortly before Christmas, while they were wrapping presents together, Mary asked her husband what was the correct garb for riding a camel. The distinguished but forgetful physician, racking his brain over where he'd hidden somebody's carefully chosen gift, replied vaguely, "What camel?"

Mary didn't care what camel. Oddly enough, each knew what the other was talking about, they'd been thinking for a while now that a trip to Egypt was just what they needed. Stanley had been through a rough time with the Veterans' Bureau and his near-fatal accident. Mary was in even worse shape than he. She was finished as a writer. Her brain refused to function, she couldn't even hold a pen.

Needless to say, that was not how things would work out, as Mary later demonstrated in *My Story* and in an often hilarious travelogue, some of which is repeated here partly or entirely verbatim through the generous permission of Mary's grandson, George H.D. Rinehart, and the family of Mary Roberts Rinehart.

They sailed late in January 1925. Stanley, always protective, watched over his wife with tenderness, compassion, and hidden alarm as she, usually so sociable, bullied herself out of shying away from her fellow passengers. When she could no longer keep up the empty chatting and laughing, she would go down to her stateroom and lie there in the dark, fighting a crazy impulse to get it over with. She herself realized what Stanley surely knew, that her mood was largely hysteria. Still, he must have been worrying about a possible suicidal gesture that could have terrible repercussions.

By the time they reached Egypt, however, Mary was beginning to mend. Finding that she could pen a legible letter to her children was a step in the right direction. She was able to discuss rationally with Stanley how they'd manage to get by on their savings now that she could no longer contribute the large sums of money that they'd come to take for granted. Having had it proved to her own satisfaction that they wouldn't be beggars, Mary sneaked out and bought a notebook. As to what she'd do with the notes, she had no idea. She'd always taken notes on her trips, and it just didn't seem right not to make any this time.

Once they'd seen the sights of Cairo, the Rineharts had planned to go up the Nile by boat. However, they got invited to a party in the desert to which the guests all arrived on camelback, and that was that. Why loll around on the deck of a dahabeah watching the crocodiles slither off the sandbanks when they might instead be pitching and rolling aboard a true ship of the desert? Camels they must have and camels they got, through the good offices of their invaluable cicerone, whose name was Ashour Abdul Karim El-Gabry. Mary's desert ship, by happy coincidence, was named Dahabeah. Stanley's was Missouri because, said Ashour, this camel always had to be shown. They were charmed to come upon this scrap of American folklore so far from home.

The question of what to wear on a camel came up again in Cairo. Ashour suggested that the Rineharts would perhaps be more comfortable in native dress, so they went and bought some. Mary chose a golden sheath to wear under a turquoise silk *aba*, a yellow head scarf, and a white silk nose veil that she found herself inhaling and exhaling with every breath. Stanley was relatively subdued in a brown undergarment, a green-and-white striped *aba*, a white turban, a colorful scarf that draped over it, and a gilt cord to anchor the scarf to the turban.

Back at their hotel, they dressed up in their new outfits and stepped out on the balcony, only to be dazzled by each other's splendor and disconcerted by the stares from passers-by. Perhaps this was not the kind of native garb that Ashour had had in mind for his patrons, though, as Mary commented, it might have suited King Solomon and the Queen of Sheba just fine.

Riding boots and breeches, while appropriate for horses, didn't work well on camels either, they found. Stanley settled for his golf knickers and Mary, all else having failed to satisfy, wore her best tailor-made suit and a pair of bedroom slippers. She remarked that her tailor in New York had taken great pains with the "expression" of the skirt, but that after a few days in the desert, its expression was both pained and shocked.

Ashour noticed early on that Mrs. Rinehart was not in the best of shape, he assured her that after having slept in the desert she would be "strong as a lions." Mary was all for being a lions; this experience was to be a far cry from any camping trip that Howard Eaton had ever put together. She and Stanley rode ahead on their camels. Both animals were females, which were alleged to have better dispositions than the males and to give a softer, smoother ride despite the looks of hatred that Dahabeah kept casting toward Mary.

Ashour came next in line, on a gray donkey named Gazelle. The cook and the butler traveled on foot, as did the men in charge of the four huge male camels that carried their handsomely decorated tents, their iron camp beds, springs, mattresses, pillows, and bedding; the washstands, bowls, pitchers, bathtub, dishes, stove, kitchenware, water tanks, dining table, folding chairs both straight-backed and steamer length, food in Lucullan abundance, assorted beverages, oriental rugs to keep the sand out of the tents, and a variety of other items that Mary forgot to mention. This would be something to tell the boys at the ranch, if they ever got back to Eaton's.

After a day's ride, the three tents were immediately set up and tea and cakes served to the intrepid travelers. Two hours or so later, after Mary and Stanley had refreshed themselves with cooling sponge baths and either a restful lie-down on a comfortable bed or a pleasant flop in a steamer chair with a book and a scotch and soda for company, dinner would be served by candlelight on an elegantly appointed table. A typical meal would be an excellent soup, an entrée, roast meat with vegetables and appropriate wine, salad with roast quail, and dessert followed by Turkish coffee and assorted sweetmeats out under the stars.

If the Rineharts didn't eat everything set before them, the cook's feelings might be hurt but the food wouldn't go to waste. Anything their entourage couldn't finish would be rolled into a package and left for any needy wanderer who might come along; the dry heat of the desert would keep it from spoiling. All this opulence may seem like excessive coddling, but after a day on camelback, an exercise much like shooting the rapids in a cranky canoe without a paddle, Stanley and Mary must have felt that they'd earned all the luxury they could get.

They could even have used a little more coddling. Flu had been prevalent during their stay in Cairo; after they'd been in the desert for about a week, both Mary and Stanley came down with it. Riding a camel on a long day's trek while running a fever, running at the nose, and running out of clean handkerchiefs proved too much for Mary. As soon as the men had got her tent and cot set up, she crawled into bed still wearing her by now thoroughly disgruntled skirt, and refused to budge.

Stanley was no gentle patient either. As his temperature mounted, so did his ire. Ashour prayed with ever-increasing fervor for the speedy recovery of his patients and most fervently of all for the improvement of Dr. Rinehart's disposition.

When they reached Fayum, the first oasis in the Libyan Desert, the two invalids spent a blessed day in bed, working crossword puzzles and ignoring the snarls and grunts of Dahabeah and Missouri outside their tent. This respite must have been just what the doctor ordered; as his fever subsided, his temper improved. Mary, though not yet quite ready to take on lions, was recovering from more than her touch of influenza. The vast silence of the desert had brought her a deep sense of peace, of acceptance and thankfulness. It had also brought back her urge to write.

Nomad's Land, the book that would come out of her automatic note-taking, turned out to be Grade A number one Rinehart, lively and merry, meticulously observed and expertly told. After 124 pages of Egypt, the text moves on to Baghdad. Mary called that segment of the book "Hunting Trouble"; her opening sentence compared the joys of that mystical city to a toothache, a punctured tire, or waking up to find burglars in the house. Back in the states, their friend Douglas Fairbanks was having a great run in *The Thief of Baghdad*. Mary waxed acerbic about how all he'd had to do was romp around the set all day, then go home to a hot shower, a good dinner, and Mary Pickford.

She and Stanley were experiencing a genuine Baghdad, complete with clouds of mosquitoes, squalor galore, and Panzer divisions of small birds who swooped in through the unscreened windows to steal the dreadful food that the Rineharts were trying to choke down for want of anything more palatable. There was nothing to do except shop for things they didn't want and go to outdated movies with scrambled subtitles in various languages that they couldn't understand. Mary gave Baghdad only forty-two pages containing few good words.

One thing that Mary mentioned in *My Story* but omitted from *Nomad's Land* was a brief return to Cairo during which they met the king of Egypt, but not the queen. She, like every respectable Egyptian woman, led a life of sequestration. The Rineharts didn't dare mention that their Royal Highnesses' daughter, married to the first Egyptian minister to America, would inevitably find it not only impractical but downright impossible to retain her veil and her privacy in Washington. When Mary met her later on, the princess confessed that wearing Western clothes and appearing unveiled at mixed gatherings had been an ordeal at first. She'd got over it, however, and had become an important asset to her husband in his new role; Mary doubted that the king ever knew what a diplomat the princess could be.

Mary and Stanley might have stayed in Egypt a little longer

had they not received a cablegram from Alan. He was engaged to be married. The formal announcement would be delayed until his parents got home, but he wanted to know if it was all right with them.

Of course it was, and it was high time they went back to tell him so. The night they arrived in New York, Alan brought his fiancée to their hotel suite. The poor girl was understandably nervous. It must have been a strange introduction, seeing her future in-laws sashaying around in their Egyptian finery and Alan's brothers rigged out in whatever grotesqueries they could contrive from the materials at hand, all the Rineharts making, as usual, a tremendous racket.

Mary and the doctor heard the romantic story of how Alan's love affair had begun. They also solved the mystery of how a window had got broken in their Washington garage shortly before they'd sailed for Egypt. Alan and a charming debutante whom he'd recently met and been eager to know better had slipped away from a ball to go for a ride. Alan had sneaked the girl into his family's drawing room to wait while he got out one of the family cars, having surmounted the minor obstacle of a locked garage by smashing a pane of glass with the leather heel of his dancing shoe.

The girl was Gratia Houghton, daughter of a co-owner of the Corning Glass Company and niece of Alanson Houghton, who was at that time America's ambassador to the Court of Saint James. The wedding took place in a private chapel on the Houghton estate, but the bride and bridegroom were barely noticed in the society column writeups. Whereas Stanley Junior's marriage had been headlined DAUGHTER OF PUBLISHER MARRIES SON OF NOVELIST, Alan's came out as SON OF NOVELIST MARRIES NIECE OF AMBASSADOR. Several years later, Ted's wife, Betty, would complain on the birth of their daughter Cornelia, Mary's fifth grandchild, that from the way the papers wrote up the story, readers must have drawn the conclusion that it was Grandmary, as she'd come to be known to her grandchildren and daughters-in-law, who had produced the latest Rinehart.

A family as close-knit as the Rineharts can too easily become a juggernaut that overwhelms the more personal relationships within its various components. At this point in their lives, there was no special reason why Mary and the doctor could not have moved to New York and enjoyed themselves playing full-time patriarch and matriarch. They chose the wiser course, stayed in Washington, and built themselves a poolroom.

They'd had one in Sewickley; everybody from the children's friends to guests at their allegedly formal dinner parties had tended to wind up at the pool table there, having a glorious time. They would see nothing strange in some Washington VIP's showing up in swallow-tailed coat and top hat, only to be found a while later in his shirtsleeves, chalking his cue and casting a calculating eye at the corner pocket.

Mary and Stanley often played pool when they were alone and not too busy with more serious matters. She had been deeply embroiled for quite a while with a novel that reflected a phenomenon she'd noticed on various occasions at the dude ranch. She called her new book *Lost Ecstasy*. It dealt with a rich society girl from the East who had fallen madly in love with a handsome young cowhand. In real life, these romances usually come to nothing; Mary's heroine, however, was foolish enough to marry her dream man. Once the stardust was out of her eyes, she would wish desperately that she hadn't.

The *Saturday Evening Post* gave Mary Roberts Rinehart $50,000 for the serial rights and didn't lose a penny on the deal. Response to the book was overwhelming. Mary noted with surprise that fully half the fans who wrote to her were male: doctors, lawyers, ranchers, all sorts and conditions of men, all of them praising her work to the skies. The critics were less gracious. Some of them were downright bitchy, following the pattern set by Edgar Allan Poe, who never reviewed a book unless he could bolster his undernourished ego by ripping it to pieces.

Mary lamented the bad reviews, but her husband told her that in his opinion (he seems actually to have said "humble" opinion, but he probably didn't mean it) reviews didn't amount to a hill of beans because books were sold primarily by word-of-mouth recommendation. Dr. Rinehart was absolutely right. As every author should know, word of mouth is still the best advertising. Doran bought the hardcover rights to *Lost Ecstasy* for an undisclosed sum and Mary sold the movie rights for another $15,000. Naturally, Hollywood changed the title. *I Take This Woman*, starring Gary Cooper and Carole Lombard, was released in 1931.

Mary had started the book back in March; its progress had been fraught with difficulties. In April, Stanley Junior's wife had had to undergo surgery and Grandmary got to ride herd on little Bab. By early summer, Mary was heading for the ranch where she could find a quiet place to write. Stanley Senior joined her a few weeks later. He'd picked the wrong time to come.

Even the carefully bowdlerized version of her married life that Mary presented in *My Story* makes it obvious that the union had never been roses all the way. How could perfect harmony ever have been possible? Here were two well-nigh irresistible forces, sometimes working together, too often pulling in opposite directions, driven each by a personal demon to perform at the peaks of their separate powers. Both were charismatic characters who'd never lacked admirers, but only one was an international celebrity. Only one was raking in money by the millions, only one had to deal every week with sacks of mail from adoring, scolding, begging fans and nonfans, people with bushels of importunings to speak, to shine, to donate to worthy and unworthy causes, to serve on government committees. Paradoxically, that was the one who required long stretches of peace and quiet in which to do the work that had brought fame, fortune, and the constant strain of having to sparkle and slave for a relentlessly worshiping public.

But what of the other one? The surgeon who'd had to quit operating because of his own increasingly troublesome medical problems, the successful head of a flourishing tuberculosis clinic who'd resigned to serve his country as an army doctor and never got beyond the rank of major, who had been given an important government position only to have the rug pulled out from under him by a high official who'd turned out to be a self-seeking rogue? Now, if ever, Stanley Marshall Rinehart needed some tender, loving care, but where was he going to get it?

Too bad, but there it was. Just what they fought about, Mary never said. All we know is that, after a major battle, Stanley got back on the train for Washington.

Whoever was at fault, whatever the provocation, this was not the end. Mary and Stanley had worked hard and long at keeping their marriage together despite the many strains to which it had been subjected. Their love had survived too many storms, their need for each other was far too deep, there were their sons and their grandchildren to think of. Diplomatic negotiations were opened, with sighs of relief at both ends. By the time Washington cooled off, so had the Rineharts; October found them back in the social swing and happy to be there.

Dinner at the White House was no longer a great thrill, just another excuse for Mary to wear a far too expensive diamond necklace that Stanley had told her she was crazy to buy. The Rineharts had dined with Warren G. Harding and his Duchess before he escaped the full force of the deluge by dying on an Alaska cruise; now they dined with the Coolidges. There was a legend around the District that Mrs. Rinehart had once actually succeeded in making Silent Cal crack a smile.

CHAPTER 31

A Time to Remember

Despite the popular outpouring of kudos for *Lost Ecstasy*, 1927 hardly seems to have been Mary's happiest year. During the winter, she and Stanley had taken a trip to Hawaii. On her first day there, she'd slipped in the hotel bathroom and broken a rib. The injury didn't bother her at first so much as the unromantic way in which she'd hurt herself. Later on, however, she developed a chronic pain in her side that kept her on the chaise longue a good deal.

Remembering how Aunt Sade and Aunt Ella had gone, being the inveterate dramatist she was, Mary almost managed to talk herself into wasting away from cancer. It was in the midst of such gloomy ratiocinations that she decided to write her autobiography, not for publication but for her children to have as a remembrance after she had passed beyond the veil.

Making the notes that would, within the next few years, evolve into yet another best-seller must have been effective therapy. Since so much of the material in this book is derived from Mary's own record, there seems little point in discussing what she wrote, except to say that it still makes excellent reading. That any literary effort of Mary Roberts Rinehart's could remain a family secret was a quaint conceit, of course; the book that she called *My Story* turned out to be a benefit to her children in more ways than she'd intended.

After Ted had overcome his early feeling of obligation to be a doctor and followed his elder brother into publishing, Mary had, as she'd done for Stanley, given him money to buy a small share in George Doran's company. In 1929, the boys announced that they were leaving the company that was by then Doubleday Doran to join with John Farrar in forming their own publishing house.

It was, and remains, generally believed that Mrs. Rinehart not only set her sons up in business but also was a principal in the company. In fact, she held no office and took no part in the publishers' operations. The infinitely more important role that she did play for the rest of her life, which would span three more decades despite the pain in her side, was to give the boys exclusive publishing rights for all her future hardcover books.

Farrar & Rinehart's opening list was an impressive one, carefully eclectic in content to attract a wide span of readers, featuring high-caliber writers of whom, naturally, Mary was one. On hearing her sons' decision, her first question had been, "What can I do to help?" They'd suggested she write a new mystery; she immediately started one that would be called *The Door*. Of course *The Door* could not be got ready for publication in so short a span of time, but the boys did manage to put together a collection of their mother's short stories that they dubbed *The Romantics*. This would be followed in 1930 by the *Mary Roberts Rinehart Mystery Book*, containing *The Circular Staircase, The Man in Lower Ten*, and *The Case of Jennie Brice*; all of which had been out of print long enough to be rediscovered by a new generation of readers, and *The Confession*, a novella last published by Doran in 1917. But the real bonanza was *The Door*. It had been five years since *The Red Lamp*, and readers were hungry for a new Rinehart mystery. Astute promoter that she was, Mary also did an article for *Publishers Weekly* in February of that year called "The Increasing Repute of the Crime Story."

Whether a publishing house launched just before the crash of 1929 could have survived without the prestige of the Rinehart name and contributions is moot. The fact is that the venture did survive; Farrar & Rinehart kept on turning out successful books. Among the best-sellers were new Mary Roberts Rinehart releases, others were anthologies of Mary's short stories or reissues of earlier books, three or four bound together in one big volume.

While the sons were cashing in on their mother's backlist, Mary and the doctor were not doing so well. During the twenties, the stock market had been on a wild upward sweep. Everybody from the plutocrat to the trash collector was getting rich, on paper. Then came that fateful day in November 1929 when the fairy gold faded away.

The crash was not the immediate total wipeout that many have pictured it to be. The Rineharts were not reduced to penury overnight; they were, however, badly hit. Dr. Rinehart, who had in recent years been managing the money that his wife was so good at making and so totally hopeless at keeping, blamed himself bitterly.

Mary wrote in *My Story* that she felt her husband's failure to foresee the crisis that also got by so many allegedly expert financiers had been a factor in hastening his death. Perhaps she was right, but it had been a long time now since Dr. Rinehart had been forced to give up surgery because of his arthritis. The disease, for which there is so far no cure and were then few palliatives, had continued its relentless progress. Unlike his wife, who was anything but stoical about her many complaints, Stanley had maintained his stiff upper lip and carried on. Now he was showing all too plainly the effects of his long struggle.

In March 1929, when the goose still hung high and the Rineharts were building a twenty-second room on their Washington house for some reason that may have made sense at the time, they had also bought themselves a twenty-eight-foot twin-cabin power cruiser that they called the *Greyhound*. Evidently there was still enough in the kitty a year later to afford them the summer rental of what Mary described as a modest house on one of the small rivers that feed into Buzzards Bay, where the boys and their families could visit them on weekends. Stanley's was still the firm hand on the helm when he and Mary decided in June of 1930 to take the *Greyhound* to Massachusetts.

It must have been one of those deceptively halcyon days when they started out. Amateurs that they were, they didn't think to check the weather reports, though one might have thought that the doctor's rheumatics would have given him a twinge of what was coming. They were still in Chesapeake Bay when the hurricane struck. While far bigger vessels went bottoms up, the *Greyhound* wallowed around in the dark, seeking only to avoid being swamped by the tumultuous waves.

Somehow, Stanley's steering and what Mary later referred to as the luck of fools and amateurs got them through. The family parrot, which they'd brought along to give a Long John Silver touch to the expedition, became terribly seasick but the manuscript of *My Story*, what there was of it at that stage, didn't even get damp around the edges. Mary noted that they burned out a motor in the Delaware River, got stuck on a sandbar off New Jersey, ran out of gas in New London, found Buzzards Bay all right, but wound up somehow in one of the tiny harbors that were considered unnavigable to powerboats.

Somebody or other piloted them safely out of their impossible berth to the modest cottage, and the clan began to gather. Mary drew a gallant picture of the family's soldiering on in the teeth of adversity, grandchildren crowding aboard the *Greyhound* to be taken for rides around the bay, everybody gathering to watch Reyes the cook, a tall, quiet man from the Philippines who was married to Peggy the parlormaid, carving the ham and filling the plates in his tall chef's cap, white coat, and impeccable apron.

During one of these weekends, a daughter-in-law who'd been reading some of the Rinehart books remarked that Mary didn't seem to like women. It's easy to see where she got the idea. A surprising number of the Rinehart novels contain perfectly awful female characters, and the longer Mary wrote, the rottener they got. *The Swimming Pool*, her very last mystery, features a woman who'd have made Medea look like Anne of Green Gables.

A psychologist could draw all sorts of interesting conclusions from this, and no doubt some of them have. What a fellow writer sees is an experienced professional who was also a dramatist of the first water, introducing bitchy wives and rapacious mothers to ginger up her plots and give her feisty young heroines a chance to shine by contrast.

Mary could hardly not have realized while she was writing *My Story* that she herself had been a lifelong role-player, and that she'd always, ever since her childhood playlets, chosen to be the star. This Leonine propensity to shine would inevitably have attracted many people to her, even if she hadn't welcomed their approaches. According to family members still living, Mary also kept in touch with her own relatives, no matter how busy she was. There is an interesting parallel here to Queen Mary of England, writing solicitously and warmly to far-flung relatives even while she was up to her neck in helping King George to rule Britannia's waves.

At this stage, in *My Story*, Mary claimed not to have told anybody what she was working on, or even that she'd gone back to work. Conditions were not just then ideal for dredging up memories. Stanley Junior had left Mary's old friend George Doran, his too-young marriage to Doran's daughter was falling apart. Little George was staying with his grandparents. One afternoon, Grandmary had just finished tucking the baby in for his afternoon nap when a New Bedford taxi rolled into the dooryard. Its passenger was a young man whom Mary immediately recognized as Arthur McKeogh, sent by his boss, Mr. Bigelow of *Good Housekeeping* magazine, to find out whether there was any truth in the rumor that M.R.R. was writing her autobiography. McKeogh had been brash enough to bring a big suitcase and trust that the Rineharts would have a bed for him.

Along with his skill as a cadger of free lodging, McKeogh was an expert nagger and bully. After considerable hounding, he managed to extract from Mary an admission that the rumor was grounded in fact, and even persuaded her to let him read the messy, handwritten first draft of what she'd accomplished so far. This was enough. After spending a day or so picking his way through the scratchings-out and puttings-in, McKeogh wheedled

Mary's promise of first refusal. Ultimately, *Good Housekeeping* would buy the serial rights for $45,000, to the expressed chagrin of the *Saturday Evening Post*.

Once the cat was out of the bag and a contract signed, Mary's reaction was one of relief at having a substantial sale locked up. What with the deepening Depression and her own sense of befuddlement, she had been concerned as to how much longer she'd be able to keep not just the *Greyhound* but the whole Rinehart menage afloat.

Talking with some of her author friends after the crash, Mary had found them all experiencing the same feelings of emptiness and confusion as she was. Since writing fiction in such an atmosphere seemed all but impossible, she'd allowed the *Ladies' Home Journal* to talk her into doing a year's worth of editorials, the first of which appeared in May 1931 under the headline THOUGHTS. The $2,500 that she was getting for each "thought" disturbed her a good deal; with her brain in its current shape, she didn't feel capable of thinking up $2,500 worth of anything. It was a relief—at least she claimed it was—when, in April 1932, the *Journal* felt the fiscal pinch so badly that they lowered her fee to $2,000.

In the meantime, Reyes kept on slicing ham until, in September 1930, Grandmary and "Maje," as his grandchildren had dubbed Major Rinehart, went back to Washington. Here, it was all too easy to notice that Mr. Herbert Hoover's exhortations about prosperity's lurking just around the corner and now being the time to buy were not falling on receptive ears. As yet, the long lines soon to be a familiar sight outside employment offices were not forming; but the freight cars rolling south were loaded with men and boys hoping to find work in a kinder climate.

Mary got the bright idea of offering these no doubt hungry transients meal tickets, to be given out by policemen and redeemed at one or another of a local restaurant chain at her expense. Her noble gesture proved a dud; Mary thought that other charities must be filling the hobos' needs, or else they just weren't getting off the trains in Washington. It doesn't seem to have occurred to her that the transients might be steering clear of cops on general principles, or that the designated restaurants were not eager to encourage an influx of unwashed, unshaven indigents who'd probably scare away their paying customers.

Everybody in the District, it seemed, was walking around with a chip on his shoulder. Political wrangles could suddenly turn into fistfights. Those elegant dinner parties that had laid so many pitfalls for Washington hostesses were no longer being held. Mary missed them; now she had no place to wear that ridiculously expensive diamond necklace her husband thought she should have had more sense than to buy. She never told Stanley that she'd bought it as an act of rebellion against his strenuous efforts to keep some kind of rein on her reckless spending, though he might have guessed.

Anyway, owning the extravagant bauble afforded Mary little real pleasure. It stayed in a bank vault most of the time and was a source of apprehension on those rare occasions when she took it out to wear. Eventually she decided to sell the overelegant bone of contention; but even this became a long, tedious pain in the neck. After hawking her great mistake around for a few years without success, Mary finally got a bid for about a third of what she'd paid, and took it.

Any anxiety over the necklace would have been a mere flea in the mink; Mary's overwhelming concern was Dr. Rinehart. Early in 1931, it became obvious to Mary that her husband's physical condition was worsening to an alarming degree. The coming of spring brought on increasingly acute bouts of pain from his arthritis, the sweltering humidity of a Washington summer would exacerbate other disturbing symptoms that may well have stemmed from his heavy smoking. They decided to rerent the house at Buzzards Bay.

New England's morning fogs and unpredictable east winds were probably not the best medicine. Mary tried to keep her husband comfortable but he battled his infirmities as savagely (her word) as he'd carried on his lifelong guerilla warfare with inanimate objects. Strong men didn't get sick, there was nothing the matter with old S.M. He just wished his wife would quit projecting her nervous fancies on him and go write a book or something.

Stanley did, however, spend an unprecedented amount of time that summer stretched out on the living room couch. He'd take Mary for a short spin in the *Greyhound* or go crabbing with her in the marshes, then he'd struggle back to the house looking gray around the gills and flop down again. For all his bravado, Dr. Rinehart was too astute a physician himself to put up much of an argument when Mary begged him to stop in New York on the way home and get examined by an expert specialist.

The results of this examination were, at the outset, highly reassuring. The boys were there to lend their father moral support, they said there was really no reason for their mother to hang around New York. Mary was willing to leave, she had a "Thought" to write for the *Journal*. Moreover, after all these arid months, she felt the preliminary tingle of a plot coming on. The house in Washington was getting its prefall housecleaning, and Mary no longer had a downtown office to go to. She took a two-room suite at the Homestead in Hot Springs and requested a big desk in her sitting room.

Most people who check in at health resorts are inclined to ask for bridge tables or wheelchairs, so the only generous work space Hot Springs could provide was a nine-foot banqueting board propped up on trestles. That would do. Mary unpacked the necessities: a quart bottle of ink, a stack of yellow paper, and her ever-trusty fountain pen. From out of the mists of time had come floating back to her a cap, an apron, a nurse's uniform, and a name snitched from the redoubtable Pinkerton men.

When Mary filled her fountain pen and took the first virgin sheet from her stack of paper, all she could remember from two short stories she'd written back in 1914 was that Miss Hilda Adams, nicknamed Miss Pinkerton, had been a trained nurse who took private patients with dark, mysterious secrets and worked undercover with an inspector of police. What more did she need? The rest would come.

The way Mary told it, for three weeks she never left those two rooms, eating meals brought up on a tray and admitting a masseuse once a day to rub away the writer's cramp. One of the letters cited by Jan Cohn in *Improbable Fiction* mentions an allusion to shopping for her winter wardrobe, but Mary probably did most of her work in a nightgown and robe. Not getting dressed is a double benefit for a writer; it allows the ideas to flow without such irritating constraints as a tight waistband and also keeps the author from traipsing off on some pretext or other instead of sitting there doggedly dredging up the elusive *mot juste* and getting it down on paper before the slippery syllables slither away.

At the end of her three-week stay, Mary staggered forth wan and trembling, on the brink of a nervous collapse, a poor advertisement for a spa but a triumphant author. She'd achieved her "Thought" and would carry back to Washington a complete first draft of *Miss Pinkerton*. There was life in the old brain yet, the creative spark could still be fanned, prosperity had crept a step or two closer to the corner. In 1932, *Miss Pinkerton* earned $50,000 from the *Saturday Evening Post* for the serial rights, $30,000 from Warner Brothers for a film starring Joan Blondell and George Brent, and provided Mary's publisher sons with a golden opportunity to cash in on their mother's unorthodox rest cure.

CHAPTER 32

Crossing the Great Divide

Preparing *Miss Pinkerton* for publication took longer than Mary had expected. She'd hoped the *Post* might pay her as much as $30,000 for a novella; the $50,000 they actually paid meant having to expand her original draft to full book length. That was fine with the author; doing the extra work helped to keep her mind off the country's steadily worsening economic situation and her husband's noticeably failing health. The dauntless doctor was still not willing to give in, however; he insisted on traveling by himself to the West Coast. Alan was working as a scriptwriter for Paramount; Stanley wanted to visit him, Gratia, and their two daughters before Christmas.

Mary was heartened by her husband's show of enterprise; she was still trying to convince herself that his illness stemmed in part from financial worries. In 1929 he had insisted on using his personal savings to cover his wife's market losses, for which he'd somewhat quixotically felt himself responsible. Mary decided that her Christmas gift to him would be enough money to cover his own stocks. She thought a dose of prosperity might be Stanley's best medicine, that and a little quiet cheerfulness in the Musgrove family manner as described by Jane Austen.

Back from his visit to sunny California (as it was then), Stanley felt well enough to escort his wife to Vice President Charles Curtis's dinner for President and Mrs. Hoover. Mary served as one of Lou Hoover's ladies-in-waiting at a Christmas tea. The Rineharts gave a tea of their own. In a letter to his son, Stanley was feeling merry enough to explain that "tea" was poetic license for more potent beverages.

Alan and Gratia didn't come east for the holidays, but Stanley Junior was there on Christmas Day with Bab and George. So were Ted and his beautiful Betty, the only one of the three boys' original wives who would not only stay married to a Rinehart but outlive her husband by a good many years. Mary had arranged a surprise for the major: a portable bar that could fold up to look like a small table. While the rest were at Christmas-morning breakfast, Stanley Junior and Ted were to sneak into the music room and set up the bar beside the tree, with the proper accoutrements. After breakfast, when it was time to open presents, the Head would find Reyes there in his white coat, shaking up some poetic license behind the bar.

The holiday revels seem to have done Dr. Rinehart some good. He was said by the family doctor to be showing improvement but given the usual caution to take it easy. The younger Stanley had already set up a trip with his father to the Florida Keys, for some fishing. Mary found this situation heartening enough to pack her own bags for a visit to Alan after the holidays. On the day when she was to catch her train for Hollywood, Stanley's doctor confessed to her that there was no hope of a recovery. The only advice he could give was to keep Dr. Rinehart from finding out that his illness was terminal and to go on with the scheduled plans as if there were nothing wrong.

Stanley Marshall Rinehart was nobody's fool and certainly no coward. More than likely, that Washington doctor was only telling Mary what her husband had known all along. Mary wrote in *My Story* that Stanley himself had driven her to the station, that being away from him had been a nightmare, and that she'd cut her visit to Alan and his family as short as she'd dared. Stanley was home before her; whether it was his Florida tan or her own wishful thinking, Mary decided he looked a little better. Why shouldn't they two go back to Florida and fish some more?

By late April, Mary had to face the fact that not even fishing was doing her husband any good. All his doctors could suggest now was a trip to Baden-Baden; the German spa and the German physicians might somehow be efficacious in alleviating his symptoms. Of course Stanley could not go alone, nor could Mary have borne to be parted from him. She canceled her contract with the *Ladies' Home Journal* and packed their steamer trunks.

The voyage over was hell. Most of the time, Stanley lay in a coma, and Mary thought he was going to die. By the time they reached Germany he'd dropped twenty-five pounds and couldn't even sit up in bed. They had to stop in Heidelberg for a week or so before he was able to go on to Baden-Baden. There, they naturally got an encouraging prognosis. If the *Herr Doktor* could go and live in a hot, dry climate like Egypt's, his life might be prolonged for many good years. For the present, he must stay in bed and take his medicine.

After several weeks, Stanley had gained back a little of his strength but was still having those disturbing attacks. While some of these were from his ailments, Mary suspected that others might be caused by the medication he was getting. There was nothing she could do, though, but sit around lending moral support and getting fat on German cooking. By June, Stanley was well enough to write home one of his typically humorous letters about Mary's strange relationship with the German language. According to him, she invented her words as she went along and conveyed their meanings by some kind of telepathy which everybody but himself understood perfectly well.

The Rineharts got back to the States on July sixth. Stanley was checked over by his own doctors, then it was on to the Adirondacks, where their sons had rented cottages for the family and hired a nurse to take the burden of caring for their father off Mary's shoulders. That nurse lasted four days. The one who replaced her endured the doctor's operating-room manner for almost a full week, perhaps because each of his attacks left him a little bit weaker than the one before. Mary kept trying to persuade herself that he was rallying.

On the last day of July, Stanley had to be taken to a Utica hospital. The doctor who examined him described his condition as "not so good." By the fourth of August it was critical, but on the eighth the patient was able to endure a journey back to Washington in a hired private railroad car, his wife and sons all with him.

The press was covering the story, of course. The family doctor told reporters that Dr. Rinehart was on his way to recovery. But the end was not far off; Mary knew, and so did her husband. They were back to running on bluff, Mary wiping away the tears and pasting on a smile when she went to Stanley, he pretending not to notice her reddened eyelids. It was an up-and-down situation. Sometimes Stanley would feel well enough to go out with Mary, other days he couldn't even drag himself out of bed. Only his spirit held up; after the act of writing had become too much for him, he could still dictate a letter in his old humorous style. There was no need to waste sympathy on the old man, he declared. He'd just got back from an enjoyable car ride, now he was in his easy chair reading a book and sipping a citrate of potash cocktail.

Stanley Rinehart was probably past worrying about himself by this time, but he did frequently express his concern for Mary. He had hoped to leave her well fixed enough so that she wouldn't have to keep on writing, but the stock market's failure meant things weren't going to work out that way. She told him money didn't matter, all that counted was that they still had each other.

But not for long. On the night of October 28, 1932, with his three tall sons standing over him and his wife of thirty-six years praying that his appalling struggles for breath might cease and deliver him from this final agony, Stanley Marshall Rinehart died. Hours later, Mary went into the room where her husband's body still lay. As she had done so many times before, she sat down beside him and took his cold, still hand in hers. It was not until the stillness and coldness penetrated her consciousness that she fully realized she was a widow.

Only someone who has gone through the experience of losing a long-cherished partner can understand how it feels to have half of one's inner self torn away, to be experiencing at the same time a kind of personal death and a stinging resentment at finding oneself left alive, alone.

Or perhaps not entirely alone?

Mary had often insisted that she had no confidence in spiritualists' claims about being able to make contact with loved ones who have passed beyond the veil. Stanley had been less dogmatic, the last book he'd been well enough to read was F.W.H. Myers's ponderous but intriguing work, *Human Personality and Its Survival of Bodily Death*. For years, he and Mary had been curious enough about psychic phenomena to have made some explorations in the field. They had come to the conclusion that most mediums were blatant phonies. Nevertheless, they had made a pact that whichever of them lived the longer would try to get in touch with the one who died first.

A promise was a promise; Mary could not but try. What happened was not what she'd expected. The medium was a nice young married woman, the venue a hotel room that contained nothing except two straight chairs, a table, and a stand in the corner with a vase of flowers on it. The floor was bare, the door was locked. After Mary had searched the room, the shades were drawn and the two women sat down face-to-face. Mary knew the protocol. She clasped the medium's hands and gripped the knees tightly between her own to prevent any tricks from being played.

The medium did not go into a trance. There was no moaning or thrashing about. She just sat there. Mary felt a hand on top of her head, the medium told her not to worry, just to sit still. The unseen hand moved down to touch Mary's wedding ring, then she felt two small hands on her own and told the medium, who suggested she speak to the presence. Quite calmly, Mary asked the darkness if this was who she hoped it was, and whether the entity knew what she'd brought with her. She was shocked to feel a hand, if it was a hand, thrust itself forcibly down the open neck of her dress and shake the object that she'd pinned to her underwear. The object was the little caduceus, insignia of the Army Medical Corps, that Major Rinehart had worn pinned to his uniform collar.

Mary's reaction was to clutch the medium's hands and knees even tighter, the woman asked her if anything had happened. Mary said yes, the medium expressed her satisfaction that they were having a productive sitting. Next, Mary exclaimed that she could hear something rustling the flowers on the stand. The medium said casually that it was probably invisible birds. They tended to fly in from the astral plane, she didn't know why. Seconds later, Mary felt something being dropped down her dress front and landing beside Stanley's caduceus; it was a rosebud from the bouquet across the room. Nonbeliever though she was, Mary would carry that withered bud for years in the back of her prayer book.

Having honored her vow, Mary made no further attempt. Still, the matter was not allowed to rest. A couple of years later, when she was living in New York, Mary invited the well-known English medium Eileen Garrett to tea. Mrs. Garrett surprised her hostess by saying that she herself was skeptical about conscious survival after death although, like Mary, she did believe in poltergeists. While the two women were chatting, Mary's three sons dropped in, as they'd got in the habit of doing after work. Once the men were settled, Mrs. Garrett pulled another surprise. She set down her teacup, murmured that she might as well try for what she could get, leaned back in her chair, and fell into a trance.

None of the Rineharts was much impressed by hearing the stereotypical babble from some alleged control with a hokey foreign accent. But now came the shocker. As the onlookers gaped in total bemusement, they heard Stanley Marshall Rinehart's familiar dry chuckle, saw the medium aping his mannerisms, and listened to his voice. He told Mary, "I didn't realize what had happened to me until you came in that night and sat down on the edge of the bed and took my hand."

Mary insisted in her autobiography that she had never told

anybody about that last time, in the dead of night, when she had sat alone with her husband's cooling body and faced the fact that their life together was over. At the time of Mrs. Garrett's demonstration, Mary had been willing to believe that she'd seen a genuine breakthrough. As time passed, credulity waned; but even as one doubted, one could always hope.

Major Rinehart had been given a full-dress military funeral and interment at Arlington National Cemetery. For the time being, Mary stayed on in the big Washington house, trying to adjust to being alone. She was not in total solitude, of course. There were Miguel the chauffeur, Peggy the parlormaid, Reyes the cook, all getting on in years, none of them likely to find new jobs in this straitened economy. How could she turn them away? Reyes was a problem, though. He had always regarded Dr. Rinehart as his employer. Having to take orders from a woman was a big adjustment, and not an easy one for him to make.

After Stanley's accident, the Rineharts had got rid of their saddle horses. During that first period of readjustment, Mary also sold the *Greyhound*. She got far less than her husband had paid for it but at least she wouldn't have to cope with the awful nuisance that a boat can be. As for the house, she'd worry about that later.

A presidential election in the midst of economic disaster was a distraction, and the boys did their best to keep their mother in good spirits. After New Year's 1933, Ted took Mary to Florida for a much-needed break. They were in Palm Beach, sitting on a hotel veranda after a luxurious meal among well-dressed fellow sufferers from the Depression when their newly inaugurated president's voice came over the radio.

There was nothing to fear, Franklin D. Roosevelt told them, except fear itself. Staunch Republican though she was, the widow felt a sense of relief. Life was going to be worth living, after all. There was still hope for the country, for her sons' business future, for everybody's future, even her own. But she, who had been on visiting terms with three previous presidents, would not be dining again at the White House.

Nor was Mary overcome with joy by Roosevelt's New Deal. She did not believe in what she saw as governmental handouts.

Her stern old Covenanter faith called for personal initiative, hard work, thrift (even, presumably, among those who could afford diamond necklaces and twenty-two-room mansions on Massachusetts Avenue), and what she saw generally as the old-fashioned virtues. She could not but have felt a certain incongruity among her ideas. She quoted in *My Story* a line of George Eliot's: "Mine, I fear, is not a well-regulated mind. It has an occasional tenderness for old abuses."

Come summer, Mary went back to Eaton's ranch. The visit was not a success. Though everybody was kind and sociable as always, being there by herself made her even more keenly aware of her widowhood. Now she had nobody to whom she was the most important woman in the world. Riding her horse without Stanley by her side was no fun at all. She felt tired all the time, just the short climb from her cabin to the corral left her gasping for breath. In *Professor at the Breakfast Table* Oliver Wendell Holmes remarked that he'd "died out" of his former lodgings; after so many happy visits, Mary was dying away from Eaton's ranch. She would not be taking the out trail again.

CHAPTER 33

Moving On

Before going west, Mary had written an article for the *Post* about a possible new approach to an age-old social problem. "Can Women Stop Crime?" brought amazing results. When she got back from that painful last visit to the ranch, she found a great heap of letters pressing her to mobilize a countrywide army of female crimebusters.

In those pre-TV days, the newsreel, along with the double feature and the "Previews of Coming Attractions," was an integral part of every movie show. "The Eyes and Ears of the World" came and shot some footage of Mrs. Rinehart trying to explain that she hadn't meant for women to become vigilantes but just to support and assist the efforts of the police. As a result of this useful publicity, Roosevelt's new attorney general asked her to serve as a member—typically, the only woman member—of a committee on crime. According to her, the group never did much except hold a general meeting for an international group of police chiefs and other interested persons. It did, however, mellow Mrs. Rinehart's attitude toward F.D.R. as she sat on the platform watching the new president's slow, painful, but determined struggle to reach the podium on his polio-weakened legs.

During that winter of 1933–34, Mary continued to find work her most effective therapy. She finished another mystery novel for the boys. *The Album* takes place in a heavily cushioned enclave of old houses inhabited by well-off people who have known each other too long and too well; where neither their attitudes, their habits, nor the cut of their clothes have had room to move with the times; and where a good-looking young woman could wither on the vine like some of her neighbors, unless a particularly gory murder should become, by a freak, her way to liberation.

Shortly after *The Album* had gone off to the publishers, Mary herself almost reached the end of the road. One night while she was sitting alone, reading, she was seized by a violent pain in the chest, accompanied by an icy chill. She struggled to her room, collapsed on the bed, and passed out.

Now comes the eerie part. After his father's death, Alan had moved his family to Washington. Their home was four long blocks from Mary's. At one o'clock in the morning, something impelled him to get up, go out, and walk to his mother's house. He had a key, he let himself in. He climbed the stairs to her bedroom, found her unconscious with hardly a thread of pulse, and sent for an ambulance. Sometime later, Mary opened her eyes to an anxious audience of doctors, nurses, and a haggard, exhausted son who, by heeding some inexplicable inner warning, had saved his mother's life.

The revelation that she had a damaged heart and was likely to suffer further attacks, as in fact she would do during the rest of her life, meant more changes in Mary's lifestyle but was not allowed to interfere with her writing. She wrote much of *The State vs. Elinor Norton* sitting up in bed. This book is less a mystery than a straight novel with a wide streak of melodrama; Jan Cohn appraises it as showing strong influences of both *This Strange Adventure* and *Lost Ecstasy*, which it certainly does. Like *The Album, Elinor Norton* got fine reviews, although William Rose Benét did mention some problems. He may have been referring to the somewhat too *parfitly gentil* narrator, or to the strange discrepancy between Elinor's letting herself drift into a stupid marriage with a man she didn't much like and then showing such rigid determination to stick by him after he'd proven himself altogether unworthy of her misplaced devotion.

Anyway, the book's gloomily perfervid atmosphere was the sort of writing that gets a novel hailed as "a definite contribution to serious American literature." *The State vs. Elinor Norton* netted the writer $45,000 from *Ladies' Home Journal* for the serial rights, $20,000 from Fox Films and, presumably, some healthy royalties from Farrar & Rinehart. *The Album*, more ably crafted and ringing a dramatic change on the Lizzie Borden legend, had fetched $60,000 from the *Post* for the serial rights and $20,000 from Fox, plus the hardcover sales. Whatever new trials might beleaguer Mary Roberts Rinehart, it didn't look as if penury was going to be one of them.

In the spring of 1934, Mary noticed that her hair was beginning to turn gray. Since she was within a few months of her fifty-eighth birthday, the only remarkable thing about the grizzling was that it hadn't happened sooner. She saw little use in touching it up; there was no point in trying to look young now that her grandchildren were growing up.

As to the kind of world they would live in, Grandmary was both curious and apprehensive. While the Depression had damped down the more spectacular cavortings of the jazz babies whom John Held caricatured with such wry affection and such consummate skill, it had by no means thrust them back into their grandmothers' high-buttoned boots and whaleboned corsets. A parody on a popular ballad of the thirties wrapped up the situation in ¾ time: the sweetheart of Sigma Chi was no longer a blonde but a fiery redhead. She imbibed strong waters, she inhaled the seductive fumes of tobacco, she told risqué stories in mixed company. For all her despairing serenader knew, his wayward dream girl might be dossing down with the whole fraternity, one for each night of the week.

Henry Goddard Leach of *The Forum* gave a dinner followed by a Socratic dialogue in which Mary took part along with Margaret Calkins Banning, Ruth Hale, and a few other prominent women. The subject was supposed to be Modern Marriage; it wound up in a gentle mass headshaking over the ladies' inescapable consensus that chastity before marriage was no longer a *sine qua non* for the younger generation. They attributed the change to a general breakdown of American morals brought on by the war, a lack of parental supervision, the decline in regular churchgoing, and, by inference, too much petting in rumble seats.

Mary wrote up their findings in an article for *The Forum* after she'd done some further research among her sons and their friends. One young fellow told her it seemed to him that girls had climbed down off the pedestal to join the postwar whoop-up and their younger sisters had followed their example. He thought a good many men would like to put their sweethearts back on the pedestal, but the girls didn't want to go.

Mary didn't believe for one second that any intelligent young woman of the thirties would allow herself to be shoved back into the straitjacketed life that Mamie Roberts had endured as a girl, but she was not ready to stand up and cheer for premarital sex. She referred to the concept of virginity among the unmarried as having suffered a blow and getting worse. Little did she reck that she would soon be paying a short visit to a country where, since the Bolshevik Revolution, social morality as formerly known had been kicked out the window, where churchgoing was officially frowned upon, and where getting divorced was often easier than getting married.

Her family, anxious for her welfare, had arranged a North Cape cruise. Mary would travel with a nurse-companion and theoretically would spend the time while at sea resting in her stateroom. Great was Mary's surprise when she found out that she was traveling with the Hope diamond. Living in Washington all those years, she'd got to know Evalyn Walsh McLean very well. A notorious lump of blue carbon with a curse on it was perhaps not quite the thing to take on a Nordic cruise, but that wouldn't have bothered Evalyn Walsh McLean. She always wore her diamond, though she never let anybody else touch it for fear some of the curse might rub off on the toucher. As for herself, her eldest son had been killed by a car, her husband was in a mental hospital, her daughter had committed suicide while still in her twenties. With such tragedies already borne, why should she worry about another?

Mrs. McLean was wearing the fateful necklace on the day she and Mary went fishing in Iceland. Seals bobbed around their little skiff like water spaniels, perfectly friendly and not at all inclined to upset the boat. Even in Moscow nothing awful happened, although Mary did have an exasperating time before she was allowed to go there.

At Stockholm, two agents of what was then the USSR boarded the steamer to check out the passengers. They knew who Mary Roberts Rinehart was, why had she come? Was she planning to write about their country? Would they get to see what she wrote? They kept coming back to ask the same questions, she could only give them the same answer. She would be in Moscow for only a few days, she had no idea whether she would write or not, she didn't know whether she'd find anything to write about during so short a stay. Eventually they allowed her to go ashore in Moscow, although they did require some of the other passengers, including a British army officer and his wife, to stay aboard while the ship was in port.

The stay-aboards didn't miss much, from Mary's point of view. She saw poverty and neglect everywhere, although attempts were made to impress the tourists with the progress that had been made under seventeen years of Communist government. They were met by a fleet of Lincoln cars. Mary found out from American newsmen that these cars were owned by the Kremlin and were, except for the journalists' few battered jalopies, the only automobiles in the USSR's capital city. At the hotel she was given a two-room suite. The bath didn't work, but that may have been on account of some cantrip emanation from her friend's malevolently inclined diamond.

She and the other tourists were well fed. From the way their Russian guides, all young women, tore into the food, however, it was obvious that Muscovites weren't faring so well at home. Mary's guide, a professor's wife, was paid 400 rubles a month. A ruble was worth about 2½ cents American; a cup of coffee cost eight rubles. The guide was allowed to buy material for only two dresses a year, one for winter, one for summer. She coveted Mrs. Rinehart's brightly colored silk scarf.

Mary didn't want to part with her scarf, as she'd only brought the one. She offered money instead, but her guide was afraid to take it. Receiving American dollars smacked too much of being hired as a spy and executions were all too frequent under Stalin's paranoid regime. Eventually the two women slipped off behind a wall. Mary gave the girl what at home would have been considered a generous tip. There, it amounted to almost a year's pay. Whether her guide got to keep the money, Mary never knew.

At least the sea voyage had shaken her out of the rut she'd been digging for herself. Mary began to think seriously of pulling up stakes. The Washington she'd known was gone, so were many of her old acquaintances. The New Deal had its good points, but it was attracting too many radical progressives (i.e. Democrats) for her staunch Republican taste. Mostly, though, she was just plain lonesome. In 1935 she moved to an apartment in New York.

This was the sensible thing to do. Mary would be close to her sons and their families. Living on one floor—a very spacious floor—would save wear and tear on her heart. She'd be rid of the many responsibilities that went with owning a big house. House lover that she was, however, Mary found it heartbreaking to sort over the accumulations of her life with Stanley and their sons. She had trouble deciding what to take, what to pass on to the boys, what to sell, what to dump.

One of the things she vowed to dump were any further invitations to speak in public. Never again, Mary vowed, would she face another insipid fruit cocktail, another rubber chicken, another dab of half-melted ice cream, another chairman of another meeting rising to introduce the distinguished author. It was high time for newer, younger, less incipiently shaky voices to be heard; she'd said enough.

The mail, of course, was a different matter. Mary still carried on the routine that she and her then secretary had developed back in that black-painted X-ray room across from her husband's office in Pittsburgh. Her last and longest-employed secretary, however, was a man. Amiable, efficient Bill Sladen would be Mary's faithful assistant for the last thirty years of her life. An entire day out of every week was devoted to whatever the postman brought; they never knew what would turn up. All except the crank letters got answered, but sometimes it was hard to tell which were the cranks. One polite answer to a sensible, courteous letter brought a second missive announcing that the writer had decided to kill Mrs. Rinehart so that she and he could occupy the center of space together.

This one was promptly handed over to the postal inspectors. Investigation revealed that Mrs. Rinehart's correspondent was a well-known lawyer with a brilliant mind and a happy family. His only problem was an occasional brief attack of homicidal mania. After some such prank as boarding a train, snatching up a knife from the dining car, and chasing a railroad porter down the aisle, the lawyer would be tucked away in an institution for a while. Once boredom set in, he would employ his legalistic skills to argue himself free, and invariably won his case. Since Mary never heard from the lawyer again, she concluded that he hadn't really meant it about the center of space.

Had she in fact been transported there, she might not have felt much more disoriented than she did in her new Gotham flat. From 1908 to 1923, Mary Roberts Rinehart had been familiar with Broadway and the theater district, but she hadn't written anything for the stage since those mostly wasted three years in Hollywood when she'd discovered that all she had to do was sign over the film rights to her latest novel and wait for the check to come in. By now, the movies had taken a heavy toll from the legitimate stage. Not only a number of writers but also some of the actors whom she'd known had migrated to the West Coast.

What with her husband's practice, the family, and her incredible work schedule, Mary had never found time to make many acquaintances among writers. Now that she was linked through her sons with a publishing house, she began to meet some of the authors whose work they were handling: fascinating people like Hervey Allen, Stephen Vincent Benét, and the acerbic Philip Wylie. What intrigued her was that they all loved to talk about almost anything, except their writing.

By late spring of 1935, Mary was fairly well settled into her new apartment. Even the pool table was set up and ready for business. She was not, however, intending to spend the summer in New York. At the time she'd decided to move, she'd been about halfway through a straight novel called, for reasons not hard to fathom, *The Doctor*. She planned to finish it during the summer and could think of no pleasanter place to do so than Bar Harbor, Maine, where she would find a number of people whom she knew.

Forbidden to climb stairs because of her heart trouble, Mary booked one of the little cabins attached to a hotel. Finding it too small to work in, she arranged for the use of a big circular table in one of the rooms off the lobby. The heavy plush furniture, dating back to the time when she and Dr. Rinehart had both been young and single, helped her to recall those days at the Homeopathic. She didn't know how much of what she remembered would get into the book, but at least straight novels were relatively easy to write. Those mysteries that her readers liked so well were the very devil, requiring so much more in the way of setting and character development and action, plus all that convoluted plotting and detecting and tying up of loose ends.

These days, Mary was in no shape for one of those marathon bursts during which she'd been wont to toss off a book in a few weeks. *The Doctor* didn't get finished until she'd gone back to New York. By then, the boys were insisting that their mother take a winter vacation at the resort in Florida where she and Dr. Rinehart used to go tarpon-fishing. In *My Story*, Mary drew a nostalgic picture of the palm trees along the shore, the huge turtles swimming past the boat, the thrill of that breath-stopping jerk when the huge fish struck at her hook and only the fact that she was strapped into a chair bolted to the deck kept the ardent fisherwoman from being dragged overboard.

Mary wouldn't get in much fishing this time. During her Florida stay, she discovered a small lump in her breast. Stanley and his second wife, Fay, were with her; they tried to persuade her that it was nothing to worry about. But it was. Mary checked into the hospital carrying a bottle of ink, some yellow paper, a board to write on, and two-thirds of a short story that she was planning to call *The Man Who Killed His Wife*. At eleven o'clock that night, she gave her son the finished manuscript to be typed. By the time Stanley got home, she was on the phone wanting to dictate a change in the final paragraph.

The operation was successful. The tumor had been discovered in time. Mary was now cancer-free and would remain so. Moreover, she would excise yet another shibboleth by writing for the *Ladies' Home Journal* an accurate account of her personal experience. Until Mary Roberts Rinehart broke the silence, breast cancer had been one of those unpleasant things that were simply not mentioned in print, notwithstanding the huge numbers of women who died from the disease every year. Mary hoped that, by sharing her experience, she might be of some service to other women who were either facing or fearing that same appalling ordeal.

She'd done the right thing. Her editors reported that no previous article ever published in the *Journal* had generated so overwhelming a public reaction. The Women's Art and Industries Exposition awarded Mrs. Rinehart a medal for her inestimable service in daring to cast light on a dark area where mistaken prudery had put so many human lives in jeopardy. This would not have been a bad way to wind up a distinguished career, but Mary had no notion of quitting yet. Radical surgery, a permanently impaired heart, the silent agonies of widowhood might make life more difficult, but to her they afforded no legitimate excuse for a working woman to quit her job.

CHAPTER 34

A Story Without an End

Another thing that Mary wasn't giving up was her long-ingrained urge to get out of town for the summer. She liked Bar Harbor, perhaps because in some ways it reminded her of the old days in Sewickley. Here too, in the summer colony at least, was a rather select enclave of comfortably well-to-do people who golfed, sailed, danced at the club, entertained quietly among themselves, and no doubt spent some of their abundant leisure dipping into the novels of Mary Roberts Rinehart to ascertain whether she was the sort of writer whom one might safely ask over for a rubber of bridge.

In 1936, instead of going back to the hotel, Mary rented a house and took her household staff with her. In *My Story* she let the reader know that Bar Harbor had never been the millionaires' paradise it was reputed to be. She cited a camera crew from *Life* magazine who'd come up to do a photographic essay on the town's great mansions and gone back to New York empty-handed and disgusted because they couldn't find any mansions to photograph.

There were, however, big houses, most of them wooden arks still furnished with odds and ends from before the turn of the century. A fair number were up for sale, their owners having been caught in the Crash. It need hardly be said that Mary fell in love with one of these great inflammables, bought it for a relative song, took a closer look at the amount of work her new house was going to need, and realized a little too late that she'd let herself in for a replay of the Bluff.

No matter, she had a house of her own again. Mrs. Rinehart was recognized by her neighbors as a respectable property owner instead of as a mere celebrity. Henceforth she would take umbrage at hearing the tour guide on the sight-seeing boat announce to its passengers that the next house they'd be passing was that of the famous Mary Roberts Rinehart.

This was only umbrage on a small scale, compared to a 1937 event that not only stirred her novelist's heart but roused her Anglophile's ire. Edward VIII, the still-uncrowned king who had succeeded to the throne on the death of George V in 1936, had, as one particularly unkind critic put it, abandoned his captaincy of the British Ship of State to become third mate of an American tramp. Some found the situation romantic but, generally speaking, Britons were not enslaved by the twice-divorced Mrs. Wallis Warfield Spenser Simpson, an American and, of course, a commoner.

As his father had done before him, the second son had to take over the rulership to which his elder brother had been destined, and would make a cracking good job of it. Mary could never have stayed away from such a spectacle as the Coronation. She had plenty to say about it afterward but her report of the event in her autobiography never once alluded to either King George VI or his lovely and wholly suitable consort, the former Lady Elizabeth Bowes-Lyon.

Mary did mention her delight at seeing Queen Mother Mary wearing the same jewels that were shown in the photograph she had received from Her Majesty after that never-to-be-forgotten visit to Saint James's Palace during World War I. Now another war was looming. This was no time for the head of an empire to have backed away from his hereditary responsibilities even if Edward VIII was small, unimpressive, and had shown no sign that he might be capable of leading a great people through a cataclysm such as the next war inevitably would be.

As for her own family, Mary could not feel the same anguish that had racked her when Stanley Junior and Alan had gone overseas. Her sons were too old for this one, her grandsons still too young. Heart trouble would bar Mary herself from taking any active role. Now that she had another white elephant to feed, she would have to keep her nose to the grindstone, hardly a graceful posture for the grande dame she had by now become.

Mary's grandson George, whose German nanny had been such a martinet when he was a baby and was by this time probably holding down a fairly important job in the Third Reich, remembers his Grandmary queening it at Bar Harbor in flowing chiffons and picture hats. Dr. Howard Gottlieb, curator of special collections for Boston University, recalls going downtown with his own grandmother, a long-time Bar Harbor resident, and seeing her mouth silently form the words "that's Mrs. Rinehart" when a lady majestic as a square-rigger with all sails set glided by, perhaps on her way to buy another bottle of ink.

The Wall, which Mary considered one of her best mysteries, came out in 1938, the year she'd bought her last house. The *Saturday Evening Post* must have agreed with her appraisal of the work, for they paid $65,000, the highest amount she appears ever to have received for serial rights. No doubt she found plenty of places to put the money. In 1939 she was able to move into her new house. Here was no longer a dusty relic of a former time but a spacious, airy blending of light pastel walls and pale carpets in blue, platinum, or white, accented by splashy floral printed slipcovers on the furniture.

Mary must have had little time for writing that year; she published only one piece, for which she got $1,500 from the *Post*. Its title was "Writing Is Work," a statement to which all professional writers wholeheartedly subscribe and which no layman ever believes for a minute. The article also came out that same year in a nicely bound hardcover edition from The Writer, the Boston company that still publishes the magazine of that name along with a good many other works.

Mary was particularly eloquent on the subject of the mystery, which she rightly considered the hardest kind of novel to write well and which was until recently the least apt to be regarded as anything more than a few hours' worth of mental relaxation. As readers have become more discerning, the mystery novel has come to dominate the fiction market. Those authors whom Mary Roberts Rinehart helped to educate in producing the traditional novel of manners with criminous overtones and a satisfying denouement do not always capture the limelight, but they continue to outsell the rest of the field by an impressive margin. Among the steady sellers is Mary Roberts Rinehart. Her early hardcovers are still being snatched up by Rinehart afficionados and collectors, her latest paperback reprints leaving the bookshops in the hands of yet another generation of Rinehart readers.

The same cannot be said of Mary's straight novels, or for most other straight novels of yesteryear, including erstwhile best-sellers (though the story goes that one bookseller many years ago was able to unload his dusty overstock of *David Harum* by advertising it as *David's Harem*). What is special about the Rinehart novels is that they were written over a span of half a century by an indefatigable wordsmith who could catch the tempo and flavor of life as it was happening; who had the ability to meld what she saw and felt and imagined into stories that pinned down with sometimes painful accuracy the moods, the mores, the essence of each generation as it passed. The pieces Mary Roberts Rinehart wrote, always in a rush, dipping her fountain pen in the inkwell because its tiny reservoir couldn't keep the flow coming fast enough for all the words she must put down before they got away, are now fertile browsing grounds for cultural anthropologists as well as for readers with nostalgic yearnings who like to treasure hunt in old libraries and secondhand bookshops.

By her own standards, Mary was slowing down. Many writers today would be more than satisfied to equal her 1940 output of four short pieces and a full-length mystery, *The Great Mistake*. Within the first half of that decade, Rinehart & Company published three more new mysteries: *Haunted Lady, Episode of the*

Wandering Knife, and *The Yellow Room*, as well as two short-story collections. 1946 left a blank in her bibliography, 1947 shows just one article, but that was the precedent-shattering "I Had Cancer."

The year 1947 brought another momentous happening. As has been mentioned, Reyes the cook had always deemed Dr. Rinehart his employer. After the doctor's death, Reyes had quietly appointed himself major domo. He ruled the domestic staff. He couldn't prevent Mrs. Rinehart from hiring a new butler now and then, but he could quickly get rid of any butler she hired. They hadn't had one for a long time, but that year the servant problem was desperate. Mary could not find a maid willing to come to Bar Harbor and work in so big a house, so she was virtually forced to hire a butler. As she'd expected, Reyes took her decision badly. Three weeks after the new man arrived, he gave her his notice.

He'd done this on a few previous occasions during his twenty-five years of service with the Rineharts but he'd always changed his mind by the following morning. This time, however, Reyes showed no sign of relenting. He took Mary's morning orders and her marketing list and drove into town. After he'd left, Mary found his wife, Peggy, the maid, crying in the kitchen. They'd had a bad fight, Peggy confessed. Reyes had been drinking, he was determined to quit. Peggy had been equally adamant that she wouldn't go with him.

He came back with the supplies and started preparing lunch as usual. Mary was in the library, reading. All of a sudden Reyes walked in, without the white coat that he had always been punctilious about wearing in his employer's presence. He came straight up to Mary, whipped a revolver out of his trousers pocket, and pointed it at her face.

She saw him pull the trigger. The gun misfired. To her astonishment, she was still alive. As he tried again, Mary leaped from her chair, pushed him away, and ran for her life through the living room, the dining room, into the kitchen with Reyes at her heels, totally out of his mind. Fortunately both Peggy and Ted, the chauffeur, were there. As Ted knocked Reyes down, Peggy collared the gun, handed it to Ted, then ran to get Mary a nitroglycerine tablet. The new butler, thinking that he himself was Reyes's intended victim, had already run down the drive and hailed a passing car to bring help.

Mary gulped her tablet, got her breath back, and headed back to the library to phone for the police. As she passed the front door, a tall boy whom she'd never seen before took off his cap and told her he'd come to apply for a job as undergardener. Always the lady, Mary explained that he'd have to come back later; at the moment, somebody was trying to murder her. Not surprisingly, the applicant never returned.

But Reyes did. As Mary was telephoning, she heard Peggy scream and wheeled to see the cook bearing down on her, brandishing a carving knife in each hand. Both the chauffeur and the gardener came pounding after him. As the two men knocked him down and struggled to secure his hands, getting slashed badly by the crazily flailing knives, a uniformed policeman burst in. Reyes got up from the floor and went meekly along with him. That night in the jail, Mary's long-time cook committed suicide. It was a relief to her and Peggy when the local Catholic priest, realizing that Reyes had been of unsound mind when he took his own life, allowed him to be buried in consecrated ground.

The summer of 1947 was unusually hot and dry. In October, after Mary had gone back to her New York apartment, a forest fire broke out of control. Fanned by a gale wind, it headed straight toward Bar Harbor's summer colony. For Bar Harbor, this was the end of an era. For Mary Roberts Rinehart, losing the house that she'd enjoyed for so brief a span was a bleak awakening from yet another dream.

It was not, however, the finish of her career. In 1948 came another straight novel. Mary dubbed it *A Light in the Window* and sold the serial rights to *Ladies' Home Journal* for $50,000. The Rinehart boys published both the novel and their mother's updated version of *My Story* in 1948. Two short stories for the *Post* and one for *Cosmopolitan* netted the author another $18,000, an article for *Town and Country* brought $300 and no doubt a certain cachet, not that the regal Mrs. Rinehart needed another touch of class.

And still she wrote; a few more short pieces, then, in 1952,

The Swimming Pool, one of the best mystery novels she'd ever written. A novelette, *The Frightened Wife*, appeared as a serial for the *Post* on Valentine's Day 1953, and became the lead story in another Rinehart collection.

That year Mary did a couple of pieces for *Collier's* magazine, but the old writing machine was at last running down. In 1954, the woman who had been the highest-paid author in the United States and perhaps in the entire world earned just $400, for a short story titled "The Splinter" that ran in *Ellery Queen's Mystery Magazine*.

Even then, she was not quite through. During her few remaining years, Mary worked when she felt able on a private memoir for her children and grandchildren. It contains no startling revelations but does present a franker, more vivid picture of her life as a child, a student nurse, a young wife and mother than some of the blander, rosier descriptions she'd given in *My Story*. The holograph manuscript is among the Rinehart archives at the University of Pittsburgh and it is from these largely handwritten pages that much of the earlier section of this biography has been derived.

Mary's granddaughter Connie, Mrs. B. Albert Burton, recalls Grandmary in her final years, sitting cross-legged on her bed working jigsaw puzzles, always well coiffed, always becomingly clad in a pretty negligee or bedjacket, always pleased to welcome family members. In 1958, with her eighty-second birthday approaching, Mary suffered another massive heart attack from which she never rallied. On September 22, 1958, she died.

In *The Bookman* of July 1927, author–critic Grant Overton made a bold statement. It was not, he said, Owen Wister nor Zane Grey nor any other writer of the purple sage, but a little woman from Pittsburgh who'd been the first to burn away the sentimental haze and depict the American cowboy as he really was. In *Lost Ecstasy*, Mary Roberts Rinehart, who styled herself a mere story-teller and hoped someday to be a novelist, had taken a simple story of a cowpoke and a girl and done with it what no author had ever done before. But was this literature?

Charles Dickens, Overton noted, had been shy on literary values, but that didn't make him any the less a novelist. Thomas

Hardy's plot construction was, in Overton's word, lamentable; but *Jude the Obscure* and *Tess of the D'Urbervilles* are still being taught in English classes. The list could go on and on; what it boils down to is that the art of the novel depends above all else on good characterization.

Mary probably hadn't even realized what she was doing when she'd hooked a whole nation of readers with her first published book. It was not the adroit plotting, not the headlong pace of a desperate struggle to solve a crime that kept the drama rolling on. It was Miss Rachel Innes, a feisty spinster of uncertain years reporting in her own grimly funny words, who yanked her readers into the midst of an ongoing family tragedy and kept her audience glued to their seats until the last gun was fired and the smoke cleared away to Miss Innes's complete satisfaction, and theirs.

There would be many successes to come, but by no means everything that came from Mary's ever-flying pen was worth crowing over. She was always ready to take on a fresh experiment; some worked, some didn't. Like Mark Twain, she turned out plenty of trash to keep the home fires burning when the flames of inspiration sank low, and was even more versatile than he about finding new ways to get bilked of her earnings. Whatever she had, she spent without stint: her money, her time, her deep attachment to her family, her spirit of adventure, her penchant for leaping in where angels feared to tread and coming up with a new batch of grist for her always ready mill. In her old age, when she could no longer hit the trail, she loaded herself with jewels and amused herself by playing the grande dame to the hilt. For Mary Roberts Rinehart, the game was never over till it was over.

Whether Mrs. Stanley Marshall Rinehart did in fact keep that long-standing appointment with her husband on the other side of the veil is not for us to know. As for Mary Roberts Rinehart, novelist and adventurer, there is still much to be read, much to be learned, and much more to be written about a woman whose spectacular career surely entitles her to be ranked among our national treasures.

BIBLIOGRAPHY

Books by Mary Roberts Rinehart:

The Circular Staircase. Bobbs-Merrill, 1908.
The Man in Lower Ten. Bobbs-Merrill, 1909.
When a Man Marries. Bobbs-Merrill, 1909.
The Window at the White Cat. Bobbs-Merrill, 1910.
The Amazing Adventures of Letitia Carberry. Bobbs-Merrill, 1911.
Where There's a Will. Bobbs-Merrill, 1912.
The Case of Jennie Brice. Bobbs-Merrill, 1913.
The After House. Houghton Mifflin, 1914.
The Street of Seven Stars. Houghton Mifflin, 1914.
"K". Houghton Mifflin, 1915.
Kings, Queens, and Pawns. Doran, 1915.
Tish. Houghton Mifflin, 1916.
Through Glacier Park. Houghton Mifflin, 1916.
Bab: A Sub-Deb. Doran, 1917.
The Altar of Freedom. Houghton Mifflin, 1917.
Tenting Tonight. Houghton Mifflin, 1918.
The Amazing Interlude. Doran, 1918.

Twenty-Three and a Half Hours' Leave. Doran, 1918.

Dangerous Days. Doran, 1919.

A Poor Wise Man. Doran, 1920.

The Truce of God. Doran, 1920.

More Tish. Doran, 1921. (short stories)

The Breaking Point. Doran, 1921.

Sight Unseen and The Confession. Doran, 1921.

The Out Trail. Doran, 1922.

Temperamental People. Doran, 1924. (short stories)

The Red Lamp. Doran, 1925.

The Bat. Doran, 1926. (Fictionalized anonymously by Stephen Vincent Benét)

Two Flights Up. Doran, 1926.

Nomad's Land. Doran, 1926 (travel articles)

Lost Ecstasy. Doran, 1927.

The Romantics. Farrar & Rinehart, 1929. (short stories)

The Door. Farrar and Rinehart, 1930.

My Story. Farrar & Rinehart, 1931.

Miss Pinkerton. Farrar & Rinehart, 1932.

The Album. Farrar & Rinehart, 1933.

The State vs. Elinor Norton. Farrar & Rinehart, 1933.

Mr. Cohen Takes a Walk. Farrar & Rinehart, 1934.

The Doctor. Farrar & Rinehart, 1936.

The Wall. Farrar & Rinehart, 1938.

Writing Is Work. The Writer, Inc. 1939.

The Great Mistake. Farrar & Rinehart, 1940.

Haunted Lady. Farrar & Rinehart, 1942.

Alibi for Isabel and Other Stories. Farrar & Rinehart, 1944.

The Yellow Room. Farrar & Rinehart, 1945.

My Story: A New Edition and Seventeen New Years. Rinehart, 1948.

Episode of the Wandering Knife. Rinehart, 1950.

The Swimming Pool. Rinehart, 1952.

The Frightened Wife and Other Murder Stories. Rinehart, 1953.

Other Sources:

History of Pittsburgh and Environs. New York, Chicago: American Historical Society, Inc., 1922.

Cohn, Jan. *Improbable Fiction*. Pittsburgh: University of Pittsburgh Press, 1980.

Dirckx, John H., M.D. *Dr. and Mrs. Rinehart: A Biographic and Literary Study*. Menlo Park, CA: Alpha Omega Alpha Honor Society, Spring 1987.

Edwards, Julia. *Women of the World*. Boston: Houghton Mifflin Company, 1988.

Green, Anna Katharine. *Hand and Ring*. New York: Dodd, Mead and Company, 1926. Copyright 1883, 1911, 1926 by Anna Katharine Green.

Lewis Allen, Frederick. *Only Yesterday*. New York: Harper & Brothers, 1931.

Means, Gaston B. *The Strange Death of President Harding*. New York: New York Guild of Publishers, 1930.

Myers, F.W.H. *Human Personality and Its Survival of Bodily Death*. New York: Longmans, Green and Company, 1903.

Overton, Grant. *Mary Roberts Rinehart: a Study in Career*. New York: The Bookman, George H. Doran, July 1927.

Pope-Hennessy, James. *Queen Mary 1867–1953*. New York: Alfred A. Knopf, 1960.

Russell, Francis. *The Shadow of Blooming Grove*. New York: McGraw-Hill, 1968.

B   MacLeod, Charlotte.
Rinehart
M   Had she but known.

DATE			